REVEALING REVELATION

AMIR TSARFATI

WITH DR. RICK YOHN

HARVEST PROPHECY
AN IMPRINT OF HARVEST HOUSE PUBLISHERS

Cover design by Faceout Studio, Molly von Borstel

Interior design by KUHN Design Group

For bulk, special sales, or ministry purchases, please call 1-800-547-8979.
Email: Customerservice@hhpbooks.com

This logo is a federally registered trademark of the Hawkins Children's LLC. Harvest House Publishers, Inc., is the exclusive licensee of this trademark.

Revealing Revelation
Copyright © 2022 by Amir Tsarfati
Published by Harvest House Publishers
Eugene, Oregon 97408
www.harvesthousepublishers.com

ISBN 978-0-7369-8524-6 (pbk.)
ISBN 978-0-7369-8525-3 (eBook)

Library of Congress Control Number: 2021949962

Printed in the United States of America

22 23 24 25 26 27 28 29 30 / BP / 10 9 8 7 6 5 4 3 2

I dedicate this book to God, whose perfect plan revealed in Scripture is what gives me peace in a tumultuous world.

I dedicate this book to my family, friends, and ministry partners. It is your love, prayers, and support that give me the strength and resources to carry out that to which God has called me.

I dedicate this book to the brave pastors who are out there still boldly teaching Revelation with the same excitement and enthusiasm they have for teaching the rest of the Bible.

ACKNOWLEDGMENTS

First and foremost, I want to thank the Lord for giving His Word. I harbor a deep love for Scripture and count it a humbling privilege to have been called by God to both study and teach biblical truth.

I want to thank Dr. Rick Yohn for his wisdom and understanding of Scripture, which have proven invaluable not just during the creation of this particular book, but at many times through the years. Your friendship is a true blessing to me. Also, thank you to Steve Yohn for your assistance in the writing of this book.

My love and appreciation go out to my wife, Miriam, my four children, and my daughter-in-law for your love and encouragement through the long workdays and the extended absences.

Thank you, Behold Israel team, for your love, support, and dedication—Mike, H.T. and Tara, Gale and Florene, Donalee, Joanne, Nick and Tina, Jason, Abigail, Jeff, Kayo, and Steve. Also, thanks to all your spouses and children, who often sacrifice their family time with you to further the spreading of God's Word.

Thank you to Bob Hawkins, Steve Miller, and the wonderful team at Harvest House for all your hard work in making this book happen.

Finally, thank you so much to the hundreds of thousands of followers, prayer partners, and ministry supporters of Behold Israel. This ministry would not exist without you.

CONTENTS

WELCOME
TO THE TOUR

Revelation was written to be read.

That may seem like an obvious fact, but when it comes to the last book of the Bible, many people forget that truth. Sure, they know that it should be read by someone, maybe theologians or pastors or prophecy teachers. But they conclude that for the ordinary church person, it's just too complicated or weird or scary. "Best to leave it for the professionals," they say.

The problem is that so many of the "professionals" are not reading it themselves. For some, it's because their seminaries barely touched on this important book during a New Testament overview course. So they have no real idea what the apostle John wrote. Others prefer to dodge the book, incorrectly claiming that there are no personal applications in it. Really? What they are saying is that Revelation is essentially irrelevant. If that is true, then why is it in the biblical canon? I challenge you to show me one book of the Bible that is not applicable in some way—one part of Scripture about which you can say, "You know, I kinda think that God was just padding His word count with this passage." This kind of Revelation avoidance is very sad, because way too many people in the church are missing out on all the blessings that God Himself promises to those who read it.

It is because I want everyone to experience these guaranteed blessings that I've written this book. It's true that, at first, Revelation can be intimidating. However, once you start reading, you'll be shocked at how easy it is to understand. Again, God wrote it to be read—not just by the professionals, but by you.

For many years, I was a tour guide in Israel. When I took a group to a location like Caesarea Philippi or En Gedi or Gethsemane, my goal was to make sure that by the time our bus departed, everyone knew all that they needed to know about that particular site. That is my goal as we roll up to Revelation. I want to be your tour guide, and together we will discover all the wonderful knowledge, promises, and blessings found in this letter.

This is not a commentary. It is a tour. My hope is that everyone who gets to the last page will say, "Okay, now I get it. What an awesome plan God has." This book is written for the common person, the everyday student of God's Word. If you want to dig deeper, let me encourage you to check out the accompanying workbook that I have written with a man who has been teaching Bible prophecy for decades and whose name shares the cover of this book, my good friend Dr. Rick Yohn.

Now, my friends, step up into the bus and find a seat. We are now departing, and the sites you are about to see will amaze you.

A Long Letter

In our age of technology, we no longer make a habit of sending letters to one another. Instead, we use email, texts, and social media. For me, my use of social media allows me to reach hundreds of thousands of people in real time with updates about events that are taking place in the Middle East. This would be impossible if we were still in the old nondigital days. In John's time, he didn't have any of those fancy options. If you wanted to communicate something to someone and you couldn't be there yourself, your one choice was putting pen to paper.

We should be very thankful that social media did not exist in the first century. Why? Because posts are usually short, to the point, and often meaningless. Can you imagine Paul, rather than writing the letters to the church in Corinth, spending his time trolling the accounts of

Apollos and Peter or creating memes that take jabs at the "super apostles" of 2 Corinthians 11–12? What if, rather than penning the amazing visions he was given of the throne room of God, John had spent his time on Patmos posting pictures of beach life and the lunch he had made of the tiny crabs he caught in the tide pools?

The first-century Roman Empire was a letter-writing society, and twenty-two of the twenty-seven New Testament books take that form. All of Paul's writings are letters, as are the writings by Peter, John (except for his Gospel), the anonymous writer of Hebrews, and James and Jude, the brothers of Jesus. In fact, once you finish the Gospels and Acts, everything from that point on might well have been stuffed into an envelope with a church's address scrawled on the front.

Revelation is no different. In a glorious moment on a rocky island, John was commissioned by Jesus Christ to send a letter to seven of His churches. Some of the content was dictated by Jesus while John furiously scribbled; some of it the apostle would witness firsthand. But all of it was a direct message from God to His people.

How is it, then, that so many Christians and their pastors turn their backs on this precious part of God's truth? There's no doubt that the churches that first received this letter didn't follow the same path by reading it over, shaking their heads, then tossing it aside and saying, "Yeah, that John was always a little bit off."

Instead, we can picture the church at Ephesus gathered for service. A hush comes over the congregation as the seal is broken and the letter is unrolled. All are on the edge of their seats. These may have been the first words they had received from their former pastor—the man who had married and buried so many of the congregation, the one whose teaching they had sat under for years, the apostle who had been one of the inner circle of the disciples of the Savior, Jesus.

The current pastor scans the faces of the people. He has a serious look on his face, but a tear is visible in the corner of his eye. He begins:

The Revelation of Jesus Christ… (Revelation 1:1).

Just those five words. They say it all. How could you not want to read the rest? Jesus Christ, God Himself, is about to reveal something to the world. What was unknown is about to be made known. What was unclear is about to be made clear. The Lord, in His infinite wisdom, determined that He had some things that He needed to lay out for His church, and here they were written out.

Yet there are believers who don't take time to read this letter.

And there are pastors who refuse to preach it.

That's amazing! How can anyone possibly think that is a wise decision?

The church at Ephesus would have soaked it in. Every word would have been like music to their ears and honey to their palate. This would have been true even of the bitter words, words that convicted them as a congregation, because they would have recognized that they were all part of "the Revelation of Jesus Christ." The message in this letter would have been the topic of conversations for weeks, months, years to come.

Without reading this letter, you cannot know the Lord as He is today and has always been. There will be a gaping hole in your knowledge of His character. You cannot know the future He has prepared for you. You will be ignorant of His plans for the rest of the world. The Lord is the Great Communicator, and He has made Himself known through the ages in dreams, visions, signs, wonders, and His Word. How can we demote any part of His Word to the level of null and void?

This sixty-sixth book of the Bible not only completes all that God wanted us to know about His plans, but also tells us the rest of the story about our Messiah. We know Jesus as our suffering Savior who took our place on the cross. We know Jesus as the risen Christ who has gone to prepare a place for us. But what then? Does His story end there? What is Jesus doing now? Is He pacing around in heaven, waiting until it's time to once again set foot on the Mount of Olives? Is He anxiously watching global events, looking for a chance to jump back in and become relevant again? And what about the church, the bride of Christ? Is there a future for us? Are we going to experience the days during which God pours out His wrath upon this world?

All these questions are answered in the book of the Revelation. God does not want you to live in ignorance of His plans. He doesn't want you to live in a state of anxiety, wondering if you will experience the time of judgment. Revelation makes it perfectly clear that the answer to that worry is no. If you are part of the church, you will not be here when the hammer comes down.

Despite its daunting reputation, this lengthy letter is a message of hope, and it is a message of promise. By the time you finish, you will know that Jesus is risen as promised, Jesus will return to take us home as promised, Jesus will return to Jerusalem with us accompanying Him as promised, Jesus will reign over the world as promised, and Jesus will judge unbelievers just as He promised.

If you, as one of God's children, read Revelation all the way to the end, I can guarantee that you'll finish with a smile on your face. So, let's dive into this final book of the Bible, which contains the very last written words of our God and Creator. We'll begin with an overview of Revelation and then move on to the first chapter, where you will learn that, like the rest of life, it's all about Jesus.

A Choice of "-ists"

Whenever you begin reading a book, you do so with a set of presuppositions. If you pick up a work of history, you will turn to the first page expecting to read about events that actually happened. If you open a novel, you will anticipate enjoying a story that did not occur 100 percent as written. Otherwise, you would be reading history.

Presuppositions make all the difference when it comes to how we read. Down through the centuries, believers have approached the last book of the Bible with varying sets of presuppositions. It is those presumptions that determine whether one believes that what is written in Revelation will take place literally or if it is simply a picture representing some other time or various theological truths. There are four primary presuppositional approaches to John's letter.

The preterist, which comes from a word meaning "past," views this book as history. It is a symbolic picture of the early centuries of the church. Most preterists believe the book of Revelation was written between AD 64–67 and the events were fulfilled in the horrific year AD 70 when Jerusalem and the temple were destroyed by Rome. But to make that work, they are forced to "allegorize" or "symbolize" many of the chapters, like chapters 20–22, which talk about the new Jerusalem and the new heaven and new earth. My house is an easy drive from Jerusalem, and I am there quite often. You can find a lot of things covering the streets of the great city; gold is not one of them. The result of this approach is that Revelation becomes a book of exaggerated, unsubstantiated history rather than a book of prophecy.

The historist says that John's letter refers to the events and conditions of the church up through the millennia until now. If Revelation ended after the first three chapters, I might agree with them. However, once chapter 4 comes along, you won't find the church mentioned again until chapter 19. Everything from the time John reaches heaven (in Revelation 4:1) onward would have to be disconnected from reality. Revelation would simply be a complicated and confusing stage play of strange nonevents that somehow communicated to you deep truths about God and the church. What are those deep truths? Ask seven historists, and they'll come up with seven different opinions. Once you say that the Bible's words don't mean what they normally mean, then understanding it becomes a matter of one's own interpretation.

The idealist says that Revelation is a grandiose picture of the great clash between God and Satan. In a sense, it is John's epic account of the eternal struggle between good and evil, similar to J.R.R. Tolkien's Lord of the Rings, only with fewer Hobbits. In the end, good wins, we all breathe a sigh of relief, and enjoy forever in the eternal kingdom. But the Bible is not a work of fiction. While there are short stories in the Bible, such as Jesus' parables, they are always brief, plainly identified as stories, and have a clear point.

Finally, there is the futurist, who says that everything in chapters 4–22, except for a few "signs" that are clearly identified as such, talks about actual future events. Jesus said to John at their encounter on Patmos, "Write the things which you have seen, and the things which are, and the things which will take place after this" (Revelation 1:19). Only the futurist can say that they have held true to this admonition without allegorizing, rejecting, or conveniently ignoring any part of this biblical book. This is the "-ist" interpretation that I hold to.

It's All About Jesus

If you were to ask a group of churchgoers what the theme of Revelation is, you would likely hear a variety of responses. "It's about the end times." "It's about the nasty stuff during the tribulation." A well-studied member of the group might even say, "It describes God's punishment on the nation of Israel and the people's ultimate salvation." All of them would be right.

But there is one central theme that carries through this wonderful letter of pain and hope, wrath and love, and judgment and grace, and it is not a *what* but a *who*. The book of Revelation is all about Jesus Christ. From beginning to end, He is there carrying out the will of the Father. It took John only four words to get to the name that is above all names. So, as you read, remember that the ultimate focus of this letter is not the rapture, nor the tribulation, nor Israel, nor the church, nor the new heaven or the new earth. It is the King of kings, the Lord of lords, the powerful Lion of Judah, and the spotless sacrificial Lamb.

PART 1

JESUS AND HIS CHURCH
(Revelation 1–3)

CHAPTER 1

A SERIES OF INTRODUCTIONS

REVELATION 1:1-8

John is about to send to the churches what he knows is a letter that is unique from all its predecessors. As he is writing, it is well past the time that Paul and Peter put pen to paper. In fact, they had been dead for decades. He knew their writings. He also would have read the letter to the Hebrews and the one that James, the brother of Jesus, had written. He was even familiar with the letter that another of the Lord's brothers had penned—Jude, whose short missive at times went a little to the unusual. But even Jude's occasional obscurity was nothing compared to what John was about to hit the church with.

Because of the nature of what Revelation would contain, when the Lord inspired John about what to write, He probably decided He had better ease the readers in. They needed a good series of introductions before He got to the visions—an introduction to the letter, to the writer, and to the Author. So, picking up his pen, John, led by the Spirit, began to write:

> The Revelation of Jesus Christ, which God gave Him to show His servants—things which must shortly take place.

And He sent and signified it by His angel to His servant
John, who bore witness to the word of God, and to the testimony of Jesus Christ, to all things that he saw. Blessed is
he who reads and those who hear the words of this prophecy, and keep those things which are written in it; for the
time is near.

John, to the seven churches which are in Asia: Grace
to you and peace from Him who is and who was and who
is to come, and from the seven Spirits who are before His
throne, and from Jesus Christ, the faithful witness, the
firstborn from the dead, and the ruler over the kings of
the earth.

To Him who loved us and washed us from our sins in
His own blood, and has made us kings and priests to His
God and Father, to Him be glory and dominion forever
and ever. Amen. Behold, He is coming with clouds, and
every eye will see Him, even they who pierced Him. And
all the tribes of the earth will mourn because of Him. Even
so, Amen. "I am the Alpha and the Omega, the Beginning
and the End," says the Lord, "who is and who was and who
is to come, the Almighty" (Revelation 1:1-8).

Revelation! The revealing of something that was previously unseen
or unknown. Interestingly, the Greek word used here is *apokalypsis*,
from which we get the word *apocalypse*. Think of those two words—
revelation and *apocalypse*. They each give off very different emotions.
Revelation is a happy, exciting word that envisions opening a gift or
discovering if the confetti is pink or blue at the gender reveal party.
But *apocalypse* is very different. It feels like it should have its own
"dom-dom-dommmm" sound effect every time that it is mentioned.
Sadly, this is likely a product of popular books and Hollywood. Apocalyptic literature is its own genre and Francis Ford Coppola's *Apocalypse Now* is about as far from that celebratory gender reveal party as
you can get.

This understanding of apocalypse is a modern interpretation. Back
when the pastor read the first line of John's letter to his congregation,

the people didn't scream, "Apocalypse?" and dive under their seats. There would have been excitement because a mystery was about to be revealed. That which was hidden was preparing to be unveiled.

That's why it is sad that so many believers know so little of this Revelation. God has revealed something very special to His church, yet so very few church members know it or understand it. Yet they bear only part of the blame. As we saw in the preface, too few preachers preach this book from the pulpit and too few seminaries teach it in their classrooms. Paige Patterson, former president of the Southern Baptist Convention, wrote:

> If there is something more regrettable than the treatment of the Revelation by enthusiastic friends, it is its abject neglect by most evangelical preachers. Partly as a reaction to the unbridled sensationalism of reckless interpreters and partly as a result of intellectual and exegetical laziness, the average evangelical pastor just never gets around to the Apocalypse.[1]

I had never planned on writing a book on Revelation. But people need to get this information somehow. Wondrous events are revealed to the Lord's church in this letter. And at the center of all of them stands one man: Jesus Christ.

Jesus—the Author and Focus of the Letter

I was tempted to call this first chapter "The Jesus Letter." The reason is because, as I mentioned above, Jesus is the central figure in Revelation. Yes, John the apostle is the writer of the letter, but he wrote only what the Lord directed him to write. This letter is from Jesus, and from front to back it is about Him.

It is easy to forget that this is a letter. First, because we often call it the book of Revelation, and second, it is longer than any other New Testament letter. However, it also doesn't look like a letter—at least not in any modern form. Our letters today usually begin with "Dear Mr. Smith." We first address the person to whom we are writing, and end the letter with our name as the sender. However, in biblical days, the reverse was true. Consider the following letters from the apostle Paul to the church at Corinth, and Peter, when he wrote to the Jewish dispersion:

> Paul, called to be an apostle of Jesus Christ through the will of God, and Sosthenes our brother, to the church of God which is at Corinth… (1 Corinthians 1:1-2).

> Peter, an apostle of Jesus Christ, to the pilgrims of the Dispersion in Pontus, Galatia, Cappadocia, Asia, and Bithynia… (1 Peter 1:1).

The opening of Revelation is even more confusing to today's letter readers because it includes the subject of the missive even before it gets to the greetings:

> The Revelation of Jesus Christ, which God gave Him to show His servants—things which must shortly take place. And He sent and signified it by His angel to His servant John, who bore witness to the word of God, and to the testimony of Jesus Christ, to all things that he saw (Revelation 1:1-2).

John made it clear from the beginning that the ultimate author is Jesus Christ. A great early twentieth-century blues classic sings of "John the Revelator," but there is no John the Revelator. Jesus is the Revelator. John is just the guy with the pen.

Revelation—the Content of the Letter

The word "of" in the first phrase of the letter leads to a question. Is this a revelation about Jesus or from Jesus? Is He the Revealed or the Revealer? The answer is both. Again, He is the Revelator. He is the One who dictates to John chapters 2–3 of the letter, and He is the superintendent of the revelation of the events in the rest of the chapters. He launches with a command: "What you see, write in a book and send it to the seven churches…." (Revelation 1:11). And He concludes with an affirmation of the message: "I, Jesus, have sent My angel to testify to you these things in the churches. I am the Root and the Offspring of David, the Bright and Morning Star" (Revelation 22:16).

Again, Jesus is the central figure in this book. Yes, it talks about the end times, but the first chapter begins with Jesus and the last chapter ends with Jesus. Chapter 1 sees Him making a surprise appearance, and chapter 22 calls out for Him to make a surprise reappearance.

The letter, though, isn't just about Jesus showing up unexpectedly, although He does do that several times. It is also about Him bringing judgment upon the world. You might say, "Come on, Amir, Jesus is all about love. He's not about judging and punishment." You're right, He is all about love. That is why His return is still yet to come. The desire of God is that all will come to Him. Paul wrote, "This is good and acceptable in the sight of God our Savior, who desires all men to be saved and to come to the knowledge of the truth" (1 Timothy 2:3-4).

Sadly, there are those who, despite the loving sacrifice of Jesus on the cross for the forgiveness of their sins, will choose to reject God. For them, there only awaits judgment. And who is the One designated to bring about that judgment? Jesus, the Righteous Judge. Speaking of Himself, Jesus said, "The Father judges no one, but has committed all judgment to the Son, that all should honor the Son just as they honor the Father" (John 5:22-23).

Blessing—the Benefit of the Letter

God made us, so He knows how we think and what it takes to motivate us. That is why when He asks us to do something, often He includes a carrot dangling at the end of a stick. "This is what you should do because it is in keeping with My holiness. And, for a little incentive, I'm going to include this reward for your obedience." That is what we find in Revelation 1:3:

> Blessed is he who reads and those who hear the words of
> this prophecy, and keep those things which are written in
> it; for the time is near.

Why should we read the words of this prophecy? What should be our motivation to hear these words and to keep the commands written in it? Because it's God's Word. That should be enough. But like a father who loves to give treats to his child when they are doing the right thing, He says, "By the way, when you do what you should be doing, I'm going to bless you to pieces."

This blessing comes in many forms. Among them is the fact that we can know what is coming for this world. God wants us to be aware of what is ahead. He wants us to prepare ourselves and our families for His return. In Israel, we have sirens that sound when our unhappy neighbors to the south and to the north decide to fire rockets into our country. When we hear their wail, we all scramble for the nearest shelter until the danger passes. Thus, we become doubly blessed—we have knowledge of the attack, and we have safety in the shelters.

God has given us 2,000+ years to prepare for the coming storm that will sweep the entire earth. When that happens, there will be no place to hide. Plagues, earthquakes, hail, fire, and starvation will run rampant throughout the globe. COVID will seem like a case of the sniffles in comparison to what people will be exposed to during the seven-year global catastrophe. "Blessed" almost feels like an understatement for those who will escape this time.

But safety doesn't come by standing there and listening to the sirens go off. Saying, "Uh-oh, rockets are coming" does absolutely nothing to protect us from bombs landing on our heads. We've got to get to shelter. That's where the last part of the verse comes in. It is not enough just to read and hear the words of this letter. We must "keep" them. The Greek word there is *tereo* and means "to guard, watch, protect, keep." The one who does this will take the central message of this letter and hold on to it with all they've got.

What is the central message of this book? It's Jesus. Remember, He is the Author and focus of this letter. Those who make Jesus their Savior and Lord by repenting of their sins and giving their lives to God will receive the wonderful blessing of shelter from the devastation. But this shelter will not be in an underground bunker. It will be in heaven with our Savior in the place that He promised to go and prepare for us (John 14:1-4).

Near—the Timing of the Letter

Near.

That may be the most difficult word to come to terms with in the whole passage. It has troubled readers and preachers and commentators for centuries. In fact, there are those who use this innocent little adverb to mock believers who are anxiously anticipating the return of Jesus and the rapture of the church. But that is nothing new. Even back in Peter's day, there were those who said, "Near, schmear." Peter, however, wasn't having any of it, and he pointedly corrected these doubters.

> This they willfully forget: that by the word of God the heavens were of old, and the earth standing out of water and in the water, by which the world that then existed perished, being flooded with water. But the heavens and the earth which are now preserved by the same word, are reserved for fire until the day of judgment and perdition of ungodly men.
>
> But, beloved, do not forget this one thing, that with the Lord one day is as a thousand years, and a thousand years as one day. The Lord is not slack concerning His promise, as some count slackness, but is longsuffering toward us, not willing that any should perish but that all should come to repentance (2 Peter 3:5-9).

That passage is a brilliant combination of smackdown and guilt trip. He starts with, "You don't understand 'near'? It's because you don't understand God." He finishes with, "While you're all in a rush, God is showing His amazing patience so that more and more people can flood into the kingdom." There is God's timetable and there is ours. From a human perspective, the word "near" passed its outer limits about 1,800 years ago. According to God's calendar, it's like we're only a couple of days into the wait. The time will come, though, when He will act. And when He does, He will do so very quickly.

A Fine "How Do You Do?"

Having given us that wonderful introduction, John now presents what is both a salutation and a benediction. He put himself forth as the writer of the letter, the seven churches in Asia as the recipients, and the triune God as the Author. Then, once Jesus is mentioned, the apostle just can't help himself from heaping praise upon his Savior.

> John, to the seven churches which are in Asia: Grace to you and peace from Him who is and who was and who is to come, and from the seven Spirits who are before His throne, and from Jesus Christ, the faithful witness, the firstborn from the dead, and the ruler over the kings of the earth. To Him who loved us and washed us from our sins in His own blood, and has made us kings and priests to His God and Father, to Him be glory and dominion forever and ever. Amen (Revelation 1:4-6).

John quickly gets past his part in one word. He states his name, then moves on to the recipients, whom he also quickly brushes by for now. They will be dealt with in much greater detail in the next two chapters. The writer and recipients may be important to an extent, but they are certainly secondary to the Ones who come next.

God in Three Persons—Blessed Trinity

Some have asked me, "Amir, did you know that the word *Trinity* is never used in Scripture?" That is true. But neither is the word *bacon*, yet I recognize its existence and am very thankful for it. How do I know that bacon exists? Because there is ample evidence for it, particularly at breakfast time. As one reads through Scripture, confirmations of the triune God are equally plentiful. Throughout Jesus' life, we can see the Father, Son, and Holy Spirit in His baptism, His transfiguration, His promise of the coming Counselor in the Upper Room Discourse, and the Great Commission. This Revelation salutation is not written to act as further proof of the Trinity. Instead, the fact is just accepted as truth.

Grace and peace are offered to the recipients of the letter first from the Eternal One—the Father who is, who was, and who is to come. Then, out of the normal order, the greetings are given from the Holy Spirit. Here He is described as the seven Spirits who are before the throne of the Father. The implication is that the Holy Spirit is ready to be sent by the Father in the same way that He was sent to inhabit the believers of the church on the day of Pentecost.

Finally, we come to the Son, placed in the third position so that John can more easily elaborate on Him without having to do any fancy grammatical gymnastics. What is it that we learn about Jesus in this mini-hymn of praise?

Jesus is the Faithful Witness. He perfectly represented the Father before the world. The first of the great prophets, Moses, made this promise: "The LORD your God will raise up for you a Prophet like me from your midst, from your brethren. Him you shall hear" (Deuteronomy 18:15). Because He is the Word of God, Jesus not only acted upon the words of His Father, but also spoke the words of His Father. As He told the disciple Philip, "He who has seen Me has seen the Father" (John 14:9).

Jesus is the Firstborn from among the dead. Paul wrote, "He is the head of the body, the church, who is the beginning, the firstborn from the dead, that in all things He may have the preeminence" (Colossians 1:18). He is preeminent in two ways. First, the fact that He is the firstborn indicates that there will be others to follow. Thus, through His resurrection, He has opened the door for our resurrection. He is also preeminent in that He is the perfect and only sacrifice that could be made for our sins. Not only is He the perfect High Priest, but He is the perfect offering. As the writer of Hebrews put it, "By one offering He has perfected forever those who are being sanctified" (Hebrews 10:14). As the High Priest, He laid the offering on the altar. And, as the spotless Lamb that was slain, He allowed Himself to be that sacrifice.

Jesus is the Ruler of the kings of the earth. The Bible first revealed Jesus as a helpless baby, lying in a manger. But as is true of all people, infancy is not where He remained. He grew in wisdom and stature and power, far surpassing all others. Later in Revelation, John revealed who that little baby became when he wrote, "He Himself will rule them with a rod of iron. He Himself treads the winepress of the fierceness and wrath of Almighty God. And He has on His robe and on His thigh a name written: KING OF KINGS AND LORD OF LORDS"

(Revelation 19:15-16). He is the One before whom one day every knee will bow and every person will acknowledge that He is the rightful King to the throne.

Jesus is the Lover of our souls. How many of you love your children? Hopefully, all your hands went up. We all love our children and would willingly lay down our lives for them. But how willing are you to lay down your life for someone who is your enemy—a person who hates you or who arrogantly acts like you don't even exist? Not too many of us would volunteer for that assignment. Yet the Bible informs us, "God demonstrates His own love toward us, in that while we were still sinners, Christ died for us" (Romans 5:8). Jesus sacrificed His life not just for His friends, but for His enemies too. That is the depth of Jesus' love.

Jesus is the Washer of our sins. This might be the characteristic of Christ that brings me the most peace. What once separated me from my God is now gone because of what was done on that cross. Not only has it disappeared from my life, but it is gone never to return. "He will again have compassion on us, and will subdue our iniquities. You will cast all our sins into the depths of the sea" (Micah 7:19). For those of you saying, "Well, Amir, couldn't God send an angel in some sort of spiritual submarine to bring them back up?," you're missing the metaphor. Because of the blood of Jesus Christ, we can come pure and holy into the presence of our righteous Creator, and that is a right and a privilege that will never be taken away.

Jesus is the enthroner of kings and the consecrator of priests. This same promise is reiterated in Revelation 5 by the twenty-four elders in heaven as they praise the Lamb, saying that He has "made us kings and priests to our God; and we shall reign on the earth" (verse 10). In the later passage we learn the purpose of our new roles. We will reign on the earth. Our experience after death is not one of luxurious lying around eating nonfattening bonbons. It is a life of learning, serving, and worshipping. Imagine what you will see, hear, and experience as the years pass and you fulfill your calling in the future kingdom of God. What exactly will it look like? We know that as kings, there is a political element to our leadership as we lead people. As priests, there is also a spiritual element as we act as connectors between God and humanity.

Because Jesus is the High Priest, He has full power and authority to place us in these positions.

The Seven Churches—the Recipients of the Letter

"John, to the seven churches which are in Asia…" (Revelation 1:4).

For those craving a little more specificity as to the location rather than "Asia," Jesus mentions the cities a little further down:

> What you see, write in a book and send it to the seven churches which are in Asia: to Ephesus, to Smyrna, to Pergamos, to Thyatira, to Sardis, to Philadelphia, and to Laodicea (verse 11).

These seven churches, which we will become much better acquainted with in chapters 2 and 3 of the letter, were all active congregations in John's day. As we read this list, it becomes clear that the churches are mentioned in geographical order, beginning with Ephesus, which was closest in location to John when he wrote the letter. Today, while you can't find the churches themselves, you can still visit the locations of the cities in Turkey. In fact, my wife and I spent our honeymoon in Pamukkale, known in the Bible as Hierapolis—a hot spring resort directly north of the city of Laodicea.

Today, the church that stands out from the others for those who have an archaeological bent is Ephesus. It is a gold mine for history lovers. You can spend an entire day walking through the reconstructed ruins. Particularly intriguing are the two theaters—one that seats about 1,500, while the other holds close to 25,000. For lovers of New Testament history, you can stand on the platform from which Paul wanted to quiet a riot or stroll through the *agora*—the market area—where some of Jesus' disciples journeyed and purchased their necessities.

"I Will Return"—the Groom's Promise to His Bride

It had been a while since Jesus promised, "I go to prepare a place for you. And if I go and prepare a place for you, I will come again and receive you to Myself; that where I am, there you may be also" (John 14:2-3). By a while, I don't mean weeks or months or even years. It had been decades. By this time, only John was left alive of those who had heard Jesus utter those words in the upper room the night before His crucifixion. It's understandable if some in the church were saying, "Uh, John, are you sure you heard Him right?"

The Lord knew that reassurance was needed, so that was exactly what He gave:

> Behold, He is coming with clouds, and every eye will see Him, even they who pierced Him. And all the tribes of the earth will mourn because of Him. Even so, Amen (Revelation 1:7).

When Jesus returns, it will not be by limousine or airplane or spaceship. He is coming with the clouds. This is a visual that we see in other parts of Scripture as well:

> I was watching in the night visions, and behold, One like the Son of Man, coming with the clouds of heaven! He came to the Ancient of Days, and they brought Him near before Him (Daniel 7:13).

> The sign of the Son of Man will appear in heaven, and then all the tribes of the earth will mourn, and they will see the Son of Man coming on the clouds of heaven with power and great glory (Matthew 24:30).

> Jesus said to him, "It is as you said. Nevertheless, I say to you, hereafter you will see the Son of Man sitting at the right hand of the Power, and coming on the clouds of heaven" (Matthew 26:64).

Notice the prepositions. He is coming *with* the clouds and *on* the clouds. He is not coming *in* the clouds. This is not a private return, nor is it momentary. Every eye will see Him, including those who "pierced" Him:

They will look on Me whom they pierced. Yes, they will
mourn for Him as one mourns for his only son, and grieve
for Him as one grieves for a firstborn (Zechariah 12:10).

This reassurance from Jesus did not directly address the concern
that many in the church had—"Lord, when are you returning to take
us to be with you?" That event is the rapture of the church, when Jesus
comes *in* the clouds and collects His bride.

The Lord Himself will descend from heaven with a shout,
with the voice of an archangel, and with the trumpet of
God. And the dead in Christ will rise first. Then we who
are alive and remain shall be caught up together with them
in the clouds to meet the Lord in the air. And thus we shall
always be with the Lord (1 Thessalonians 4:16-17).

Again, notice the preposition "in." The event promised in Revelation 1 is the second coming of Christ. That is when He returns to bring
judgment upon the world and to set up His kingdom, which He will
rule from His throne in Jerusalem. While that is certainly a time to
anticipate, the blessed hope of the church is not the second coming.
The rapture is our "go time." At the second coming, we will be on the
clouds with Jesus.

The Beginning and the End

This introduction ends with the following verse:

"I am the Alpha and the Omega, the Beginning and the
End," says the Lord, "who is and who was and who is to
come, the Almighty" (Revelation 1:8).

My red-letter-edition of the New King James Version attributes this
statement to the Lord Jesus Christ. But in verse 4, the phrase "from
Him who is and who was and who is to come" is attributed to God the
Father. So, is "the Lord" here referring to the Father or to Jesus, the Son?
As always with interpreting Scripture, context is key.

The verse begins with the phrase "Alpha and Omega." This title is used three times in the book of Revelation (1:8; 21:6; 22:13). The first two can be speaking of either the Father or the Son. The third is most definitely a statement coming from Jesus the Son:

> Behold, I am coming quickly, and My reward is with Me, to give to every one according to his work. I am the Alpha and the Omega, the Beginning and the End, the First and the Last (Revelation 22:12-13).

Who is the coming One? As we have already seen, it is Jesus Christ. Thus, both the Father and the Son are Ones "who are and who were and who are to come." "The Alpha and Omega" refers to God's eternity or His eternal existence. He never had a beginning, so He always was. He will never have an ending, so He always will be.

"Uh, Amir, I know you're Jewish and all, so you may not know about this thing called Christmas that celebrates when Jesus was born." Actually, I have heard of the event, and *mazel tov* to Joseph and Mary. That day in Bethlehem when the virgin gave birth was the beginning of the humanity of Jesus. But John himself, long before he wrote this letter from the island of Patmos, opened his Gospel with these words:

> In the beginning was the Word, and the Word was with God, and the Word was God. He was in the beginning with God. All things were made through Him, and without Him nothing was made that was made (John 1:1-3).

Jesus, the Word, was, is, and is to come. In this context, based on what we see in the rest of Revelation, it was Jesus who spoke the words of verse 8. If there was ever any doubt in anyone's mind whether Jesus is God Himself, He uses the title "the Almighty" to refer to Himself. That Greek word used there appears eight other times in Revelation and once outside of this letter by Paul in 2 Corinthians 6:18 when he was quoting from the Old Testament. The word is used only in reference to God. When Jesus stood before John, the disciple was looking at the face of the Almighty Himself.

CHAPTER 2

AN UNEXPECTED MEETING

I t's Sunday, the first day of the week. It used to be that John would have been worshipping with his church in Ephesus. During the opening part of the service, one, two, maybe three people would share something that the Lord had laid on their hearts. Then John—disciple, writer, evangelist, preacher—would teach the Word of God to the people.

Later in John's ministry, the canon of Scripture would have included not just the Old Testament, but the letters of Paul and Peter, the Gospels of Matthew, Mark, Luke, and his own, the letter to the diaspora Hebrews, and the epistles of James and Jude. In other words, all the Bible had been written…almost. There was one more addition yet to be written—a conclusion to touch on what had passed and what was happening at the present time, but would also focus on what God had planned for the future. Once that was included, then the message that the Lord wanted to communicate to humanity would be complete.

It's Sunday. But rather than being in Ephesus with his church, John was on a barren rock of an island in the Mediterranean Sea. Instead of his congregation, he had a choir of seagulls, along with some lizards and a handful of hermit crabs. Still, while it's wonderful to worship with Christian brothers and sisters, you don't need a congregation to praise the Lord. So John was praying and honoring God, when suddenly it all went to the next level:

> I, John, both your brother and companion in the tribulation and kingdom and patience of Jesus Christ, was on the island that is called Patmos for the word of God and for the testimony of Jesus Christ. I was in the Spirit on the Lord's Day, and I heard behind me a loud voice, as of a trumpet, saying, "I am the Alpha and the Omega, the First and the Last," and, "What you see, write in a book and send it to the seven churches which are in Asia: to Ephesus, to Smyrna, to Pergamos, to Thyatira, to Sardis, to Philadelphia, and to Laodicea" (Revelation 1:9-11).

The phrase, "in the Spirit" is a special expression. It is used thirteen times in the New Testament. The apostle Paul used it six times in his epistles, and John three times in Revelation. It refers to an individual being "possessed" by the Holy Spirit for prophecy. According to Jesus, David prophesied in the Spirit (Matthew 22:43). Old Simeon prophesied in the Spirit when he saw the infant Messiah in the arms of His mother (Luke 2:27). Now the apostle John was "in the Spirit" as he penned the prophetic words of his Savior. And while his physical location may have changed, either by vision or by reality, from Patmos to heaven (Revelation 4:2), then to a high mountain in eternity, from which he watched the New Jerusalem descend to earth (21:10), his spiritual location never changed. He was in the Spirit from start to finish.

When John slipped into this spiritual state, a voice called out with an identity and a charge. First, the speaker introduced Himself: "I am the Alpha and the Omega, the First and the Last." Immediately, John would have realized the divinity of the voice, because the words the speaker used to identify Himself would have been familiar to any Jew reared in a good Hebrew home:

> Thus says the LORD, the King of Israel,
> and his Redeemer, the LORD of hosts:

"I am the First and I am the Last;
besides Me there is no God" (Isaiah 44:6).

Listen to Me, O Jacob,
and Israel, My called:
I am He, I am the First,
I am also the Last (Isaiah 48:12).

This letter, however, was sent primarily to the Gentile church throughout the world. So, while the Jews of the church would be tipped off right away to the speaker's identity, unless they let slip a spoiler alert, the rest of the congregation would still be in the dark. John, in full author mode, seems to play up the suspense, letting it build a little longer.

Take a second and imagine the shock that ran through John's tired, old body. He was probably convinced that his days of writing were finished. He'd had a few "bestsellers" in his day, but who really cared anymore what this elderly exile trapped out on a rock had to say? There was already new blood in the church. The next generation had filled up the church and was likely in the process of passing it on to the *next* next generation. Yet God demonstrated that He was not quite finished with John. There is no retirement plan when it comes to serving the Lord. On that island, Jesus appeared to His elderly disciple and tapped him for the experience of a lifetime.

> Then I turned to see the voice that spoke with me. And having turned I saw seven golden lampstands, and in the midst of the seven lampstands One like the Son of Man, clothed with a garment down to the feet and girded about the chest with a golden band. His head and hair were white like wool, as white as snow, and His eyes like a flame of fire; His feet were like fine brass, as if refined in a furnace, and His voice as the sound of many waters; He had in His right hand seven stars, out of His mouth went a sharp two-edged sword, and His countenance was like the sun shining in its strength. And when I saw Him, I fell at His feet

as dead. But He laid His right hand on me, saying to me, "Do not be afraid; I am the First and the Last. I am He who lives, and was dead, and behold, I am alive forevermore. Amen. And I have the keys of Hades and of Death. Write the things which you have seen, and the things which are, and the things which will take place after this. The mystery of the seven stars which you saw in My right hand, and the seven golden lampstands: The seven stars are the angels of the seven churches, and the seven lampstands which you saw are the seven churches" (Revelation 1:12-20).

When John turned to see who was speaking to him, he saw seven golden lampstands. Then, as he squinted his old eyes, he also saw a figure—"One like the Son of Man." This descriptive term appears 189 times in the Old and New Testaments. The prophet Ezekiel is responsible for almost half of those because that is the nickname that God gave to him. But with the next book of the Bible, Daniel, a shift occurred. What once was either a generic term for humanity or a moniker for a prophet became a descriptive name for one person.

I was watching in the night visions, and behold, One like the Son of Man, coming with the clouds of heaven! He came to the Ancient of Days, and they brought Him near before Him. Then to Him was given dominion and glory and a kingdom, that all peoples, nations, and languages should serve Him. His dominion is an everlasting dominion, which shall not pass away, and His kingdom the one which shall not be destroyed (Daniel 7:13-14).

The Messiah, the Son of Man, coming with the clouds of heaven! Isn't that what we are all waiting for, the day when Jesus will come to establish His kingdom? This title became well known for the coming Messiah, which is why it was so powerful when Jesus took the name for Himself in the Gospels. Nearly eighty times we read of Jesus using the third person to refer to Himself as the Son of Man. So when John used the phrase, it wasn't out of confusion. He wasn't saying, "There was a human-looking figure standing there likely born from another human." He was saying, "I saw Jesus standing there, or at least someone who looked very much like Him."

There had been some changes to his teacher and friend. The figure that John saw standing before him looked much more like the Jesus he had seen up on the Mount of Transfiguration than the man upon whom he had reclined in the upper room or had seen ascending into heaven. The God-man was still the same God, but the man portion had experienced some major renovations. Jesus was "clothed with a garment down to the feet and girded about the chest with a golden band. His head and hair were white like wool, as white as snow, and His eyes like a flame of fire; His feet were like fine brass, as if refined in a furnace, and His voice as the sound of many waters; He had in His right hand seven stars, out of His mouth went a sharp two-edged sword, and His countenance was like the sun shining in its strength" (Revelation 1:13-16).

The change was dramatic and terrifying. The old man's knees gave out and he dropped. Then something beautiful happened. His old friend touched him. Just a simple touch and a few reassuring words were enough. John doesn't write that healing or restorative power coursed through Jesus' fingers or that the power of God lifted him to his feet. It was just the soft touch of Jesus and the comforting statement, "Do not be afraid," likely said in the same tone that the Lord had used to calm Mary Magdalene when she had gone to the tomb and found it empty. Peace flooded into John, undoubtedly along with an abundance of joy.

Jesus continued to speak:

> I am the First and the Last. I am He who lives, and was dead, and behold, I am alive forevermore. Amen. And I have the keys of Hades and of Death (Revelation 1:17-18).

Now before we go any further, let's pause here for a moment and look at the title "the First and the Last." This title, similar to the "Alpha and the Omega, the Beginning and the End" from verse 8, comes from the book of Isaiah and once again links Jesus with Yahweh or Jehovah of the Old Testament.

> Thus says the LORD, the King of Israel, and his Redeemer, the LORD of hosts: "I am the First and I am the Last; besides Me there is no God" (Isaiah 44:6).

Recall that the name of Jehovah can be translated "I AM." It was Jesus who told His Jewish listeners that He was equal with God the Father: "Most assuredly, I say to you, before Abraham was, I AM" (John 8:58).

Yes, this was John's old friend standing in front of him—the One he traveled with and fished with and laughed with and ate with. But John was also seeing Jesus in His full glory, the splendor of the Son of Man that Daniel had written about. His hair was the perfect white of purity, as opposed to old John's gray. His clothes affirmed His royalty and everything about Him spoke of strength—He looked so different than He had on that tragic afternoon six decades earlier. John saw the I AM.

But now, it seems as if there was a shift. Rather than the glory of God amongst the lampstands, there was the man at John's side. In verse 20, when Jesus referred to the stars in His hand, He did so in the past tense. Based on the context, the lampstands could easily be included in the phrase "which you saw." Here is the Rabbi saying to His disciple, "My friend, I have one more task for you, but you're going to need to get your pen and some parchment to carry it out."

> Write the things which you have seen, and the things which are, and the things which will take place after this (Revelation 1:19).

This command keeps with the theme the Lord established early on with His title "Him who is and who was and who is to come" (verses 4, 8). Here, though, Jesus changed the order so that it corresponded to the outline of the book: "things which you have seen" (chapter 1), "the things which are" (chapters 2–3), and "the things which will take place after this" (chapters 4–22).

Before this scene wrapped up, Jesus gave an explanation for this vision that John had just seen. By the way, this "explaining the vision" is something that occurs several times throughout this letter, making its interpretation much easier. If the Lord, through His proxies, says that this is what a passage means, we can be sure that it is what it means.

The seven stars, Jesus said, are the angels of the seven churches, and the seven golden lampstands are the actual seven churches. Some commentators say that the seven stars are literal angels, but I believe He is referring to the seven messengers or pastors of the churches. Why do I say that? First, because the Greek word *angelos* can mean either "angel" or "messenger." Second, the location of the stars in Jesus' hand communicates two truths. One, they are there to be used by Him—like tools ready to be put to use. That fits both angels and pastors. And two, to be in the Lord's hand is comfort and protection. Nowhere else in Scripture do we find angels safely tucked in God's hand. That is a place for His children, particularly those who are serving on the front lines of the spiritual war.

We don't know what happens next. Do John and Jesus go to the disciple's ramshackle hut? Do they have a meal together and talk about old times before getting to work? Does John already happen to have his writing gear with him and they just set to work? The narrative stops with 1:20 and doesn't pick up again until 4:1. However they were situated, we know that at some point Jesus began speaking and John began writing, and this wonderful letter of the Bridegroom to His betrothed commenced.

CHAPTER 3

AN INTRODUCTION TO THE CHURCH: AN OVERVIEW

Before I started the ministry of Behold Israel, I led tours throughout Israel. I loved that ministry for many reasons, a primary one being that it gave me the opportunity to meet so many people. As I taught them about Israel's history and God's plans for the future of the nation and the world, I began to notice a pattern in the questions they put to me. One of the queries most often asked back then and still today at my conferences is, "Where is the church during the tribulation?" It is a great question, but before we can give a good answer and before we begin to examine Revelation 2–3, we must take a step back and ask a more fundamental question: What is the church? Today, what ought to be a very basic concept to many is becoming more and more clouded.

What Is the Church?

Was Jesus a Baptist, a Presbyterian, or a Methodist? "Oh, Amir, you're just being silly," you may say. "Jesus wasn't a member of any particular church. He was nondenominational!" Well, my friend, the first part of your statement is 100 percent correct, and the second part is 100 percent wrong. Jesus was not part of any church because the church didn't begin until after His death, resurrection, and ascension into heaven.

Jesus was a Jew who grew up going to synagogue. His Bible was made up of the Hebrew Scriptures. In fact, Jesus never once quoted a New Testament verse in all His teaching! But even though He never raised His hands with the Pentecostals or sang in a Lutheran choir, He still has a very special relationship with the church. In Scripture, the word translated "church" comes from the Greek *ekklesia*, from which we get the English word *ecclesiastical*. It speaks of a people called out of the world system and into a personal relationship with God through Jesus Christ. And that is the key—the church is not a building or a religion or a denomination. The church is made up of people who have received Jesus as their Lord and Savior.

The closeness between Jesus and the church can be seen in two descriptive terms we find in the New Testament. At times the church is spoken of as the "body of Christ" (1 Corinthians 12:27), and at others as "the bride" of Christ or of the Lamb (Revelation 21:9). Both terms emphasize the intimacy and the otherness of the church.

Being the body and bride, however, doesn't mean that we are equal to Christ. Unlike what some belief systems say, we are not gods nor will we ever be. Think about it: As the bride of Christ, the church must be separate from Christ. As proof that you can find just about anything online, I found examples of both men and women marrying themselves, but not in any sense that is real or is sanctioned by any state. However, with the way culture is trending, could that be too far away? The bride and the groom must be two different people. Therefore, Jesus cannot be part of the church if the church is to be His bride. Instead, what Scripture tells us is that the Lord has a passionate, sacrificial love for those who belong to Him as His betrothed (Ephesians 5:25-27).

Knowing the love Christ has for His bride, we must ask ourselves what aspects of the harsh, violent events spelled out in Revelation 4–19 belong to the church and what belong to Israel and the rest of the world. "Whoa, whoa, whoa," some will say. "Slow down now, Amir. What do you mean 'what belong to the church' and 'what belong to Israel'? They're one and the same." This belief is held by many in the Reformed tradition who hold to what is called Replacement Theology. This view says that when the Jews rejected Jesus, God rejected them. Thus, all the promises that once belonged to Israel, apart from the promise about the land, now belong to the church.

This lie has been around from early on. Even Paul was forced to combat it head on in his letter to the Romans. Speaking of Israel as "His people," he wrote, "I say then, has God cast away His people? Certainly not! For I also am an Israelite, of the seed of Abraham, of the tribe of Benjamin. God has not cast away His people whom He foreknew" (Romans 11:1-2).

Yet there are so many well-known and well-respected pastors and theologians today who read those words of Paul and say, "Well, that doesn't really mean what it looks like it means." I addressed this "Who are you going to trust, me or your own lying eyes?" mindset at length in my book *Israel and the Church*, which is all about the distinct roles that the two play in God's plan. Let me lay out a number of the distinctions between the two.

Membership into Israel is by birth; membership into the church is by new birth. Israel is a nation made up of Jews; the church is a people made up of believers. The focus of Israel is Jerusalem; the focus of the church is heaven. Israel possesses an earthly hope in the land; the church possesses a heavenly hope in eternity. Israel began with Abraham; the church began with Pentecost.

Israel and the church are two different groups. The former is ethnic and the latter is spiritual. As we saw above, they have two distinct beginnings, and, as we will learn in Revelation, they have two distinct culminations. The removal of the church from this world will come at the rapture, and the salvation of Israel will come at the second coming of Christ, when all who are left as part of Israel will recognize the One whom they have pierced and will, as individuals, receive Him as their Lord and Savior.

That is what the plain reading of Scripture shows. The only way to unite the two entities is to set aside exegesis—"drawing out meaning from the text"—in favor of allegory and hidden meanings and opinions. When that happens, Scripture becomes "what I think it should mean" rather than what it clearly says. The Bible is no longer God's Word. Instead, it becomes words that we put in God's mouth.

The Church Today

If you are married, it's likely that you remember the period between the beginning of your engagement and the date the wedding finally arrived. It's a time filled with excitement and expectancy, planning and preparing—very much like the time we in the church are experiencing now. If we have been promised to Christ as His bride, then until the day of the marriage feast that we'll read about in Revelation 19, we are in our engagement period. The apostle Paul explains it this way: "Now He who establishes us with you in Christ and has anointed us is God, who also has sealed us and given us the Spirit in our hearts as a guarantee" (2 Corinthians 1:21-22).

The word translated "guarantee" is the Greek word *arrabon*. It is a beautiful word full of meaning. Along with "guarantee," it can have the sense of "a pledge, a down payment, an engagement." What Paul is telling us is that the Holy Spirit, in a sense, is God's engagement token to guarantee that He will complete what He has started. As the Lord said to His disciples, "I go to prepare a place for you. And if I go and prepare a place for you, I will come again and receive you to Myself; that where I am, there you may be also" (John 14:2-3).

Jesus was preparing the disciples for His departure. He wanted them to know that though He was going to His Father, they would not be abandoned. He was going to send the Holy Spirit to live within them. The Spirit inside them would guarantee that the Lord will return for His bride, the church.

Today, the Spirit inside us is our token of our engagement to our Bridegroom, the Lord Jesus Christ. And I believe we are the generation that will not die but will live to experience the rapture of the church, when Jesus will come to take His bride to the wedding ceremony.

The Church During the Tribulation

Now that we've established what the church is, let's return to our original question: Where is the church during the tribulation? Will the church experience the wrath of God as He pours out judgment upon the earth? There are many believers who are convinced that is what will happen. They feel that we as the church have not lived up to the pure and spotless bride level, so we need some straightening up. The tribulation will be a time that will soften some of our rough edges and give us a swat on the backside as punishment for the bad things that we've done.

I'm trying to understand the mindset of a groom in this situation. "My dear, I can't wait to be married to you, but I don't know if you're dedicated enough to me yet. So, I'm going to put you through some misery, so that you can learn to love me more." I'm doubting that perspective is included in most pastors' premarital counseling regimen.

But there are those who really feel that the church should endure the tribulation, and to them I say, "Be my guest!" I, on the other hand, will gladly take the first flight out of this world to meet the Groom in the clouds. Thankfully, a pre-tribulation rapture isn't just wishful thinking. It's biblical. Consider the following passages and the preposition "from":

> They themselves declare concerning us what manner of entry we had to you, and how you turned to God from idols to serve the living and true God, and to wait for His Son from heaven, whom He raised from the dead, even Jesus who delivers us from the wrath to come (1 Thessalonians 1:9-10).

> Because you have kept My command to persevere, I also will keep you from the hour of trial which shall come upon the whole world, to test those who dwell on the earth (Revelation 3:10).

The promise of Jesus, the Groom, is that He will deliver His church *from* the coming wrath. He is not delivering the church *to* the coming wrath, or even *through* the coming wrath. We will be delivered *from* "the hour of trial which shall come upon the whole world."

This is the way God works. There is precedence for such removal. Did God tell Noah that He would deliver him through the flood? "Just keep treading water. A year's time, and you'll be back on dry ground." Or what about Lot? When God rained fire and brimstone on Sodom and Gomorrah, did He tell Abraham's nephew, "Just keep dodging the fireballs. You might get a little singed, but at least you'll survive." Of course not! God delivered Noah and his family *from* the judgment of the flood by having him build an ark. God delivered Lot and his family *from* the judgment on Sodom and Gomorrah by sending angels to rush them out of the city. And God will deliver the church *from* the coming tribulation by rapturing us to meet Jesus in the clouds.

If we are delivered *from* here, where are we delivered *to*? Heaven, of course—the place that our Bridegroom promised to prepare for us. He will come for His bride and take her to His Father's house. Also, at that time, we as the church will appear before the *bema* of Christ. What is a *bema*? In ancient times, it was a raised platform where a referee, city mayor, or some other authority handed out crowns and other trophies to the winners in a race. The word is translated "judgment seat" in Scripture.

> We make it our aim, whether present or absent, to be well pleasing to Him. For we must all appear before the judgment seat of Christ, that each one may receive the things done in the body, according to what he has done, whether good or bad (2 Corinthians 5:9-10).

This judgment seat of Christ does not determine whether we get into heaven. We are already there at that time. However, it will determine whether we receive or lose rewards, depending upon our faithfulness to the Lord while alive on earth.

When seven years have passed, it will be time for Jesus' return to earth—this time coming as King and Judge. Will He be leaving us behind to take care of heaven while He's gone? Absolutely not. We will be returning with Him!

> In that day His feet will stand on the Mount of Olives,
> which faces Jerusalem on the east.
> and the Mount of Olives shall be split in two,
> from east to west,

> making a very large valley;
> half of the mountain shall move toward the north
> and half of it toward the south.
>
> Then you shall flee through My mountain valley,
> for the mountain valley shall reach to Azal.
> Yes, you shall flee
> as you fled from the earthquake
> in the days of Uzziah king of Judah.
> Thus the LORD my God will come,
> And all the saints with You (Zechariah 14:4-5).

For what purpose are we returning? One would think that once we get a taste of heaven, we won't want to come back to this planet—especially after all the destruction of the previous seven years. But we must come because an incredible event is about to take place, and we are the guests of honor.

> Let us be glad and rejoice and give Him glory, for the marriage of the Lamb has come, and His wife has made herself ready. And to her it was granted to be arrayed in fine linen, clean and bright, for the fine linen is the righteous acts of the saints. Then he said to me, "Write: 'Blessed are those who are called to the marriage supper of the Lamb!'" (Revelation 19:7-9).

After the tribulation period, the great wedding feast will begin. Both Bridegroom (Jesus) and bride (the church) will descend from heaven and come to the earth, where the wedding banquet will occur. The millennial reign of Christ from Jerusalem will include that great wedding feast.

If the church is in heaven, who is left on earth for the tribulation? The "left behind" include unbelieving Israel and the nations of the world. The tribulation was not designed by God for the church. It was designed for Israel and for the world at large. God has been patient for thousands of years because of His mercy and grace. He has held back

His wrath from mankind. It is the Lord's patience that keeps Him in heaven. But one day, the Father will say to the Son, "It's time to go get Your bride and bring her home."

The Purpose of the Tribulation

In the church, we tend to be myopic when it comes to biblical interpretation. In other words, we want to know where we fit in. That's one reason it is so difficult for some Christians to accept that most of the book of Revelation, including the seven years of the tribulation, has nothing to do with the church. It also begs the question, If the intent of the tribulation is not to purify the church, then what is its purpose?

Thankfully, God makes the answer very apparent. With just a little investigation, we can see that there are three major reasons why God is going to bring His wrath to this world. We'll begin with Israel.

The Tribulation Will Prepare Israel for Her Messiah

The tribulation is a time of turning the people of Israel to the Lord. Initially they will trust in a false Messiah, known as the Antichrist, before realizing that he is not who he claims to be. Consider the following promises God made to His people:

> From there you will seek the LORD your God, and you will find Him if you seek Him with all your heart and with all your soul. When you are in distress, and all these things come upon you in the latter days, when you turn to the LORD your God and obey His voice (for the LORD your God is a merciful God), He will not forsake you nor destroy you, nor forget the covenant of your fathers which He swore to them (Deuteronomy 4:29-31).

> Alas! For that day is great, so that none is like it; and it is the time of Jacob's trouble, but he shall be saved out of it (Jeremiah 30:7).

> At that time Michael shall stand up, the great prince who stands watch over the sons of your people; and there shall

> be a time of trouble, such as never was since there was a nation, even to that time. And at that time your people shall be delivered, every one who is found written in the book (Daniel 12:1).

> Therefore when you see the "abomination of desolation," spoken of by Daniel the prophet, standing in the holy place (whoever reads, let him understand), then let those who are in Judea flee to the mountains (Matthew 24:15-16).

Our God keeps all His promises. He has given His chosen people generation after generation to turn to their Messiah, but they have refused. So God has sent a partial blindness upon Israel. What could possibly open their minds and hearts to Christ? The terrible time of tribulation. They will discover three-and-a-half years into this period that the one who made a covenant with them and promised them that they could once again build their temple and worship as they once did has turned on them and set up himself to be worshipped in the temple.

This is the time when the full wrath of God will descend upon the earth. As destruction and calamity surround everyone, 144,000 Jewish evangelists will go forth preaching the gospel. At the conclusion of this terrible devastation, Jesus will touch down on the Mount of Olives, and every eye will see Him and they will all mourn because of Him.

> Immediately after the tribulation of those days the sun will be darkened, and the moon will not give its light; the stars will fall from heaven, and the powers of the heavens will be shaken. Then the sign of the Son of Man will appear in heaven, and then all the tribes of the earth will mourn, and they will see the Son of Man coming on the clouds of heaven with power and great glory. And He will send His angels with a great sound of a trumpet, and they will gather together His elect from the four winds, from one end of heaven to the other (Matthew 24:29-31).

This is the same promise the apostle Paul gave when he wrote the following about Israel's eventual salvation:

> I do not desire, brethren, that you should be ignorant of
> this mystery, lest you should be wise in your own opinion,
> that blindness in part has happened to Israel until the full-
> ness of the Gentiles has come in. And so all Israel will be
> saved, as it is written:

> "The Deliverer will come out of Zion,
> and He will turn away ungodliness from Jacob;
> for this is My covenant with them,
> when I take away their sins" (Romans 11:25-27).

Some critics of Israel claim that those who take this passage literally are saying that God will save the Jews because they are Jews. That
is not true at all. No one will be saved apart from a personal acceptance of Jesus as Savior and Lord. This passage says that in that day, all
of Israel will finally recognize what they have been missing all this time,
and each Jew will take that individual step to receive Jesus and trust
Him to save them.

When will this take place? Paul says it will happen when the fullness of the Gentiles has come in. The Bible speaks of both the "fullness
of the Gentiles" (Romans 11:25) and the "times of the Gentiles" (Luke
21:24). It's easy to conflate them, but they are not the same thing. The
fullness of the Gentiles refers to the time when the last Gentile comes
to faith in Christ. On the other hand, the times of the Gentiles refers
to something very different.

The Tribulation Will Bring an End to the Times of the Gentiles

The "times of the Gentiles" began under King Nebuchadnezzar
when he destroyed Jerusalem and took the people of Israel captive.
From that point until 1948, Israel has been under Gentile control. God
scattered His people throughout the nations of the world for their dis-
obedience, as He promised He would (Ezekiel 36:16-19).

Did May 14, 1948, the day of Israel's statehood, bring an end to the
"times of the Gentiles"? Some commentators believe it did. However,
Israel's present peace is only temporary because God tells us that once

again Jerusalem will be surrounded by armies as they were in 586 BC under King Nebuchadnezzar and in AD 70 under the Tenth Roman Legion, both of which destroyed the city of Jerusalem.

Israel will once again be besieged, this time by Gog, the prince of Magog, and his cohorts from Russia, Iran, Turkey, Sudan, and Libya, as described in Ezekiel 38–39. These nations will "come to take plunder" (Ezekiel 38:13), referring to the present prosperity of Israel. But God will intervene and destroy those armies.

Does that mean Israel will once again be safe? Not at all. Once those powers are removed by God's intervention, that will pave the way for the rise of the Antichrist. And, as we just talked about, three-and-a-half years into the tribulation, the Antichrist will break his covenant with Israel and set himself up to be worshipped. Eventually, armies from around the world will gather at a place called *Har Megiddo*, or Armageddon, and march up to Jerusalem to destroy her. God will once again intervene on behalf of His beloved people and will bring an end to the times of the Gentiles. This will take place when Christ descends from heaven and sets up His millennial kingdom on earth.

Jesus spoke of this time when He said,

> When you see Jerusalem surrounded by armies, then know that its desolation is near. Then let those who are in Judea flee to the mountains, let those who are in the midst of her depart, and let not those who are in the country enter her. For these are the days of vengeance, that all things which are written may be fulfilled. But woe to those who are pregnant and to those who are nursing babies in those days! For there will be great distress in the land and wrath upon this people. And they will fall by the edge of the sword, and be led away captive into all nations. And Jerusalem will be trampled by Gentiles until the times of the Gentiles are fulfilled (Luke 21:20-24).

It will be a horrific time. I don't understand the gluttons for punishment in the church who so desperately look for evidence that the bride of Christ is destined to endure those days. As Jesus explains in the Luke passage above, they are days of vengeance and times of woe. The Jews must endure this period so that they will finally turn to the Messiah. The unsaved Gentiles will face it because it is the just punishment for their sins. But for those who have already given themselves to Christ, salvation has come and all in the church have already been fully purified by the blood of Jesus. There is simply no purpose in the tribulation for the church.

The Tribulation Will Punish Mankind for Sin

How often have you heard someone ask, "Why did God allow that to happen?" or "Why doesn't He do something about man's inhumanity to man?" Well, here is your answer: He is going to do something about it. For now, He continues to patiently wait for mankind to respond to Him. But as time goes on, there is more and more rejection of God and more hatred expressed toward one another.

The time is coming when God will say, "Enough!" Then He will pour out on this planet the judgments of the seals and the trumpets and the bowls that are found in Revelation. These judgments will be just rewards for the rebellion and antipathy that this world has levelled against its Creator. Through Isaiah, God promises judgment upon the nations:

> Come, my people, enter your chambers,
> and shut your doors behind you;
> hide yourself, as it were, for a little moment,
> until the indignation is past.
> For behold, the LORD comes out of His place
> to punish the inhabitants of the earth for their iniquity;
> the earth will also disclose her blood,
> And will no more cover her slain (Isaiah 26:20-21).

This will be a time unlike any other. My friend, you do not want to be here for it. How do you ensure that you will escape this time of wrath? You become part of the church, the bride of Christ. How do you do that? Romans 10:9-10 makes it very clear:

> If you confess with your mouth the Lord Jesus and believe in your heart that God has raised Him from the dead, you will be saved. For with the heart one believes unto righteousness, and with the mouth confession is made unto salvation.

It all comes down to Jesus. Will you trust Him for your salvation? Will you make Him the center of your life? Will you follow Him by making Him your Savior and your Lord? If you will, then you can know that before all the craziness begins here on earth, you will be safe and secure with Jesus in heaven.

CHAPTER 4

LOVE LETTERS TO THE BRIDE

REVELATION 2-3

The woman came home from work exhausted, but not without a little excitement. After pulling into the driveway, she got out of her car and turned toward the street rather than the house. She rushed down to the mailbox, and, opening it, she reached in without looking—pulling out the contents and quickly closing the mailbox. Hurriedly, she retrieved her purse and her travel mug from the roof of the car and entered her house. The mug went on the counter along with her purse and keys. She sat at the kitchen table, took a deep breath, and sifted through the mail.

"Bill, bill, junk, bill…" she mumbled as one after another of the letters moved from the stack in her hand to the table. Then her breath caught. The rest of the mail was set on the table as her eyes read her name written on the envelope in her husband's distinct printing. In the top left corner was a return address that started with APO—Army Post Office. Not wanting to risk damaging its precious contents, she took the letter into the kitchen, where she used a paring knife to slice open the envelope.

"To My Dearest Love…" she read. The tears began to flow. She knew that there was no one on earth who loved her more, and that made every word she read that much more precious. When she was done reading, she took the priceless letter into her bedroom and set it on the nightstand, where it would be read several more times before she stored it with other letters in a special box she had made just for them.

What we are about to read in Revelation are love letters from the Groom to His future bride. There are words of admiration and words of admonition. The Groom encourages His fiancée, but He also challenges her. Through it all, the love Jesus feels for His church can never be questioned. We are His, and He is ours.

There is a pattern in each of the seven short messages Jesus dictated to John. We see (1) the location of the church, (2) the One addressing the church, (3) what Jesus knows about the church, (4) a word of encouragement to all but two churches, (5) a rebuke to all but two churches, (6) a challenge to repent to all but two churches, and (7) a promise to the faithful.

The Lord begins with John's home church of Ephesus, then continues in geographical order, heading north in what will become a clockwise circle. Isn't it interesting that His first love letter goes out to a church that had lost its first love?

The Church at Ephesus

Ephesus was the best of cities, and it was the worst of cities. On the positive side, it had an excellent harbor and marketplace. Its population was enormous, with a portion of it always fluctuating as sailors came into port, took some leave time, then sailed out. The reputation of Ephesus spread far and wide because it was the home to what later came to be known as one of the Seven Wonders of the World—the Temple of Diana. With columns rising sixty feet into the air, this amazing structure brought worshippers from all over the empire.

This temple, though, was also the center of the worst part of Ephesus. Diana, also known as Artemis, was a goddess of fertility. Therefore, much of the worship of her involved sexual immorality and temple prostitution. This, combined with the constant ebb and flow of sailors who had been out to sea for extended periods of time, led to Ephesus becoming a cesspool of sin and debauchery. If you sometimes wonder how you can reach out to people in a culture that is as sin-obsessed as ours is today, just think of Paul on his second missionary journey strolling into this city that makes Las Vegas look like a children's summer camp.

As usual, Paul first focused on the Jews in the synagogues—until they turned against him. "When they opposed him and blasphemed, he shook his garments and said to them, 'Your blood be upon your own heads; I am clean. From now on I will go to the Gentiles'" (Acts 18:6).

Who were these Gentiles? They were pagans who did what everybody else did in Ephesus; they worshipped Artemis. Paul didn't turn his back on them simply because they were caught up in sin and confusion. He recognized that they had been deceived by the enemy and were following the devil's lead. Paul showed them a new way, a way of truth and righteousness. For the next two years he worked with these pagan people, teaching them salvation by faith in Christ and how to live as servants of Jesus. Later, our Revelation author, John, stepped in as pastor and served in that church until his exile fifty miles west on Patmos.

By the end of the first century, the congregation of the Ephesian church was composed of theologically sound, hard-working folks. They knew what they believed and why they believed it.

> I know your works, your labor, your patience, and that you cannot bear those who are evil. And you have tested those who say they are apostles and are not, and have found them liars; and you have persevered and have patience, and have labored for My name's sake and have not become weary (Revelation 2:2-3).

What a wonderful commendation from the lips of our Lord! Most pastors would love to have such a congregation. They were active in service, moral in conduct, and sound and accurate in their theology. But something was missing. While the brain and the muscles worked in tandem, there was a heart problem. The love that the first generation of believers had for the Lord had begun to dissipate. The second generation carried on the theology and the commitment to service, but their passion was leaking like a nail-punctured tire.

> Nevertheless I have this against you, that you have left your first love. Remember therefore from where you have fallen; repent and do the first works, or else I will come to you quickly and remove your lampstand from its place—unless you repent (Revelation 2:4-5).

That had to feel like a kick in the shins to the church as they listened to the pastor reading the letter. Likely, there was a bit of spiritual pride in the congregation. After all, Paul himself had written one of his holy letters to the church a few decades previously, in which he had said, "I also, after I heard of your faith in the Lord Jesus and your love for all the saints, do not cease to give thanks for you, making mention of you in my prayers" (Ephesians 1:15-16). What had happened between those two generations of believers?

Such change often happens in the transition from the visionary and building generation to the next generation, which enjoys the fruit of all the earlier labors. The second generation doesn't know the hardships and trials; they don't have a chance for their faith to be challenged and to see the Lord at work. Think of the difference between King David and King Solomon. David was a warrior king who knew what it was like to stare death in the face. The kingship had cost him struggle and blood. King Solomon was a palace king who knew what it was like to stare a kingdom full of worshipful followers in the face. All the wisdom in the world couldn't stop the second ruler in the Davidic line from taking his love from the true God and giving it to the false-idol gods of his foreign wives.

The warning that the Groom gave to His Ephesian bride carried a severe penalty if they refused to repent of leaving their first love. He would bring an end to the church. He would remove their lampstand from its place. History tells us that the Ephesian believers must have responded positively to this warning, because they once again became a thriving church.

We can all name churches like the one Christ wrote to in Ephesus.

Or maybe you are in an "Ephesian" church. There are Bible studies galore in the church and in homes. They have several talented worship teams that rotate from Sunday to Sunday. They hold numerous services simultaneously, maybe even on different campuses, with the sermons streamed in via video. They run training classes for Christian growth and leadership, have men's and women's groups, parking-lot attendants, happy greeters, food pantries, and a large missions budget. These can all be strong elements of an active church.

But sometimes Christian activities can keep believers from spending time with Christ. Churches can be so full of things to do that there is no time for the people to simply be with the Lord. The Bible studies are big enough to move into the sanctuary. The prayer night, though, is relegated to a small children's classroom where all the participants are forced to sit on the tiny toddler chairs. Tickets need to be distributed so that everyone is assured a seat at the special guest concert, but the leader of the worship and contemplation evening has to ask everyone to move to the center section of the sanctuary so that the room doesn't feel quite so empty.

This doesn't just happen to churches. It can also happen in us. I've often heard it said that 10 percent of the church does 90 percent of the work, and I'm inclined to believe it. While we should be ever grateful for those 10 percent, they need to beware of being so busy for God that they lose touch with God. If you find yourself so diligent with church ministry that you run out of time for personal prayer and time in the Word, then you are sacrificing the great at the altar of the good. If service is not built on a foundation of close daily time with God, it becomes inevitable that bitterness, anger, territorialism, and wrong motives will creep in. Jesus taught the great "doer" Martha this truth when He said of her sister Mary that "one thing is needed, and Mary has chosen that good part, which will not be taken away from her" (Luke 10:42). What was that one thing? Mary was sitting at the feet of Jesus, learning to love Him by being in His presence.

Remember, repent, and redo—that's what Jesus was calling the Ephesian believers to. Remember your first love. Remember the excitement of knowing you are right with the Lord and your sins are forgiven.

Experience in your heart once again the removal of the fear of death and the joy of eternal life.

Repent—turn from what you were doing and begin doing the right things. Put your sin behind you and live a life of holiness. Too many people who claim to be Christians want to play it both ways. They have the "sin on Saturday and pray on Sunday" mindset. But that doesn't fly with God, because repentance doesn't come from the lips in a prayer of forgiveness. It comes from the heart in an attitude of sorrow and humility. Determine now to be done with sin so that you may live for Christ.

Then redo. The Ephesian church went from revival to rebuke. A return to revival was just a heart change away. The same is true for you. If you have let your love for Jesus wane or if you've never known Jesus well enough to establish that "first love" relationship, let today be your day of drawing near. Notice that the Lord didn't give the Ephesians a long list of penitential to-dos to get back on His good side. He simply called them back. Turn from what you're doing now and live life God's way. Spend time with Him, get into His Word, build the relationship. You'll be amazed at just how quickly your love for Him will grow.

The Church at Smyrna

The Lord's focus then moved north to Smyrna, the largest city in Asia Minor. It had a fine harbor and was the political center of the region. It was also the birthplace of Homer back in 750 BC. In the sixth century BC, the Mermnads pounded the powerful city until it was no more than a raggedy village. Three centuries later, Alexander the Great decided to restore Smyrna and give it new life. Like many other Greek cities, it had several temples and a large theater that sat 20,000 spectators.

The name Smyrna finds its derivation in the word *myrrh*, an embalming fluid that was one of this city's chief exports. Recall that it was one of the three gifts brought to Jesus by the wise men from the East. Along with the gold that was fit for a king and the frankincense that was used for worshipping gods or idols, myrrh was given to the parents of this special baby in one of the greatest acts of poetic foreshadowing of all time.

The church in Smyrna was suffering. The persecution that it was under was great.

> I know your works, tribulation, and poverty (but you are rich); and I know the blasphemy of those who say they are Jews and are not, but are a synagogue of Satan. Do not fear any of those things which you are about to suffer. Indeed, the devil is about to throw some of you into prison, that you may be tested, and you will have tribulation ten days. Be faithful until death, and I will give you the crown of life. He who has an ear, let him hear what the Spirit says to the churches. He who overcomes shall not be hurt by the second death (Revelation 2:9-11).

The Groom saw the suffering of His bride for His name's sake. He commended this church for its faithfulness amid great persecution and poverty, but He did not give Smyrna a "nevertheless" warning. There was no need.

What He also didn't add was "Don't worry, I'll protect you from the suffering" or "It's okay, I won't let them harm you." Instead, He said, "Be faithful until death, and I will give you the crown of life." Wow!

I hear so many Christians these days talking about the suffering they are going through because they can't meet when they want to meet or because the government is wanting them to wear masks or take shots. While I don't believe that it is the government's position to demand any of these things, this is not persecution! Let me say it again: The government telling you how many you can have in your sanctuary and forcing you to wear a mask may be foolish, unconstitutional, and not backed by medical science, but it is not persecution against the church! How do I know? Because the same thing is happening at temples and mosques and theaters and restaurants. Trust me, when persecution comes against the church, you'll know it.

If you want to understand persecution, talk to a Christian from South Sudan or northern Nigeria or Iran or North Korea or China. They will tell you about what true suffering is. They will also tell you how God has walked with them through the pain and loss. These dear brothers and sisters understand being "faithful until death." They continue to trust God because they know the blessed promise that comes with that admonition—"and I will give you the crown of life."

The Church at Pergamum

Continuing north from Smyrna, Jesus next focused on Pergamum, located about two miles inland from the Aegean Sea. A large city of great wealth with many temples, a university, and a 200,000-volume library, its most important export was parchment and is the city from which the animal-skin-based writing material derived its name.

Pergamum was also notable for another fact: It is where Satan had his throne.

> To the angel of the church in Pergamos write, "These things says He who has the sharp two-edged sword: 'I know your works, and where you dwell, where Satan's throne is. And you hold fast to My name, and did not deny My faith even in the days in which Antipas was My faithful martyr, who was killed among you, where Satan dwells'" (Revelation 2:12-13).

This Antipas of whom the Lord speaks was a true man of God. But, as we saw with Smyrna, that doesn't keep you from enduring suffering. The people of the city took this man and tried to force him to denounce the Lord. When he refused, they roasted him in a bronze bull-shaped altar. Despite this persecution, there were many in the church who remained faithful to God, keeping their eyes on Him and living righteously.

Unfortunately, I had to include that caveat word *many* in the previous sentence. This is because while faith was strong in the church, so was sin and theological error. There was a large contingent of church members who were living like unbelievers—eating food offered to idols and participating in sexual sin.

> But I have a few things against you, because you have there those who hold the doctrine of Balaam, who taught Balak

to put a stumbling block before the children of Israel, to eat things sacrificed to idols, and to commit sexual immorality. Thus you also have those who hold the doctrine of the Nicolaitans, which thing I hate (Revelation 2:14-15).

There were three problems in this church: (1) the doctrine of Balaam, (2) idolatry, and (3) immorality. Many only know Balaam as the guy whose donkey had a few choice words for him (Numbers 22:27-30), but he was a very important and destructive figure for the Israelites. Balak, the king of Moab, hired Balaam the prophet to curse the wandering nation. But Balaam refused to pronounce anything over God's people that the Lord Himself had not told him to say. Yet although the prophet would not curse the Israelites, he had a Plan B to bring them down. He thought, *Maybe I can't curse them, but I can corrupt them.* He taught King Balak to put forth a stumbling block encouraging the people to eat what was sacrificed to idols and to commit sexual immorality.

Prior to Moses showing up to lead the people out of Egypt, idol worship was rampant among the Hebrews. This is why they were so quick to make a calf idol when they thought that Moses was not coming back down the mountain. They were caught up in the sins of the nation in which they resided. This is exactly what the church in Pergamum, as well as all the others, was dealing with. They were former eaters of idol-sacrificed foods and participants in sexually active worship of the gods. And, like the Hebrews, it didn't take much to coax many of them back to their old ways. All it took was bringing in some beautiful foreign women who said, "You know, I worship my idols with sex. Anyone want to worship with me?" Suddenly, the men of Israel became very devout to the foreign gods.

Jesus also condemned them for holding to the doctrine of the Nicolaitans. It is very possible that the founder of this gnostic sect was Nicholas of Antioch, a leader in the early church and one of seven specially designated by the disciples to serve (Acts 6:5-6). Two early church fathers, Irenaeus and Clement of Alexandria, point to Nicholas as the founder of this heresy, and Hippolytus, in his *Refutation of All Heresies*, said that Nicholas had "departed from sound doctrine, and was in

the habit of inculcating indifferency of both life and food." Hippolytus was referring to the gnostic belief that the flesh isn't real, so whatever
you do with your body is fair game because it doesn't really count as sin.

Sadly, this Nicolaitan belief isn't much different than what we are
finding in the church today. Abortion is becoming more accepted
within many denominations. Heterosexual and homosexual immorality are rampant. Recently, a transgender person was installed as a
bishop in the Evangelical Lutheran Church. The trend is moving far
away from Scripture. If you remain faithful to biblical morality, you
will soon find yourself the minority in the church.

As believers, we must be very careful that we don't slip into our old
ways. Often, it takes only one act to trigger former habits or begin new
ones. We must be diligent. We must be committed to righteousness.
And we must be in the Word and in prayer each and every day, because
we cannot fight the world, the flesh, and the devil on our own. But
we also know that, as John himself reminded us, "He who is in [us] is
greater than he who is in the world" (1 John 4:4).

The Church at Thyatira

When Paul, Silas, and Timothy reached Philippi on Paul's second
missionary journey, they went down to the riverside, where they met a
group of women—one of whom stood out from the others.

> Now a certain woman named Lydia heard us. She was a
> seller of purple from the city of Thyatira, who worshiped
> God. The Lord opened her heart to heed the things spo-
> ken by Paul. And when she and her household were bap-
> tized, she begged us, saying, "If you have judged me to be
> faithful to the Lord, come to my house and stay." So she
> persuaded us (Acts 16:14-15).

As one who was from Thyatira, it is no surprise that Lydia dealt
in purple cloth. Her home city was well known for the wool and dye
industries. Located southeast from Pergamum on the Lycus River, Thyatira was small but incredibly wealthy. It was also well organized, with
every artisan in the city being required to belong to a guild.

The Thyatiran church was quite active in serving others, seeming to carry on the hospitality of its first member.

> I know your works, love, service, faith, and your patience; and as for your works, the last are more than the first (Revelation 2:19).

Works, love, faith, service, and perseverance. What more could any church want from its members? Most churches today would love to hear these words of commendation from the Lord. But this church had one glaring problem—it tolerated sin.

> Nevertheless I have a few things against you, because you allow that woman Jezebel, who calls herself a prophetess, to teach and seduce My servants to commit sexual immorality and eat things sacrificed to idols. And I gave her time to repent of her sexual immorality, and she did not repent. Indeed I will cast her into a sickbed, and those who commit adultery with her into great tribulation, unless they repent of their deeds. I will kill her children with death, and all the churches shall know that I am He who searches the minds and hearts. And I will give to each one of you according to your works. Now to you I say, and to the rest in Thyatira, as many as do not have this doctrine, who have not known the depths of Satan, as they say, I will put on you no other burden (Revelation 2:20-24).

The church in Thyatira allowed an individual who called herself a prophetess to teach and influence others. Like Jezebel of old, the wife of the notorious King Ahab of Israel, this woman encouraged the worship of other gods, along with the immorality that was practiced by many of the religious cults of that time. Not only had she led many in the congregation to follow her, but they were brazenly refusing to repent of their actions. This was a moral rebellion, and the congregation was either unwilling or unable to do anything about it.

Notice what Jesus said to the church: "I gave her time to repent." Our God is long-suffering and takes no joy in discipline. He would much rather we turn to Him on our own accord after recognizing our sin and repenting. However, there is a point when God will eventually say, "That's enough. You have had time. I have given you many opportunities to change your attitudes and your actions, but you have refused. Therefore, this is what I am about to do." You don't want to get to that place in your church, and you don't want to get to that place in your life. God is holding out forgiveness to you no matter what you have done or are currently doing. Make the change now. Let Him cleanse you of your sin. Put yourself on the path of righteousness, hope, and joy.

The Church in Sardis

Jesus continued His southeast direction another 30 miles to Sardis. Once the capital of the ancient kingdom of Lydia, Sardis was one of the noblest and greatest cities of the East. Along with textile manufacturing, dyeing, and jewelry making, another of its greatest trades was human wisdom. Known as a center of philosophy and study, Thales, the great Greek philosopher, made his home in Sardis. But as often happens, along with the study of mysteries came cults and idolatrous worship. Sardis was plagued with the orgies and depravity that are part of the practices of this kind of paganism.

The church in Sardis had a great reputation. Jesus, however, knew just how undeserved their status was.

> To the angel of the church in Sardis write, "These things says He who has the seven Spirits of God and the seven stars: 'I know your works, that you have a name that you are alive, but you are dead. Be watchful, and strengthen the things which remain, that are ready to die, for I have not found your works perfect before God'" (Revelation 3:1-2).

Ouch! Like a Christmas tree that looks festive and beautiful on the outside but inside is rapidly dying, the veneer of health that covered the church at Sardis was hiding the rot inside. Jesus very easily could have christened them with the same epithet He gave to the Pharisees: "whitewashed tombs" that are beautiful outside, but full of death inside (Matthew 23:27).

This is true of many churches today. How do we know whether we are in a healthy church? Look for signs of life. Is there love in the church for one another and for those outside? Are there factions in the church? How welcoming is the church to visitors? Don't just look for activities. A robot can carry out many of the same tasks as a human, even though there is no heart inside. When you walk into your church, is all that you see a beautiful building or a likable pastor or a well-rehearsed band? Or do you see Jesus—in the warmth of the people around you, in the passion of the leaders on stage, in the commitment of the pastor to the Word of God?

While you are examining your church for life, take time to inspect yourself. Is there evidence of Christ in you? James challenged the readers of his letter, "Show me your faith without your works, and I will show you my faith by my works" (James 2:18). Are you spending time in prayer and in the Word? Are you using your spiritual gifts to bless the church not out of obligation or guilt but out of love? Are you sacrificially giving to support God's work? Is your faith evident in your life?

The Church in Philadelphia

After hearing the scathing rebuke given to the church at Sardis, the Philadelphians had to be nervous. They knew geography. They knew they were next on Jesus' list.

Philadelphia was about 30 miles southeast of Sardis. Situated at the gateway to the central plateau of what is now Turkey, the city was the center of a great vineyard district and had a thriving business in wine. No stranger to adversity, the city had to be rebuilt several times after earthquakes had caused severe damage.

When the pastor of the church read the words, "To the angel of the church in Philadelphia write," it's likely everyone stiffened. But as the words came, they relaxed and maybe even a little hoot or holler sounded out. As bad as it had been for Sardis, it was that same level of good for Philadelphia. Jesus had nothing positive to say about the former; He had nothing negative to say about the latter.

> I know your works. See, I have set before you an open door, and no one can shut it; for you have a little strength, have kept My word, and have not denied My name. Indeed I will make those of the synagogue of Satan, who say they are Jews and are not, but lie—indeed I will make them come and worship before your feet, and to know that I have loved you (Revelation 3:8-9).

As the apostle Paul moved from place to place to spread the gospel, he asked others to intercede for him so that God would open new doors of ministry:

> Continue earnestly in prayer, being vigilant in it with thanksgiving; meanwhile praying also for us, that God would open to us a door for the word, to speak the mystery of Christ, for which I am also in chains, that I may make it manifest, as I ought to speak (Colossians 4:2-4).

This was the type of doorway that was wide open for Philadelphia. Because of its location, this church was at the entrance to the kingdoms of Lydia, Mysia, and Phrygia. Any merchants traveling to and from these locations had to pass through the city. This gave the church at Philadelphia a great opportunity to reach many people across the Roman Empire with the gospel. The door for evangelism was wide open for them, and the Philadelphians were making great use of it.

This should be a prayer for all of us. "Lord, open a door of opportunity for me to love others and share the truth of Your gospel." Can you imagine what would happen throughout the world if those within the church would look for "open doors" to make Him known to those who live without hope? The majority of this earth's population have no awareness that Jesus will return one day. We know the truth, and we are called to be His heralds to a lost world.

The Church in Laodicea

Finally, Jesus reached the southernmost of the seven churches. Located along the Lycus River, Laodicea was a wealthy city that was known for its production of wool cloth. In AD 60, Laodicea was decimated by an earthquake, but its population was able to rebuild the city without needing any help from Rome. Located nine-and-a-half miles northwest of Colossae, it was the Colossians' richer, more popular sister city. Although Paul never visited the churches in either Laodicea or Colossae, he deemed both worthy of a letter from him, although only one was prompted by the Holy Spirit's inspiration, making it worthy of being made part of the Bible (Colossians 4:16).

High above Laodicea are mountains capped with sparkling white snow. Below flows a hot-water spring that rises out of the earth. As the snow melts and ice-cold water cascades down the mountain, the flow merges with the hot springs. The result? A lukewarm river of *meh*.

Unfortunately, just like dog-owners sometimes appear to take on the physical characteristics of their dogs, the Laodicean church took on the spiritual characteristic of their geography. Jesus wrote to them:

> I know your works, that you are neither cold nor hot. I could wish you were cold or hot. So then, because you are lukewarm, and neither cold nor hot, I will vomit you out of My mouth (Revelation 3:15-16).

That graphic visual clearly communicates the Lord's frustration with casual Christians. When Jesus talked about discipleship, He set the standard high: "If anyone desires to come after Me, let him deny himself, and take up his cross, and follow Me. For whoever desires to save his life will lose it, but whoever loses his life for My sake will find it" (Matthew 16:24-25).

If you are looking for a recipe for the greatest life you can live, Jesus' words to His disciples give it. The deceiver says, "Think of what you will be giving up. Think of the sacrifice. Don't you have that bucket list you want to get to?" What he doesn't tell you is that the life of discipleship is what we were created for. It is a perfect fit for us. It provides everything needed to give us joy and peace and purpose. There is no loss in denial; there is only gain. If you are trapped in the Laodicean *meh*, it's time to get hot, turn it on for Jesus, and live the life you were made for.

PART 2

A JOURNEY TO HEAVEN

(Revelation 4–5)

CHAPTER 5

HEAVEN'S OPEN DOOR

REVELATION 4

The captain ran with the members of his crew close behind. Hot on their tails was the enemy—strange-looking creatures with advanced weapons. A scream sounded from behind, and the captain turned and saw a red-shirted crewman fall to a laser blast. The moment had become critical. There was no way they would be able to escape their pursuers, especially not on the enemy's terrain. Reaching to his belt, the captain snatched his communicator. Flipping it open, he cried, "Beam us up, Scotty!"

The remaining members of the crew began to dissolve into a million little pieces before disappearing, leaving behind a confused contingent of creepy creatures. The next moment, in the USS Enterprise's transporter room, the million little pieces of people reappeared and soon coalesced in the transported crew. Captain James T. Kirk had once again narrowly escaped certain doom.

Something happens to the church between chapters 3 and 4 of Revelation. The word "church" occurs 19 times in chapters 1–3, then not again until chapter 22. Where did we go? Quite simply, we've been "beamed up." The word we use is *rapture*, and, yes, for those of you who quickly shot your hands up into the air, the rapture is a concept that is in the Bible. Paul wrote:

> The Lord Himself will descend from heaven with a shout,
> with the voice of an archangel, and with the trumpet of
> God. And the dead in Christ will rise first. Then we who
> are alive and remain shall be caught up together with them
> in the clouds to meet the Lord in the air. And thus we shall
> always be with the Lord (1 Thessalonians 4:16-17).

After the dead in Christ have been resurrected to Him, those in the church who are still alive on earth will be "caught up" with our formerly dead brothers and sisters in the Lord and we will meet our Savior in the clouds. The Greek word translated "caught up" is *harpazo*. When the New Testament was translated into Latin, the word became *rapturo*, which is where we get the word *rapture*. While it won't be Scotty at the controls, when the time comes, the church will be removed from the earth as Jesus fulfills His promise to His bride to "come again and receive you to Myself; that where I am, there you may be also" (John 14:3).

John gives us a sneak peek at what being caught up looks like when he writes,

> After these things I looked, and behold, a door standing
> open in heaven. And the first voice which I heard was like
> a trumpet speaking with me, saying, "Come up here, and
> I will show you things which must take place after this"
> (Revelation 4:1).

One moment John was standing solidly on terra firma and the next he was in the presence of God Himself. What a glorious day it will be when Jesus says to us, "Come up here, and I will show you the place that I have prepared for you."

Moving On Up

So far, we have focused on "the things which you have seen" (chapter 1) and "the things which are" (chapters 2 and 3). Now it is time to turn our attention to "the things which will take place after this."

John finds himself transported upward, where he arrives in the throne room of God. Imagine what an experience that must have been! John had heard about heaven and preached about heaven. But now he is seeing the home of God and the glorious One sitting on His throne. Only a handful of people in history have been invited to witness this most holy of locations, and with each instance, more detail is added to the description of God's throne room.

One day the prophet Isaiah entered the temple of the Lord. It wouldn't have been his first time inside, but it was certainly his most memorable.

> In the year that King Uzziah died, I saw the Lord sitting on a throne, high and lifted up, and the train of His robe filled the temple. Above it stood seraphim; each one had six wings: with two he covered his face, with two he covered his feet, and with two he flew. And one cried to another and said: "Holy, holy, holy is the LORD of hosts; the whole earth is full of His glory!" (Isaiah 6:1-3).

We don't know how many seraphs there were—maybe five, maybe 5,000, maybe 500,000. Each one was calling out praise for the holy God whose train from His robe filled the inside of Solomon's great temple. Unfortunately, the vastness of God's attire and a smoke-filled room are really the only details we get of the One on the throne and the great chamber in which He sat.

About a century later, Ezekiel filled in some of the gaps. In a vision, the prophet was transported back from exile to the temple in Jerusalem. There he saw four creatures, which, in a later chapter, he identified as cherubim, each with four faces and four wings (Ezekiel 10:14). Above them was an expanse in the sky—a split in the physical atmosphere that opened into the spiritual dimension.

> Above the firmament over their heads was the likeness of a throne, in appearance like a sapphire stone; on the likeness of the throne was a likeness with the appearance of a man high above it. Also from the appearance of His waist and upward I saw, as it were, the color of amber with the

appearance of fire all around within it; and from the appearance of His waist and downward I saw, as it were, the appearance of fire with brightness all around. Like the appearance
of a rainbow in a cloud on a rainy day, so was the appearance of the brightness all around it. This was the appearance
of the likeness of the glory of the LORD (Ezekiel 1:26-28).

Colors, fire, rainbow—do you get the feeling that Ezekiel was
grasping at words to try to describe the awesomeness of what was
before him? It was like trying to describe the feeling of love or the color
green. Some visuals are simply beyond words.

Then came Daniel, and his view took us from simple color TV to
high-def. He was a contemporary of Ezekiel but had a very different
position. Ezekiel was a prophet to the people, whereas Daniel was an
advisor to the kings. But the writings of both were directed to the Jews
with a wider future audience of all who belong to God. It is because
of this end-of-all-times focus that it was so important for both to be
reminded that God is on His throne. No matter what vision they communicate to their readers, no matter how violent and chaotic it may
sound, there is no reason for anyone to panic. The Lord is in control,
just as He has always been.

Daniel's vision took him to a courtroom and introduced him to
the Ancient of Days:

> I watched till thrones were put in place,
> and the Ancient of Days was seated;
> His garment was white as snow,
> and the hair of His head was like pure wool.
> His throne was a fiery flame,
> its wheels a burning fire;
> a fiery stream issued
> and came forth from before Him.
> A thousand thousands ministered to Him;
> ten thousand times ten thousand stood before Him.
> The court was seated,
> and the books were opened (Daniel 7:9-10).

But Daniel's image didn't end with God on His throne and His vast multitude of angelic servants. Someone else entered the scene; Someone who would one day come to earth and change everything:

> I was watching in the night visions,
> and behold, One like the Son of Man,
> coming with the clouds of heaven!
> He came to the Ancient of Days,
> and they brought Him near before Him.
> Then to Him was given dominion and glory and a kingdom,
> that all peoples, nations, and languages should serve Him.
> His dominion is an everlasting dominion,
> which shall not pass away,
> and His kingdom the one
> which shall not be destroyed (Daniel 7:13-14).

The preincarnate Jesus had entered! But what was He doing there in the throne room in the presence of the Ancient of Days? The Old Testament left that question hanging. Even in the New Testament we aren't given an answer to what the Son of Man was doing there. The apostle Paul may have witnessed "the rest of the story" when he was caught up (*harpazo/rapturo/raptured*) to heaven, but the things he saw he was not permitted to talk about (2 Corinthians 12:2-5). It wasn't until John was invited to "come up here" that we finally get a full view of that incredible throne room, the Father who is on the throne, and the Son of Man, who stepped into His rightful place in the redemptive plan for mankind.

> Immediately I was in the Spirit; and behold, a throne set in heaven, and One sat on the throne. And He who sat there was like a jasper and a sardius stone in appearance; and there was a rainbow around the throne, in appearance like an emerald (Revelation 4:2-3).

John saw heaven in brilliant colors. The One sitting on the throne had the appearance of jasper and sardius, which is a variety of carnelian.

Though jasper is often a brownish color, in 21:11, the jasper is said to be clear like crystal. Carnelian is red, like a ruby. The jasper and carnelian stones are the first and last stones on the high priest's breastplate (Exodus 28:15-20). Surrounding the throne was a rich green rainbow that John compared to a beautiful emerald.

Because John doesn't give a physical description of the One on the throne as Daniel did, there are those who say John saw Jesus, not the Father. But when we look at the next chapter, we will see Christ enter the room to take a scroll from the One on the throne. So, unless Jesus is handing something to Himself, it is best to understand that it is God the Father who is ruling from that lofty position.

The Elders in the Room

The Father was not alone in the room. He had an extensive entourage sitting with Him.

> Around the throne were twenty-four thrones, and on the thrones I saw twenty-four elders sitting, clothed in white robes; and they had crowns of gold on their heads (Revelation 4:4).

Twenty-four elders surrounded the throne. Each one with a golden *stephanos*, a victor's crown, upon his head. Of course, the question is, Who are these men? Some believe they represent the church. Others divide the twenty-four into two groups of twelve—the tribes of Israel and the apostles of the church. To add to the confusion, there are those who don't see these as people at all, but as a special group of ministering angels.

Those who say that the elders represent the church first speak of the relationship these men have to the Lamb of God. Often, they will point to Revelation 5:9, which, in the New King James Version, has the elders saying to the Lamb, "You are worthy to take the scroll, and to open its seals; for You were slain, and have redeemed us to God by Your blood." Stanley Toussaint, a former professor of New Testament at Dallas Theological Seminary, disagrees that this is evidence of a special relationship primarily because that word "us" is not in the oldest and best Greek manuscripts. Most modern translations say that the Lamb ransomed "people" or purchased "men" or something similar, making it apply more broadly to what the Savior did for the entire world as opposed to these specific elders.[2]

Second, proponents of the church view also point to the crowns. They are victors' crowns, which speaks of the church overcoming the world. Then we see them casting their well-deserved crowns at the feet of the Lamb. There are problems with both points. Taking the latter first, we see that when the elders fall down to worship the Lamb in 5:8, they have already cast their crowns down before the Father in 4:10. Also, these elders are not the only ones who wear the golden *stephanos*. The Antichrist wears one in 6:2, as possibly do the locusts that come out of the abyss in chapter 9. While crowns certainly can speak of the church, there are too many other "crowned" options to be definitive.

Additional evidence that these elders might represent the church is found in the fact they are wearing white garments. However, angels also are seen in the same attire (John 20:12). So, once again, the one doesn't necessarily equal the other. Toussaint's conclusion is to say that they are heavenly beings with authority, but that is the extent of our knowledge.[3] Because we will only assert with certainty that which we can be certain about, on this issue we will be comfortable in our uncertainty knowing that one day soon we will have an answer to the question.

Seven Lamps, One Sea, and Four Creatures

John adds another intriguing detail that was not mentioned by any of the previous prophets:

> From the throne proceeded lightnings, thunderings, and voices. Seven lamps of fire were burning before the throne, which are the seven Spirits of God. (Revelation 4:5)

Seven lamps burned, representing the seven spirits of God. In Revelation, we first met these spirits back in the letter's salutation: "John, to the seven churches which are in Asia: Grace to you and peace from Him who is and who was and who is to come, and from the seven Spirits who are before His throne, and from Jesus Christ, the faithful witness, the first-born from the dead, and the ruler over the kings of the earth" (Revelation 1:4-5). They appear again with Jesus in His shout-out to Sardis (3:1) and as eyes on the Lamb, whom we will meet in the next chapter (5:6).

The seven spirits that John describes represent the Holy Spirit. The number seven throughout this book communicates completeness or perfection, so in the throne room of God, the fullness of the Holy Spirit is in evidence. What is the sevenfold character that makes up the Holy Spirit? Isaiah lists it this way:

> The Spirit of the LORD shall rest upon Him,
> the Spirit of wisdom and understanding,
> the Spirit of counsel and might,
> the Spirit of knowledge and of the fear of the LORD
> (Isaiah 11:2).

The Father on the throne and the Holy Spirit in front! Can you imagine the sight? But John wasn't finished describing what he witnessed. Also before the throne spread a sea of glass clear as crystal, and surrounding it were four very strange-looking creatures:

> Before the throne there was a sea of glass, like crystal. And in the midst of the throne, and around the throne, were four living creatures full of eyes in front and in back. The first living creature was like a lion, the second living creature like a calf, the third living creature had a face like a man, and the fourth living creature was like a flying eagle. The four living creatures, each having six wings, were full of eyes around and within. And they do not rest day or night, saying:
>
> "Holy, holy, holy,
> Lord God Almighty,
> Who was and is and is to come!" (Revelation 4:6-8).

Before we look at the creatures, I want to take a closer look at their words. The very first focus of heaven's praise is the holiness of God. That is His character; it's who He is. He lives completely apart from sin. When Isaiah was invited to witness the throne room of God, he heard the same praise from the seraphim, who cried out, "Holy, holy, holy is the Lord of hosts; the whole earth is full of His glory!" (Isaiah 6:3). It is this absolute "otherness" to sin that embodies the perfection of God and that will always elude us this side of eternity.

The second part of the heavenly praise of Revelation comes a few verses later and is spoken by the twenty-four elders:

> You are worthy, O Lord,
> to receive glory and honor and power;
> for You created all things,
> and by Your will they exist and were created
> (Revelation 4:11).

What we see is a perfect picture of praise. It begins with who God is—holy and worthy—then moves to what He has done. He has created all things flawlessly. For just a hint at the brilliance of creation, tap on a hard surface. Now think of the molecular makeup that it took in both your hand and within that surface to make a hard tap happen. The combination of intelligence, creativity, and power necessary to go from nothing to who we are and the world we live in is mind-blowing.

Back to the creatures—what are these things that are hovering around the throne? If you have studied Old Testament prophecy at all, then there is likely something pinging in the back of your mind saying, "Hey, I think I've met these guys before." If that is happening, then listen to your ping. It is correct. Ezekiel was down by the River Chebar when he encountered the creatures described here in Revelation:

> I looked, and behold, a whirlwind was coming out of the
> north, a great cloud with raging fire engulfing itself; and
> brightness was all around it and radiating out of its midst
> like the color of amber, out of the midst of the fire. Also
> from within it came the likeness of four living creatures.

> And this was their appearance: they had the likeness of a man. Each one had four faces, and each one had four wings. Their legs were straight, and the soles of their feet were like the soles of calves' feet. They sparkled like the color of burnished bronze...As for the likeness of their faces, each had the face of a man; each of the four had the face of a lion on the right side, each of the four had the face of an ox on the left side, and each of the four had the face of an eagle (Ezekiel 1:4-7, 10).

What are these strange-looking beings? Unfortunately, as is the case for other questions that arise in the course of reading this wonderful book of Revelation, there is no "proof text" that provides an exact answer for us. If the Lord wanted us to know without a doubt, He would have made it as plain as John 3:16. Let me lay before you four possible interpretations, and then I will tell you which one I think is best.

Option one is that these creatures represent the attributes of God. The four faces are those of a lion, calf, man, and flying eagle. The lion shows majesty and strength. The calf or ox is a servant, revealing God's sacrificial nature. Recall Jesus' words when He said that He "did not come to be served, but to serve" (Matthew 20:28). The face of a man reveals intelligence and sovereignty. That of a flying eagle reveals God's sovereignty and supremacy. It all makes sense and fits into a nice, easy package. The problem with this view is that you have to read into the text quite a bit to come up with this explanation. Like we said with the crowns, just because something is similar does not mean "this equals that."

Option two is that these creatures represent the four Gospels. The lion represents the Gospel of Matthew, which was written to Jews about their King as the Lion of the tribe of Judah. The ox or calf represents the Gospel of Mark, showing Jesus as a servant doing the will of His Father. The man represents the Gospel of Luke, which was written to mankind in general and shows Jesus as the Son of Man. The eagle is seen as representative of the Gospel of John, which reveals Jesus as

God. This argument sounds persuasive, and I have used it myself when teaching the four Gospels. However, not everyone agrees about the audience each writer is addressing, nor that the nature of each Gospel can be so succinctly categorized. The other difficult question is God's motive for representing all four Gospels separately and distinctly as the creatures surround Him.

Option three sees the creatures as symbolizing the twelve tribes of Israel. When the Israelites were wandering in the desert prior to entering the Promised Land, they set up their camps in a fashion similar to what we read about the arrangement of the creatures in Revelation. Numbers 2 tells us that on the east side was the tribe of Judah, along with Simeon and Gad. The symbol of Judah was a lion. On the south was Reuben, Simeon, and Gad, under Reuben's symbol of a man. Ephraim, Manasseh, and Benjamin were to the west and Ephraim was symbolized by an ox. And, finally, to the north were Dan, Asher, and Naphtali. Not surprisingly, Dan's symbol was that of an eagle. This is a very compelling and logical connection to make, until you realize that the symbols for each tribe do not come from the Bible, but from tradition. There is no telling when and from where the tradition finds its origin.

Option four sees a special group of angels in the creatures. These angels' focus is not only on serving the Lord, but on worshipping Him as well. This fits perfectly what we know of angels and their purpose. This also fits the wider biblical context. When Isaiah saw the throne, he saw it surrounded by seraphim (Isaiah 6:2-3). When Ezekiel saw the creatures with the wheels outside the temple, he was sure they were cherubim (Ezekiel 10:20).

Based on biblical context and the activities of these creatures, the idea of them being angels makes a lot of sense. They are there to highly exalt and worship the Lord, and to be ready to serve at His beck and call. Robert L. Thomas summarizes:

> A merging of these four aspects results in the following identification of the four living beings of the Apocalypse: they are of an exalted angelic order engaged in worship,

who bear a special relationship to those angelic beings described in Ezekiel and Isaiah and whose special function in the context of the Apocalypse is the administering of divine justice in the realm of animate creation.[4]

The scene will now shift slightly. More individuals will be introduced, and the action will intensify. It reminds me a bit of the flash mob fad of a few years ago. Someone would walk into a busy public place and begin singing loudly. Not many would pay her notice initially, but then out of the crowd two or three more would join in the song—possibly incorporating choreography. Then out of the crowd more and more would join until there was a large group of performers surrounded by admirers, most with their cell phones out recording the event.

The first groups have started the song, and the praise is building. Very soon, the performance is going to hit its crescendo as a special guest makes His appearance and brings down the house.

CHAPTER 6

THE LION
AND THE LAMB

REVELATION 5

The worship service in the throne room of God was enough to shake the ceiling, assuming the room has a ceiling. Cries of "Holy" and songs of praise filled John's ears, and his eyes continued to behold in wonder the beauty of his surroundings. Then, a crisis occurred. It was a situation troubling enough to cause John to break down not in tears of joy but of sorrow.

> I saw in the right hand of Him who sat on the throne a scroll written inside and on the back, sealed with seven seals. Then I saw a strong angel proclaiming with a loud voice, "Who is worthy to open the scroll and to loose its seals?" And no one in heaven or on the earth or under the earth was able to open the scroll, or to look at it. So I wept much, because no one was found worthy to open and read the scroll, or to look at it (Revelation 5:1-4).

As the beautiful sounds of worship dissolved, the apostle turned his attention to the One sitting on the throne. There was something in His right hand—a scroll with writing on the inside and the outside. Typically, one would only find writing safely secured in the privacy of the inner-facing side. Holding it closed were seven seals. Roman wills of that day were sealed with seven seals, so it is quite possible that this was a legal document that could not be opened until the death of the person for whom it was written.

Curious as to its contents, John waited for the scroll to be read. A voice called, "Who is worthy to open the scroll and to loose its seals?" John looked around for who would step forward. But nothing happened. Stillness. Silence.

The tragedy of God's plans being brought to a screeching halt hit John hard. He began to weep at the unworthiness of the Lord's creation. Maybe he wept in guilt at his own sinful history that removed his name from the "Worthy" list. But just when it looked like his heavenly visit might be cut short due to a lack of qualified personnel, John heard one of the elders say to him, "Do not weep. Behold, the Lion of the tribe of Judah, the Root of David, has prevailed to open the scroll and to loose its seven seals" (Revelation 5:5).

Immediately, John's mood would have changed. He recognized those messianic titles that had been so popular and so powerful from the time of his youth. First, there is the Lion of the tribe of Judah. When the patriarch Jacob was on his deathbed, he gathered his sons around him. One by one, he pronounced a blessing upon each. When Judah approached his father, Jacob said,

> Judah, you are he whom your brothers shall praise;
> your hand shall be on the neck of your enemies;
> your father's children shall bow down before you.
> Judah is a lion's whelp;
> from the prey, my son, you have gone up.
> He bows down, he lies down as a lion;
> and as a lion, who shall rouse him?
> The scepter shall not depart from Judah,
> nor a lawgiver from between his feet,
> until Shiloh comes;
> and to Him shall be the obedience of the people.

Binding his donkey to the vine,
and his donkey's colt to the choice vine,
he washed his garments in wine,
and his clothes in the blood of grapes.
His eyes are darker than wine,
and his teeth whiter than milk (Genesis 49:8-12).

Judah is the royal tribe. While Israel's first king came from the tribe of Benjamin, David's line of kingship came from Judah. This was the permanent line, as evidenced by Jacob's promise that "the scepter shall not depart from Judah." This is why the crowds were so excited that day when Jesus rode into Jerusalem on the colt of a donkey. They hailed him as their king, their lion. But when Jesus didn't bare His teeth and overthrow the hated Romans, the people quickly became disillusioned. That is why cries of "Hosanna" so soon turned to "Crucify Him!" The people failed to realize that the coming of the Lion would have to wait until His return. Jesus' first time here was focused on a very different role.

The second messianic appellation pronounced by the elder was the Root of David. This title narrowed Jesus' lineage from tribe to family. He wasn't just a Jew from the tribe of Judah; He was part of the royal line. This title had Messiah written all over it from the time that Isaiah first pronounced it: "There shall come forth a Rod from the stem of Jesse, and a Branch shall grow out of his roots" (Isaiah 11:1). Jesse was the father of King David. It is this offspring that Isaiah spoke of upon whom the Holy Spirit would rest and who would judge with righteousness and justice.

Lion of Judah, Root of David—John knew these were titles for the Messiah. So when he followed the elder's outstretched finger, he was ready to see his Savior, Lord, Friend in all His deserved glory. But the figure his eyes saw was something quite different.

The Worthy Lamb

Like the Jews at the triumphal entry, John had let his expectations focus on the Warrior King. Instead, he saw the Sacrificial Lamb.

> I looked, and behold, in the midst of the throne and of the
> four living creatures, and in the midst of the elders, stood
> a Lamb as though it had been slain, having seven horns
> and seven eyes, which are the seven Spirits of God sent out
> into all the earth. Then He came and took the scroll out
> of the right hand of Him who sat on the throne (Revela-
> tion 5:6-7).

A Lamb—one of the most helpless and docile of creatures. It provides wool for a while until the time comes for its slaughter. Jesus,
God Himself, "made Himself of no reputation, taking the form of a
bondservant, and coming in the likeness of men. And being found in
appearance as a man, He humbled Himself and became obedient to
the point of death, even the death of the cross" (Philippians 2:7-8). The
all-powerful God made Himself powerless. The sovereign Lord made
Himself subservient. He provided wisdom and teaching for a while
until the time came for His slaughter. Just like the lamb's flesh provides
for physical life, Jesus' flesh and His blood provide "eternal life, and
[He] will raise him up at the last day" (John 6:54).

John would have recognized Jesus in this role. He had seen the Savior on the cross—torn, battered, bloody. Jesus entered the room as the
redemptive sacrifice. The slain Lamb was a reminder to everyone of the
justice of what was about to take place. Jesus had suffered and died on
the cross so that every person who was about to experience the coming
wrath would have an opportunity for redemption. But they rejected
the free gift that cost the Savior so much and turned their backs on
God's mercy. Whatever they were about to face, it would be based on
their own choice.

Another reason for Jesus coming as the Suffering Servant and the
Sufficient Sacrifice was to visually show the full character of God, the
all-powerful Lord on the throne who became one of us, as stated in Philippians 2:7-8. Perfect sovereignty and perfect humility. The One who
rightfully accepts praise and honor and who willingly gave Himself
over to slaughter. The God who is love putting His love on full display.

The Lamb was standing at the throne surrounded by the four living creatures and the elders. There were some unusual physical properties to the Lamb—seven horns, which represent His complete power, and seven eyes, which are the seven spirits of God, or the Holy Spirit, whom we spoke of earlier. Reaching toward the One who sits on the throne, the Lamb removed the scroll from His hand.

The place erupted!

The wondrousness of seeing the Son who has the Holy Spirit resting on Him receiving the scroll from the hand of the Father dropped creatures and elders alike to the ground. The triune God united in person and purpose right before their eyes. Spontaneously, worship burst forth. The creatures and elders each held "golden bowls full of incense, which are the prayers of the saints" (Revelation 5:8). Who are these saints whose prayers offer such a pleasing aroma to the Creator?

Stanley Toussaint names them as believers from the present church age who are praying for God's kingdom to come. In the Lord's Prayer, our request is that "Your kingdom come. Your will be done on earth as it is in heaven" (Matthew 6:10). In the original Greek language, this request is more of a command. It is an emphatic appeal for God to "bring Your kingdom to the earth!"[5] Toussaint sees these prayers as the voices from two millennia of church-age Christians calling for the events that the Lamb is about to set in motion.

A second option is that these are the prayers of the saints who appear in Revelation 7. These saints had been martyred by the Antichrist. Even though the seals were still on the scroll, the persecution against these tribulation saints had already begun. Again, we cannot be completely certain of either option.

In a great balancing feat, the creatures and elders held the bowls of incense in one hand and a harp in the other. With a divinely given skill, they began to pluck the strings. Then the voices joined together in a melody that is part awestruck hymn and part love song:

> You are worthy to take the scroll,
> and to open its seals;
> for You were slain,
> and have redeemed us to God by Your blood

> out of every tribe and tongue and people and nation,
> and have made us kings and priests to our God;
> and we shall reign on the earth (Revelation 5:9-10).

This chorus of worship begins to expand and grow. Close your eyes and imagine that you are sitting in the David Geffen Hall in New York City's Lincoln Center. The warm-up for the New York Philharmonic Orchestra has just finished and the maestro has walked out. He taps his music stand with his baton, then raises his hands. All instruments ascend into position.

Pointing to the strings, he gently moves his hands. The violins begin a soft, sweet melody. Soon, the violas and cellos enter the musical score, along with the string bass. As the symphony picks up in tempo and volume, he looks to the woodwinds. Flutes sing in, followed by oboes, clarinets, saxophones, and the reedy depth of the bassoons. The melody is in full swing, and the conductor flings an arm toward the brass. Trumpets pierce the fabric of the song, surrounded by the alto range of the flugelhorns and trombones, the deeper baritones, and the low bass of the tubas. By this time, the conductor's hair is bouncing and his arms are flailing as the orchestra crescendos toward the score's conclusion. Finally, both hands reach for the percussion. The tympani echo as the cymbals crash, culminating in a heart-quivering *bong* of mallet to gong.

The dynamic worship service John found himself in similarly began reservedly but quickly escalated. What began with the creatures and elders expanded to "many angels," which became "ten thousand times ten thousand, and thousands of thousands" (verse 11). The song they sang was pure love and praise for the Lamb:

> Worthy is the Lamb who was slain
> to receive power and riches and wisdom,
> and strength and honor and glory and blessing! (verse 12).

The worshippers praised the Lord for His worthiness. This is the very definition of worship. The word *worship* comes from Old English *weorþ* ("worthy") and *scipe* ("ship"). When we worship our Savior, we are acknowledging that He is the One who was, is, and always will be worthy of our adoration and allegiance.

This led to the ultimate crescendo that included "every creature which is in heaven and on the earth and under the earth and such as are in the sea, and all that are in them" (verse 13). There is not one person, mammal, bird, reptile, fish, or insect that did not participate in this next chorus. I admit that I do not know what this will look like. Will every person be singing and every dog barking and every bird tweeting and every fish glugging and every insect buzzing the following words? Will the supernatural fact of their creation and very existence cry out this refrain? Will they suddenly all become like Balaam's donkey and sing with the voices of humans? I have no idea, but I can't wait to hear it.

What is it that this creation-wide choir sang?

> Blessing and honor and glory and power
> be to Him who sits on the throne,
> and to the Lamb, forever and ever! (verse 13).

When the gong sounded and the symphony came to rest, the creatures closed the celebration with a fitting "Amen!" The elders, though, weren't ready to let go of the blessed time. They dropped back down to the ground and "worshiped Him who lives forever and ever" (verse 14).

A Sad Goodbye

It's hard to leave Revelation 4 and 5. They are the highlight of the book. A holy, heavenly worship service like none we've ever experienced before. It's also difficult to depart because of what is ahead. The scroll is in the hands of the Lamb. The seals are about to be opened. God's hammer of justice and wrath is about to fall. While it is true that we who are part of the church will not experience any of what we are about to read, it is still difficult to picture those whom we love—and even those we may not love quite as much—going through what will be unleashed by the opening of the seals and the sounding of the trumpets and the pouring of the bowls.

Before we move on, let's take a moment to remind ourselves of what John has experienced to this point. In chapter 1, the "disciple whom Jesus loved" received an incredible surprise. A voice called to him, and he turned to find his glorious Savior and dear Friend walking among the seven churches, holding the seven pastors or leaders in His hand. For each of those churches of Asia, He had a special message—usually both good news and bad news, but not always.

Having completed the "what was" and "what is" portions of the letter, John was now transported into the throne room of God to begin to record "what will be." Surrounding the throne where the Lord sat was beauty and music and praise and adoration like nothing that can be experienced this side of eternity. Just when it seemed the worship couldn't get any better, the Guest of Honor arrived—the Lion of Judah who is also the Lamb that was slain. He alone, it was discovered, was worthy to open the seven-sealed scroll. That truth not only unleashed a torrent of praise in heaven, but also from every creature on earth.

I hope you enjoyed the celebration, because now it's all going to get very dark very fast.

THE JUDGMENTS OF THE LAMB

(Revelation 6–18)

CHAPTER 7

THE LAMB
OPENS THE SEALS

REVELATION 6

Try to think back to where you were when you first heard of COVID-19. Can you remember what you were doing when the news of this virus reached you? If you can't, don't worry. I would suspect you are in the majority. COVID didn't hit us like 9/11 or the start of the Yom Kippur War or the assassination of President John F. Kennedy. The virus was stealthier and more gradual. But look at what it has done to this world.

Since the beginning of 2020, the people of this planet have gone COVID-crazy. You listen to the words of some people and watch their actions, and it is easy to think that the virus attacks the brain as much as it strikes the body. And all this is for one virus! Can you imagine what this world is going to look like when the Lamb begins opening the seals of the scroll and the plagues and pestilences begin multiplying? Picture your country with six or seven viruses more deadly than COVID, then add to that food shortages, economic collapse, and natural disasters on a scale never before seen since the flood.

That is why it is so difficult to write these next chapters. This is not just theoretical. Real people will be experiencing these real events, and many of them may be people who we are close to, who we love, who we gave birth to, or who gave birth to us. Billions of people will die, and billions of others will survive to endure the righteous judgment of God. As you read these next chapters, let them serve as a motivation to speak to those around you of the hope that is in Christ. If they've rejected you before, try again. Any persecution or alienation you receive is well worthwhile if the result is that one of your loved ones is spared from the seven years of God's wrath.

A Mood Change

The attitude of this letter changes as we enter the sixth chapter. We have just experienced an amazing and uplifting worship experience—praise, reverence, and shouts of "Worthy is the Lamb." But now the Lamb has taken the scroll from the hand of the One sitting on the throne and His thumb is ready to break the first seal.

There are three series of seven judgments that we will encounter in chapters 6, 8–9, and 16—the seal judgments, the trumpet judgments, and the bowl judgments. They are all linked together as the seventh seal and the seventh trumpet each open the next series. During the tribulation, just when the world thinks that maybe the worst is over, the next series of judgments will come.

Each successive set of judgments will be worse and more devastating than its predecessor. The seal judgments will kill one-third of the world's population. The trumpets will take another one-third and will devastate the earth. Finally, the bowls will come, which John describes as "the seven last plagues, for in them the wrath of God is complete" (15:1). They will bring unimaginable sores and blood and darkness and misery until a voice mercifully calls out from heaven, "It is done!" (16:17).

One more time before the Lamb breaks the first seal, let me implore you to get yourself right with God! If you don't know Jesus as your personal Savior, these judgments will come upon you. And remember, these punishments will last for only seven years. After that comes a day when all those who have rejected the grace and mercy of Christ will be judged for their rebellion and sentenced to an eternity separated from God and all that is good. That final state will make what we are about to read seem like child's play.

The Horsemen Cometh

All eyes were on the Lamb. He stood before all no longer as the prisoner under the false accusations of the Jewish Sanhedrin or the violent hand of the Roman government. This is the Lamb restored to His proper place with all authority because of His character, His position, and His person. He alone is worthy to open the seals on the scroll. And that is what He proceeded to do:

> Now I saw when the Lamb opened one of the seals; and I heard one of the four living creatures saying with a voice like thunder, "Come and see" (Revelation 6:1).

What John saw at the creature's behest was the first of a quartet of personages who have become legendary. The four horsemen of the apocalypse have come to represent strength, terror, and impending doom, and can be seen in everything from literature and comic books to television shows and movies, and even an infamous foursome who wreaked havoc from Notre Dame's football backfield in the 1920s. This fictionalization has allowed the world to relegate these riders to tall-tale status. But when they gallop forth from heaven, all will know that they are very real.

This is not the first time that we see horsemen of this type. In Zechariah 1, the prophet sees "a man riding on a red horse, and it stood among the myrtle trees in the hollow; and behind him were horses: red, sorrel, and white" (verse 8). When he asked what the horsemen were, he was told that they were ones who wandered to and fro throughout the earth. Later, in chapter 6, we see four chariots, and "with the first chariot were red horses, with the second chariot black horses, with the third chariot white horses, and with the fourth chariot dappled horses—strong steeds" (verses 2-3). Like the earlier horsemen, these chariots pulled by colored horses roamed throughout the earth.

Now, when riders show up again, their job has changed. Rather than scouting the earth so that they can bring a report back to the throne, they are being sent out from the throne to bring judgment to the earth. Are these the same horsemen Zechariah saw? It is unlikely, particularly because of the identity of the one on the white horse.

> I looked, and behold, a white horse. He who sat on it had a bow; and a crown was given to him, and he went out con-quering and to conquer (Revelation 6:2).

Before the rider of the white horse left heaven, he was given a *stephanos*. Remember, this is the victor's crown, not the crown of a king. He goes out to conquer and becomes victorious over much of the world. Who is this rider? It is the Antichrist. "But, Amir, what is the Antichrist doing in heaven?" Good question. He's not in heaven. This rider is a representation of the Antichrist and his campaign of deception and intrigue that earns him global loyalty and devotion, including that of the Jews.

To say that the rider is a representation of the Antichrist is very different than the allegorizing that amillennialists use to water down the book of Revelation. The amillennial camp says that what you are reading in the letter is actually symbolic and figurative language that relates to spiritual events that are currently taking place in the kingdom of God. The judgments you read about are not to be taken literally. You have to look deeper, between the lines and behind the words to find out what John really meant when he wrote them. For the amillennialist, the "what will be" portion of Revelation doesn't really begin until chapter 20.

But Revelation cannot be allegorized. It is an account given by God to John of what He has planned for His future judgment on this world. It must be interpreted using a literal method. Yes, there are times when symbolism appears in Revelation, but they are few and the context helps to make those instances clear. So when I say the rider on the white horse represents the Antichrist, I am saying it in the same way that the rider on the pale horse represents death. Although he is given the name

Death, he is not death itself. Death is not a person who walks around in a shroud carrying a sickle. *Death* is simply a word that we use to describe the moment that a life ends. The four horsemen are not going out as the judgments themselves, but as the ones representing the factual, tragic times that are about to befall the world.

> When He opened the second seal, I heard the second living creature saying, "Come and see." Another horse, fiery red, went out. And it was granted to the one who sat on it to take peace from the earth, and that people should kill one another; and there was given to him a great sword (Revelation 6:3-4).

There are two Greek words for sword. One is *rhomphaia* and describes a large sword used in battle. This is the kind of weapon that protrudes from the mouth of Jesus as He comes to strike down the nations (19:15). The second word is *machaira*, which describes a short sword or dagger. Rather than being used in major battles, it was employed in close-contact violence and assassinations. The short sword is what the rider of the red horse is carrying. This is why the translation of the Greek adjective *megas* as "great" makes more sense than the "large" or "huge" that appears in a number of Bible versions. The weapon this horseman wielded was great in its power; it was not a huge short sword.

When the rider of the red horse comes, he will not be ushering in World War III. Instead, he will bring division and subterfuge and civil unrest. The phrase "people should kill one another" has a very personal, one-on-one meaning to it. Peace will disappear—not just between nations, but within cities and neighborhoods and homes.

> When He opened the third seal, I heard the third living creature say, "Come and see." So I looked, and behold, a black horse, and he who sat on it had a pair of scales in his hand. And I heard a voice in the midst of the four living creatures saying, "A quart of wheat for a denarius, and three quarts of barley for a denarius; and do not harm the oil and the wine" (Revelation 6:5-6).

Many of us experienced shortages in our local grocery stores when COVID hit. Big-box stores had lines snaking through the whole building as people tried to purchase basic staples and paper goods. When the black rider comes, the world's population will be longing for the days when they could find anything on the shelves.

The third horseman will bring with him hunger and famine. World currencies will crash, and inflation will skyrocket. A quart of wheat is enough for one person to sustain life, and a denarius is one day's wage. How will a person feed their family if they are earning enough money to feed only one mouth? And that is for those who are lucky enough to still have jobs. For those thinking, *Well, I'll just skip the wheat and get the barley at the three-for-one bargain price,* understand that it takes three quarts of barley to provide the same nourishment as one quart of wheat. The oil and wine may remain unharmed, but who will have any money left over to buy them?

When the supply lines for food go down, chaos will ensue. Other than a small handful of people, the world's population will not be prepared to provide for itself. First will come protests, then looting, then violent theft of basic supplies. Anarchy will prevail, and government leaders will be utterly without solutions.

> When He opened the fourth seal, I heard the voice of the fourth living creature saying, "Come and see." So I looked, and behold, a pale horse. And the name of him who sat on it was Death, and Hades followed with him. And power was given to them over a fourth of the earth, to kill with sword, with hunger, with death, and by the beasts of the earth (Revelation 6:7-8).

As the next riders came forward, a shiver must have crept up John's spine. Why two riders instead of one? Each has a part in the departure of a person from this earth. Death claims the body, while Hades takes the soul. As they ride a circuit around the world, they will take with them a fourth of the people on the earth. Think of that. The current global population is just about eight billion. That means that during the period of the seal judgments, two billion people are going to die. COVID deaths are in the millions, and look at what that has done to our world. Picture it—for every one person that has died in this pandemic, another 500–1,000 will die just during the seal judgments.

What will bring about this massive loss of life? Four tactics are given to this deadly pair. Violence, whether due to warfare, civil unrest, or crime, will bring about a bloody slaughter. Famine and hunger will lead to millions dying of starvation. This scarcity will not be limited to third-world countries. Lack will replace the plenty of first-world nations, and highly populated cities will experience some of the worst deprivation when stores stop being replenished.

The next is translated in the New King James Version as "death." But to say that people will die by means of death is like saying that a bird will fly by means of flight. The Greek word here is *thanatos*, which normally does mean "death." However, it can also mean "pestilence," which, when we look at the context, makes the most sense. As we talked about earlier, as tragic as COVID has been for so many people, it is nothing compared to what is coming.

For me, the final lethal foe that the world will face is the most frightening. Because of the lack of food due to environmental havoc to come, the predators of the animal kingdom will have to find alternative sources of food. They will find their new prey massed together in the cities or wandering the countryside in search of provisions. Packs of hungry dogs will roam neighborhoods looking for quarry. "Lions and tigers and bears" will not just be a cute little ditty. It will be a warning parents will give to their children before they exit the house.

With all this happening, you might think that people would be turning to God en masse. But the opposite is true. Rather than turn to God, most will turn against God's people.

Death of the Just vs. the Justice of Death

When the fifth seal is lifted from the scroll, the lid comes off a dirty secret of the tribulation. While God has been bringing His just punishment upon the wicked, the Antichrist has been prosecuting his unjust persecution upon the righteous.

> When He opened the fifth seal, I saw under the altar the
> souls of those who had been slain for the word of God and
> for the testimony which they held. And they cried with
> a loud voice, saying, "How long, O Lord, holy and true,
> until You judge and avenge our blood on those who dwell
> on the earth?" Then a white robe was given to each of them;
> and it was said to them that they should rest a little while
> longer, until both the number of their fellow servants and
> their brethren, who would be killed as they were, was com-
> pleted (Revelation 6:9-11).

When it comes to our salvation, there are two deadlines approaching. One is death. That deadline is final. If you have not received Jesus
as your Savior and Lord by the time you die, it will be too late. There
are no second chances.

The second deadline is the rapture. If you have not given your life to
Christ by the time Jesus removes His church from the earth, you will be
left behind. However, while there will be no second chance for the rapture, there will be a second chance at salvation. When true Christians
are removed from the world, some of those who remain will recall the
words that they learned in church as children or that they heard from
loved ones about Jesus and His forgiveness. Some of them will recognize the error of their rebellion and repent of their sins. God, in His
grace and mercy, will accept them into His family based on their trust
in His Son, Jesus Christ.

Now, however, these new Christians will find themselves in the
worst of all physical situations. Not only will they be suffering the
violence, deprivations, and disasters of the tribulation, but they will
be hunted and executed for their faith. Trust me, you do not want to
put off giving your life to Christ now, thinking, *Well, if I miss the rapture, I can just accept Christ during the tribulation.* Remember, the fifth
seal reveals a crowd of martyrs in heaven. No one becomes a martyr by
dying of old age.

This group of tribulation saints are described as being "under the
altar." Why are they stashed away there? First, you have to put them

someplace. I'm not meaning to be snarky. But these new believers are not part of the church. That ship has already sailed. Jesus came and took His bride away while these men and women were still in their sins. Therefore, there is no place that Jesus has gone to prepare for them like the one He told the disciples about in the upper room (John 14:1-4). They are not invited to the bema seat judgment, nor are they one of the principles in the upcoming wedding. While they are still loved by God and accepted as part of His family, they have escaped, as Job put it, "by the skin of [their] teeth" (Job 19:20).

Second, while under the altar may appear to be a strange place to tuck them away, I think it makes a lot of sense. In both the earthly tabernacle and the temple, there were two altars. There was the bronze altar, which was the place where the blood was shed and the sacrifices were made. A second altar was inside the Holy Place near the Holy of Holies. This was the golden altar of incense, the smoke of which was a wonderful aroma before the Lord. These martyred saints have already shed their blood for their testimony and walk with Christ. Now they stand under the altar of incense crying out their prayers, which were, as we already saw in 5:8, an offering up to the throne of God.

The content of their prayers was a plea for justice against those who had murdered them for their faith. God's answer is as wonderful as it is typical of His character. He didn't say, "I'm holding off my final judgment because I must make the wicked suffer longer." Instead, He said, "I'm delaying the end because I'm still waiting for more sinners to turn to Me." Yes, He knew what that would mean for the new converts—a violent martyr's death. But God always sees the big picture. The death may be harsh, but the ensuing life would be beautiful.

The opening of the sixth seal pulled triggers both under the earth and over the earth:

> I looked when He opened the sixth seal, and behold, there was a great earthquake; and the sun became black as sackcloth of hair, and the moon became like blood. And the stars of heaven fell to the earth, as a fig tree drops its late figs when it is shaken by a mighty wind. Then the sky receded

as a scroll when it is rolled up, and every mountain and island was moved out of its place (Revelation 6:12-14).

A massive earthquake will shake the entire world. If you have ever experienced an earthquake, you know that it feels "great" no matter the number on the Richter scale. This one will be notable both for its reach and its intensity. Buildings will collapse and landslides will occur. Many of those who live near oceans will be washed away by the resultant tsunamis. As destructive as this sixth seal earthquake will be, there will be at least three more earthquakes during the tribulation that will be greater yet (8:5; 11:13; 16:18-19).

It's not just the earth that will be affected. The sun will be darkened and the moon reddened like blood. This takes us back to the prophecies of the prophet Joel:

> The sun shall be turned into darkness,
>   and the moon into blood,
> before the coming of the great and awesome day
>   of the Lord (Joel 2:31).

Later, he pairs these cosmic events with a shaking of the earth:

> Multitudes, multitudes in the valley of decision!
> For the day of the Lord is near in the valley of decision.
> The sun and moon will grow dark,
>   and the stars will diminish their brightness.
> The Lord also will roar from Zion,
>   and utter His voice from Jerusalem;
> the heavens and earth will shake;
> but the Lord will be a shelter for His people,
>   and the strength of the children of Israel (Joel 3:14-16).

This describes a massive shaking of the ground. Then the earth will be pummeled by meteors. It will be like being in a catastrophe sandwich, with devastation coming from below and above. It's no wonder that the sun and moon will be obscured by the smoke of all the resulting fires. Add to that the volcanic eruptions that will blast ash up into the atmosphere, further darkening the sun and the moon and affecting weather patterns.

How will the people on earth react to this devastation? As is so often the case, rather than running to God, they will run away from Him.

> The kings of the earth, the great men, the rich men, the commanders, the mighty men, every slave and every free man, hid themselves in the caves and in the rocks of the mountains, and said to the mountains and rocks, "Fall on us and hide us from the face of Him who sits on the throne and from the wrath of the Lamb! For the great day of His wrath has come, and who is able to stand?" (Revelation 6:15-17).

Many people will recognize the cause of the calamity. They will understand that they are experiencing physical judgment because of their spiritual sin. But rather than saying, "God, we have sinned—forgive us! We repent and will follow You!" they will try to hide from the all-seeing, all-knowing, all-powerful Judge. What would have happened if instead, they had thrown themselves on the mercy of God? Remember what God said to the martyrs. During the tribulation, the Lord will delay final judgment until the full number of converts is complete. For those alive on earth during this time, salvation will be only an arm's length away. But they will choose the darkness of the caves rather than the light of Christ.

CHAPTER 8

THE FIRST INTERLUDE

REVELATION 7

A question was posed at the end of Revelation 6: "Who is able to stand?" John is about to give an answer.

This chapter is the first of three interludes in the book of Revelation (7:1-17; 10:1–11:13; 12:1–14:20). It interrupts the flow of the seal judgments, but not necessarily the flow of the book. During the judgments, just as even greater devastation is about to occur, God calls a time-out.

> After these things I saw four angels standing at the four corners of the earth, holding the four winds of the earth, that the wind should not blow on the earth, on the sea, or on any tree. Then I saw another angel ascending from the east, having the seal of the living God. And he cried with a loud voice to the four angels to whom it was granted to harm the earth and the sea, saying, "Do not harm the earth, the sea, or the trees till we have sealed the servants of our God on their foreheads" (Revelation 7:1-3).

Four angels were poised to unleash the next blow to the earth. "The four corners of the earth" is not a biblical claim to the earth being flat. It is simply an ancient idiom that refers to every part of the globe. Before these angels were sent out to do their business, another angel cried out, "Wait! There's something that has to be done first!" It is here we are introduced to the first answer to the question, "Who is able to stand?"

144,000 Jewish Evangelists

Second to the four horsemen in the category of "Revelation Groups Most Talked About and Least Understood" are the 144,000 Jews who are sealed for service to God. Rather than seeing this mass of young Israeli men, John hears about them:

> And I heard the number of those who were sealed. One hundred and forty-four thousand of all the tribes of the children of Israel were sealed:
>
> of the tribe of Judah twelve thousand were sealed;
> of the tribe of Reuben twelve thousand were sealed;
> of the tribe of Gad twelve thousand were sealed;
> of the tribe of Asher twelve thousand were sealed;
> of the tribe of Naphtali twelve thousand were sealed;
> of the tribe of Manasseh twelve thousand were sealed;
> of the tribe of Simeon twelve thousand were sealed;
> of the tribe of Levi twelve thousand were sealed;
> of the tribe of Issachar twelve thousand were sealed;
> of the tribe of Zebulun twelve thousand were sealed;
> of the tribe of Joseph twelve thousand were sealed;
> of the tribe of Benjamin twelve thousand were sealed
> (Revelation 7:4-8).

Despite God's righteous judgments upon mankind, the Lord continues to give people the opportunity to return to Him. This is a demonstration of both God's justice and His love. He is just to hold humanity accountable for their sinful actions. And yet, He remains merciful and loving enough to provide 144,000 Jewish evangelists to take the message of salvation to the world. Even while pouring out His wrath, God continues to draw people to Himself.

When you think of it, what more could God have done to bring His creation into a personal relationship with Him? In the Old Testament, God introduced the way into His presence through the furniture in the tabernacle and then the temple, beginning with the bronze altar, where animals were sacrificed to cover the sins of the owner. And then He sent His one and only Son to the cross to pay the price of sin on our behalf.

Furthermore, God raised up prophets, apostles, evangelists, and Bible teachers to share the message of salvation and to instruct humanity in proper living. But the world wanted nothing to do with God. Mankind was captured by the pleasures of sin and has done everything possible to reject God. And so, God must deal with humanity's depravity. However, He continues to offer salvation throughout the entire tribulation by sealing this group of Jewish men to carry the message of the gospel to the world.

These 144,000 Jewish evangelists will be sealed with God's mark of protection. Just as no one could harm the Lord Jesus Christ until "His time," so no one will be able to harm these missionaries.

Although the passage specifically names the twelve tribes of Israel, there are some interpreters who believe these 144,000 individuals make up the church. This is what happens when you spiritualize a passage to make it fit your doctrinal beliefs rather than reading it at face value. What is the square doctrine these interpreters are trying to fit into the round hole of this passage? It is their Replacement Theology, which says that the church has taken Israel's place in God's plans. The only way to make this Reformed doctrine fit into Scripture, especially when it comes to prophecy, is to allegorize and spiritualize many parts of the Bible. A literal reading of the Word of God simply will not allow for this understanding.

Think of the ramifications if God has replaced Israel with the church. First, God's everlasting covenant with Abraham is no longer everlasting. If God's covenant with Abraham is no longer everlasting, then His promise of everlasting life for believers cannot be trusted to be everlasting.

In addition, if God has removed His hand from Israel, then how can we explain the fulfillment of so many Israel-oriented prophecies in

Scripture? Ezekiel prophesied that God would prepare the land for Israel's return (Ezekiel 34:26; 36:8-9). Before the Jews began their return in the late nineteenth and early twentieth centuries, the whole area was a wasteland filled with scrub and malarial swamps. Even when Israel became a nation in 1948, only 14 percent of the land was capable of growing produce.[6] Today, it is agriculturally self-sufficient and Israel is a great exporter of food.

Through the same prophet, the Lord promised to return the Jews to their land from all the nations into which He had scattered them (Ezekiel 34:13-16; 36:24; 37:12-14, 21). Since Israel's independence, the population of the nation has grown from 806,000 to 9,246,000 in 2020.[7]

God said that He would prosper Israel when the Jews were in their own land (Ezekiel 36:11-12). Today, Israel is an established global power and is the envy of the Middle East.

In Isaiah 66:8, God promised that He would create the nation of Israel in one day. That day was May 14, 1948, when the country declared its independence. He also has been protecting Israel from its enemies through all the wars and attacks since.

It's not just Old Testament promises that affirm a continued Israel. The term *Israel* is used seventy times in the New Testament and always refers to ethnic Israel. In Galatians 6:16, Paul uses the phrase "Israel of God" to refer to those Jews who have placed their faith in Jesus Christ and have not depended on circumcision to get them to heaven. To apply that phrase to the church is inconsistent with the way "Israel" is used throughout the New Testament.

John F. Walvoord strongly disagrees with the idea that the church has replaced Israel. He wrote:

> The fact that the twelve tribes of Israel are singled out for special reference in the tribulation time is another evidence that the term "Israel" as used in the Bible is invariably a reference to the descendants of Jacob who was first given the name Israel. Galatians 6:16 is no exception. The prevalent idea that the church is the true Israel is not sustained by any explicit reference in the Bible, and the word Israel is never

used of Gentiles and refers only to those who are racially descendants of Israel or Jacob.[8]

Likewise, Robert L. Thomas wrote the following:

> The term Israēl must be referred to the physical descendants of Abraham, Isaac, and Jacob. This is the natural understanding and the word's normal usage in the NT as well as the OT. This accounts for the detailed division of the people of God into twelve families answering individually to the twelve tribes of Israel in vv. 5-8, and is the explanation favored by the earliest Christian tradition. A tie-in of the term to the church through the twelve apostles (cf. Matt. 19:28) is improbable because Rev. 21:12, 14 makes a clear distinction between the two groups of twelve. It is also in harmony with Paul's clear distinction between two groups of God's people, Israel and the church, as developed in Romans 9–11.[9]

Will there really be 144,000 of these young men? There are those who want to put an "-ish" at the end of the number. They say that it just means a whole lot of guys. In fact, one Reformed commentator wrote:

> The number is too exact and artificial to suppose that it is literal. It is inconceivable that exactly the same number—precisely twelve thousand—should be selected from each tribe of the children of Israel. If literal, it is necessary to suppose that this refers to the twelve tribes of the children of Israel. But on every supposition this is absurd. Ten of their tribes had been long before carried away, and the distinction of the tribes was lost, no more to be recovered, and the Hebrew people never have been, since the time of John, in circumstances to which the description here could be applicable.[10]

I have to chuckle when I read this. This commentator used the word *inconceivable* when talking about the possibility of there being exactly 144,000. It is as if he were saying, "Sure, God is sovereign and all-powerful and has created all things from nothing and has sustained and maintained the universe ever since and has provided a perfect plan of salvation for all mankind. But gathering exactly 12,000 Jews from each tribe? Inconceivable!"

The commentator goes on to say that it is absurd to think that these are even real Jews being discussed because the Jews are lost—scattered to the four winds. It would be impossible to think of that many Jews gathering together, he says. I will give the commentator a little slack on this point. He wrote his Reformed commentary in the mid-nineteenth century. Therefore, he was not around to see the way that God miraculously gathered His people back from every corner of the globe as He promised He would in Ezekiel 36–37. The commentator did not hear of the creation of Israel in one day in 1948. He was gone before the country's population grew to nine million, seven million of whom are Jews all gathered once again in the Promised Land. For God to fulfill His promise to the Jews seemed impossible to him, so he allegorized the promise. Then God made Israel a nation again.

A close look at the list of tribes has caused some to wonder why both Joseph and his son Manasseh are mentioned, but Joseph's other son Ephraim is left out. And where is the tribe of Dan? As you look through Scripture, you will discover several tribal listings of Israel that do not all jibe with one another (Genesis 35; 1 Chronicles 4–7; Ezekiel 48; Revelation 7). It's possible that Ephraim was left out because it was the most idolatrous of all the tribes or because its name became interchangeable for the northern kingdom during the period of the divided monarchy. However, the tribe of Ephraim is not fully excluded because they would have been included under the heading of Joseph.

Charles C. Ryrie takes the same "not to worry" stance when it comes to the tribe of Dan. He explains,

> Whatever the reason for Dan's omission from the list of tribes from which the 144,000 elect will come, this is not the end of God's dealings with that tribe. The Danites will receive a portion of the land during the millennial

kingdom. Indeed, in Ezekiel 48:1 Dan heads the list of the tribes as the inheritance is divided to them (cf. also 48:32). So the exclusion here is not permanent, for the gifts and calling of God with regard to His people, including Dan, are without repentance.[11]

We briefly touched on the "sealing" of these evangelists. What exactly is this? We can get a clue by looking back to the Old Testament when the glory of the Lord was about to depart from the temple in Jerusalem:

> Now the glory of the God of Israel had gone up from the cherub, where it had been, to the threshold of the temple. And He called to the man clothed with linen, who had the writer's inkhorn at his side; and the LORD said to him, "Go through the midst of the city, through the midst of Jerusalem, and put a mark on the foreheads of the men who sigh and cry over all the abominations that are done within it." To the others He said in my hearing, "Go after him through the city and kill; do not let your eye spare, nor have any pity" (Ezekiel 9:3-5).

When judgment came, those who had been marked by God were spared. The rest faced the just rewards for their sins. Similarly, the 144,000 in Revelation 7 will be sealed to indicate their ownership by God and to protect them from those seeking their harm.

Why would anyone want to harm them? Because they will stand apart from all others in their dedication to righteousness and purity. They will be living examples of the failure of the world's moral code. People will hate them because they will represent everything that is wrong with their own lives. As Jesus told His disciples in the upper room, "If the world hates you, you know that it hated Me before it hated you. If you were of the world, the world would love its own. Yet because you are not of the world, but I chose you out of the world, therefore the world hates you" (John 15:18-19).

Yet it is in part due to the testimony of this first group of people who "will be able to stand" that we are able to be introduced to the second.

A Multitude of Martyrs

How relieved are you to know that you will not have to survive the terrors of the tribulation? Just imagine the joy of those who were caught up in months or years of the tribulation because of their sin, but now find themselves safe and secure before the God whose grace reached through the judgment and pulled them from the fire. It's no wonder that we find ourselves in the middle of another spontaneous worship service.

> After these things I looked, and behold, a great multitude which no one could number, of all nations, tribes, peoples, and tongues, standing before the throne and before the Lamb, clothed with white robes, with palm branches in their hands, and crying out with a loud voice, saying, "Salvation belongs to our God who sits on the throne, and to the Lamb!" (Revelation 7:9-10).

This great multitude of martyred tribulation believers is made up of both Jews and Gentiles. Those hostile to God killed them. Then the Lord welcomed them into His presence. They went from hell on earth to the throne room of heaven. Like the martyrs of chapter 6, they are calling out to the Lord. However, the message of this group is not a petition for more judgment but praise for their salvation.

Although the physical predicament of this multitude may be different from ours, our spiritual situation was exactly the same as theirs. We were all once destined for an eternity apart from God. Then, because of the sacrifice of Jesus, our eternal death became eternal life. The prophet Isaiah stated it so beautifully:

> All we like sheep have gone astray;
> we have turned, every one, to his own way;
> and the LORD has laid on Him the iniquity of us all.
> He was oppressed and He was afflicted,
> yet He opened not His mouth;
> He was led as a lamb to the slaughter,
> and as a sheep before its shearers is silent,
> so He opened not His mouth (Isaiah 53:6-7).

A true recognition of God's love and our salvation will lead to worship. It's impossible for it not to. I can't help but smile as I picture all these men and women and children from all the nations of the world gathered in one chorus before the Lord. It reminds me of conferences that I speak at across the globe. In many, I don't even speak the language of those who live there, but I still join in the worship, letting my Hebrew merge with their language. Even though the words may be different, it all blends together in joyful adoration of the One who has given us new life. This is why it is not surprising to see what happens next.

The angels and the elders and the creatures are all so overwhelmed at the purity and sincerity of the martyrs' worship and the reminder of the greatness of the grace of God that they drop to the ground and join in with another sevenfold doxology similar to the one we read in 5:12:

> All the angels stood around the throne and the elders and
> the four living creatures, and fell on their faces before the
> throne and worshiped God, saying:
>
> "Amen! Blessing and glory and wisdom,
>   thanksgiving and honor and power and might,
>   be to our God forever and ever.
> Amen" (Revelation 7:11-12).

Genuine praise leads others into genuine praise. Many times I have been in churches where the worship service felt like a big production. The band may be excellent and the singers may have beautiful voices, but they are performing instead of worshipping. They honor God with their lips, but their hearts are far from Him (Isaiah 29:13). As a result, the congregation also honors God with loud voices but with empty hearts.

True worship begets worship, and the worship from this group of martyrs was enough to bring the house to its knees. Who exactly is this praising group? We've already tipped our hand, but John is still in the dark.

> Then one of the elders answered, saying to me, "Who are
> these arrayed in white robes, and where did they come

from?" And I said to him, "Sir, you know." So he said to me, "These are the ones who come out of the great tribulation, and washed their robes and made them white in the blood of the Lamb. Therefore they are before the throne of God, and serve Him day and night in His temple. And He who sits on the throne will dwell among them. They shall neither hunger anymore nor thirst anymore; the sun shall not strike them, nor any heat; for the Lamb who is in the midst of the throne will shepherd them and lead them to living fountains of waters. And God will wipe away every tear from their eyes" (Revelation 7:13-17).

There are several interesting insights we can glean from this passage. First, notice that these are tribulation saints, not church saints. They have come out of the great tribulation. The church is already enjoying the place that Jesus had prepared for His bride. Second, they serve the Lord day and night in His temple. Heaven is not a place where believers sit on clouds and play harps. It is a place of service. It is an eternity of expressing our gratitude to our Lord through fulfilling whatever responsibilities He has tasked us with.

Third, they will forever be in the presence of the Lord, for He will dwell among them. They will never have to worry about food or water anymore. They will never be cold again, nor suffer melanomas due to overexposure to the sun. Nor will they face loss and shed tears because a loved one has been taken from them.

In Revelation 7, we see 144,000 on the earth and a multitude in heaven. What do they have in common? They all belong to the Lord. Whether they are sealed on the forehead or clothed in white robes, God has His eyes on them. He has chosen them and called them into His service whether standing as a testimony of righteousness in an unholy world or as a testimony of praise in the holiness of the throne room of the Lord.

As we move to the next chapter, the seventh and final seal will be opened, triggering a very unexpected result.

CHAPTER 9

THE TRUMPETS SOUND

REVELATION 8-9

Silence.

After all the singing and the calls of praise. After the tumult of creatures and elders and martyrs and tens upon tens of thousands of angels lifting their voices up, the Lamb breaks the seventh seal, the plug is pulled, and even the heavenly crickets go quiet.

> When He opened the seventh seal, there was silence in heaven for about half an hour (Revelation 8:1).

Can you imagine silence in heaven? This must be a first. The reason for the silence is not given to us. The Lamb of God still holds the scroll. Six of the seven seals have been opened. Every angel is in place to carry out more judgments. But no commands are heard. No one is speaking.

A Moment of Peace

When you read through Revelation, you discover a lot of sights and sounds. In fact, there is a "sights and sound" formula throughout this book.

Around the throne were twenty-four thrones, and on the thrones I saw twenty-four elders sitting, clothed in white robes; and they had crowns of gold on their heads. And from the throne proceeded lightnings, thunderings, and voices (4:4-5).

Then the angel took the censer, filled it with fire from the altar, and threw it to the earth. And there were noises, thunderings, lightnings, and an earthquake (8:5).

Then the temple of God was opened in heaven, and the ark of His covenant was seen in His temple. And there were lightnings, noises, thunderings, an earthquake, and great hail (11:19).

And there were noises and thunderings and lightnings; and there was a great earthquake, such a mighty and great earthquake as had not occurred since men were on the earth (16:18).

These sights and sounds are a reminder of the power and magnificence of God. The people of Israel saw something like this at Mount Sinai.

Then it came to pass on the third day, in the morning, that there were thunderings and lightnings, and a thick cloud on the mountain; and the sound of the trumpet was very loud, so that all the people who were in the camp trembled. And Moses brought the people out of the camp to meet with God, and they stood at the foot of the mountain. Now Mount Sinai was completely in smoke, because the Lord descended upon it in fire. Its smoke ascended like the smoke of a furnace, and the whole mountain quaked greatly. And when the blast of the trumpet sounded long and became louder and louder, Moses spoke, and God answered him by voice. Then the Lord came down upon Mount Sinai, on the top of the mountain. And the Lord

called Moses to the top of the mountain, and Moses went
up (Exodus 19:16-20).

Having seen and heard the power of God, the Israelites were terrified. "You speak with us, and we will hear; but let not God speak with
us, lest we die," they implored Moses (Exodus 20:19). How often are
we like that? We love to have a powerful God around when we are in
trouble. But in the day-to-day when His strength and holiness can
remind us of our own weakness and unrighteousness, we'd rather have
Him in the background. "Let the pastor talk with Him and tell us what
He said." How much did the Hebrews miss out on by demanding there
be a middleman between themselves and a holy God?

> When He opened the seventh seal, there was silence in
> heaven for about half an hour. And I saw the seven angels
> who stand before God, and to them were given seven trum-
> pets. Then another angel, having a golden censer, came
> and stood at the altar. He was given much incense, that he
> should offer it with the prayers of all the saints upon the
> golden altar which was before the throne. And the smoke
> of the incense, with the prayers of the saints, ascended
> before God from the angel's hand (Revelation 8:1-4).

Heaven may have been quiet for those thirty minutes, but it wasn't
still. Seven angels were standing before God. The Greek word translated "stand" is *histemi* and is in the perfect tense. What that means is
that those angels have been standing there for some time. They were
waiting there, and they continue to wait there anticipating the moment
when they are called to carry out their special assignment. In prepara-
tion for that moment, each of them was given a trumpet.

Then another angel comes with an incense censer. What is the
incense? As we've seen before, it is the prayers of the saints. The fact
that the angel is given much incense means that this is not the prayers
of a few individuals, but of a multitude. What prayer was it that the
multitude of martyrs was offering up before the Lord? "How long, O
Lord, holy and true, until You judge and avenge our blood on those

who dwell on the earth?" (Revelation 6:10). At the end of heaven's half-hour break, the Lord said, "Now!"

> Then the angel took the censer, filled it with fire from the altar, and threw it to the earth. And there were noises, thunderings, lightnings, and an earthquake (Revelation 8:5).

When the heavenly time-out ended, it did so with a bang. What an amazing visual of the power of prayer! God assured the martyrs that He had heard their petitions to Him, but that it was not time yet. He promised that when the proper number of people had repented and come to Him, then He would unleash His recompense against their executioners. At the end of the half-hour of peace, the number was reached. The prayers of the tribulation saints were gathered and hurled toward the earth.

The Sounding of the Trumpets

The first angel put his trumpet to his lips and blew. What followed was unimaginable.

> So the seven angels who had the seven trumpets prepared themselves to sound. The first angel sounded: And hail and fire followed, mingled with blood, and they were thrown to the earth. And a third of the trees were burned up, and all green grass was burned up (Revelation 8:6-7).

With the sounding of that first trumpet, one-third of the world faces irreversible damage, beginning with the vegetation. Today, when we hear about forest fires, the damage is measured in acres or miles. When the first trumpet sounds, the damage will be measured by countries, maybe even continents. The ecology of the entire earth will be turned upside down. Economic collapse will ensue, along with food shortages and massive property damage from the fires. If you happen to work for an insurance company, you'll probably need to start looking for a new job.

> Then the second angel sounded: And something like a great mountain burning with fire was thrown into the sea, and

a third of the sea became blood. And a third of the living creatures in the sea died, and a third of the ships were destroyed (Revelation 8:8-9).

The song of the second trumpet will bring saltwater devastation. A massive, poisoned, burning something will be thrown into the sea. It could be a meteor or the contents of a volcanic eruption. Whatever it is, we know that it is not a natural disaster. Natural disasters are the random results of an impersonal world. This is intentional. The fact that it is "thrown" means that someone had to throw it. The resulting tsunami will be large enough to overturn, sink, or carry far onto shore a third of all ships. In 2016, the number of ships on the ocean at any given time was around 50,000.[12] That means that nearly 17,000 ships and their crews will be be destroyed in this one cataclysmic act. The damage to supply lines would be irreparable.

But what's significant is not just the size of this "great mountain," but its composition. There is something about it that will cause the sea to turn to blood and one-third of all sea life to be destroyed. Fishing companies will have to close their doors. The economies of many coastal countries will implode. The world will be reeling. And only two trumpets will have sounded up to this point.

> Then the third angel sounded: And a great star fell from heaven, burning like a torch, and it fell on a third of the rivers and on the springs of water. The name of the star is Wormwood. A third of the waters became wormwood, and many men died from the water, because it was made bitter (Revelation 8:10-11).

The third trumpet blares its note and freshwater devastation follows. A star called Wormwood crashes to the earth. This could very well be a meteor strike. In Scripture, wormwood is used to illustrate bitterness, as seen in the words of the prophet Jeremiah: "He has filled me with bitterness, He has made me drink wormwood" (Lamentations 3:15). One-third of all fresh water will be tainted by the star. The fact that "many men died from the water" indicates that either the taint is too

strong for modern decontamination techniques or the water purifica-
tion systems in many cities and countries no longer exist. While the
destruction of food sources will start claiming victims in weeks, the
loss of potable drinking water will begin taking lives on a massive scale
within a few days.

> Then the fourth angel sounded: And a third of the sun was
> struck, a third of the moon, and a third of the stars, so that
> a third of them were darkened. A third of the day did not
> shine, and likewise the night (Revelation 8:12).

When the fourth angel sounds his trumpet, the skies as we know
them will be changed forever. A third of the sun, moon, and stars will be
darkened. This is a fascinating judgment to contemplate. The first part
of the verse makes it sound like one-third of the sun is now dark, one-
third of the moon is now dark, and one-third of the stars no longer shine,
and that seems like an impossibility. The earth would freeze immediately
if one-third of the sun stopped burning. The second part of the verse may
hold the key to what is happening: "A third of the day did not shine, and
likewise the night." I think that it is very possible that for one-third of
the day and one-third of the night the earth will be plunged into utter
darkness. During those hours the light of the sun is gone, its reflection
on the moon is gone, and the light from the heavenly hosts is obscured.

The First Woe

It's hard to imagine John's feelings as he is witnessing the suffering
upon humanity. Sure, there is the understanding that God is just, and
they are receiving the wages of their own sins. But one would have to
be very cold-hearted to not empathize at least to some extent with the
plight of those remaining on earth. John knew, though, that it was only
going to get worse. After all, there were three angels near him who had
not yet blown their trumpets. And there was now another angel that
flew by to remind everyone that the worst is still yet to come.

> I looked, and I heard an angel flying through the midst of
> heaven, saying with a loud voice, "Woe, woe, woe to the

inhabitants of the earth, because of the remaining blasts of the trumpet of the three angels who are about to sound!" (verse 13)

In the book of Revelation, not only are there three series of judgments, but there are also three woes. The word translated "woe" is the Greek term *ouai*. It is an expression of pain and anger. It is a cry of distress. It is someone calling out who doesn't know where to turn because the governments have collapsed, the hospitals are overcrowded and undersupplied, and the volunteer organizations have all disbanded because everyone is just trying to survive.

As soon as the angel had flown by crying out "Woe, woe, woe" for those who still survive on the earth, the first of the three woes begins.

> Then the fifth angel sounded: And I saw a star fallen from heaven to the earth. To him was given the key to the bottomless pit (Revelation 9:1).

The bottomless pit is another one of those images in Revelation that culture has taken and run with, of course getting everything wrong as it does. The Greek work is *abussos*, from which we get the word *abyss*. The word is found nine times in the Bible, seven of which are in the book of Revelation. What is the abyss?

When Jesus went to the Gentile side of the Sea of Galilee, he met a man who was possessed by a demonic horde. Jesus asked the name of the demons, and they answered "Legion" because there were so many of them (Luke 8:30). As Jesus prepared to cast them out, the demons became terrified and pleaded with Him not to send them into the abyss (verse 31). In an act of incredible mercy to those who were His enemies, Jesus instead sent them into a nearby herd of swine. The pigs panicked and ran down the hill into the sea, where they drowned.

Similarly, every time that we find the abyss or the bottomless pit in Scripture, it is associated with demonic forces. John tells us that the beast will ascend from the abyss (Revelation 11:7; 17:8), and at the end of the tribulation, the devil will be locked away in the bottomless pit for a 1,000-year period before being released out into the world to deceive the nations once again (Revelation 20:1-3). Thus, we can be confident that whatever goes into the abyss or comes out of it is demonic in nature.

> He opened the bottomless pit, and smoke arose out of the pit like the smoke of a great furnace. So the sun and the air were darkened because of the smoke of the pit. Then out of the smoke locusts came upon the earth. And to them was given power, as the scorpions of the earth have power. They were commanded not to harm the grass of the earth, or any green thing, or any tree, but only those men who do not have the seal of God on their foreheads. And they were not given authority to kill them, but to torment them for five months. Their torment was like the torment of a scorpion when it strikes a man. In those days men will seek death and will not find it; they will desire to die, and death will flee from them (Revelation 9:2-6).

A dark cloud fills the air. People will wonder if a weather front is moving in, maybe a thunderstorm that will pour out enough fresh water for them to ease their parched throats. But then they will notice that the cloud is very low and is moving extremely fast. Soon, the movement and the undulations of the mass will tell them that it has nothing to do with the weather—it is alive. The first locusts arrive, landing on person after person. Screams echo through the air as the attack begins. The pain of their sting will be searing, and the resulting sores will be unbearable. There will be no escaping them because they will come in the tens of millions. They will cause horrendous pain, but they will not be allowed to take anyone's life even though there will be some who will wish the locusts would put them out of their misery.

This will not be like the plague of locusts that came on the Egyptians in the time of Moses. Those locusts were directed toward the food supplies of Pharaoh and his people. The Revelation locusts will be commanded to avoid the crops altogether. They will feed on the people. Also, the Egyptian locusts only stayed for days; these tribulational locusts will remain for five months. Imagine that. Think of five months from the day you are reading this. Each and every day, between now and then, you would be afraid to go outside for fear of the locusts, who will immediately inflict you with the burning pain of more bites.

But there will be some people who very well might be picnicking in the park, playing a little Frisbee, and feeding the ducks while everyone else is cowering in their homes. The 144,000 witnesses will be bug-proof because they have received the seal of protection from God Himself. There will be many who will resent them for their immunity from the locusts and seek their harm—to no avail. But there will likely be others who will recognize that their protection is divine in nature and, as a result, turn to God.

There has been much controversy about whether these are actually locusts. John gets quite descriptive as he talks about them, and much of what he says is quite unlocustlike.

> The shape of the locusts was like horses prepared for battle. On their heads were crowns of something like gold, and their faces were like the faces of men. They had hair like women's hair, and their teeth were like lions' teeth. And they had breastplates like breastplates of iron, and the sound of their wings was like the sound of chariots with many horses running into battle. They had tails like scorpions, and there were stings in their tails. Their power was to hurt men five months. And they had as king over them the angel of the bottomless pit, whose name in Hebrew is Abaddon, but in Greek he has the name Apollyon (Revelation 9:7-11).

Crowns, faces like men, hair like women, teeth like lions, breastplates of iron, tails like scorpions. What are these things? Some commentators believe that John is describing modern helicopters, and there are elements of the description here that would fit. But unless the pilot holding the cyclic and working the pedals has little red horns and a pointy tail, it doesn't quite work. Remember, these locusts didn't come from a Sikorsky helicopter factory; they came flying up from the abyss. There is no reason to allegorize their origin. John said that these are demonic locusts, and when I read the description of these little creatures, they sound like exactly what he said they are.

One more reason to look at them as demonic creatures is the fact that they have a king leading them. He is the angel of the abyss with a very fitting name—"Destruction" or "Destroyer." What the hierarchy of the bottomless pit looks like, we don't know. This is our only peek into that demonic order. We only know what we can read here, which tells us that they were led by their king and given authority by heaven to torment humanity, but only to a certain extent and only for a specific time.

Five months of this horror qualifies as the first woe. But hold on, there is more woe to come.

> One woe is past. Behold, still two more woes are coming after these things. Then the sixth angel sounded: And I heard a voice from the four horns of the golden altar which is before God, saying to the sixth angel who had the trumpet, "Release the four angels who are bound at the great river Euphrates" (Revelation 9:12-14).

The Euphrates River is well known in the Middle East, but those in the West heard little about it until Saddam Hussein invaded Kuwait in 1990. Suddenly, the Euphrates was on every newscast. Many readers of the Bible, however, were aware of the Euphrates well before Operation Desert Storm. When God created man, He also planted a garden where he could live. This was in Eden. Flowing through the garden was a river that kept all the plants and trees lush and fruitful. Once the river exited the garden, it split into four rivers.

> The name of the first is Pishon; it is the one which skirts the whole land of Havilah, where there is gold. And the gold of that land is good. Bdellium and the onyx stone are there. The name of the second river is Gihon; it is the one which goes around the whole land of Cush. The name of the third river is Hiddekel; it is the one which goes toward the east of Assyria. The fourth river is the Euphrates (Genesis 2:11-14).

Today, the Euphrates River originates in modern-day Turkey, flows through Syria, enters Iraq, and empties into the Persian Gulf. Many people depend on it for food, drinking water, and even electricity through the Haditha Dam, which provides power to Baghdad. What few people who live along the river realize is that God has kept four demonic spirits bound along the waterway. They have been locked there for centuries, awaiting their release. At the sixth trumpet, their chains will fall to the ground.

> So the four angels, who had been prepared for the hour and day and month and year, were released to kill a third of mankind. Now the number of the army of the horsemen was two hundred million; I heard the number of them. And thus I saw the horses in the vision: those who sat on them had breastplates of fiery red, hyacinth blue, and sulfur yellow; and the heads of the horses were like the heads of lions; and out of their mouths came fire, smoke, and brimstone. By these three plagues a third of mankind was killed—by the fire and the smoke and the brimstone which came out of their mouths. For their power is in their mouth and in their tails; for their tails are like serpents, having heads; and with them they do harm (Revelation 9:15-19).

Here we see a demonic army of 200 million troops. That is something that nightmares and blockbuster horror movies are made of. This massive army may be made up of humans or demonically possessed people. It is not too difficult to see modern armor and air warfare in the descriptions. However, it's also possible that they are a supernatural force—sort of the evil opposite of what was seen by the prophet Elisha (2 Kings 6:16-17). Unlike the locusts, we don't know the origin of the army, so their makeup is dependent upon speculation. Another one-third of humanity will be wiped out by this terrible militia. That equates to a number in the billions, which makes it that much easier to see this army as not of this world.

Surely, after all the devastation that occurs after the sounding of the six trumpets, humanity would have to be on their knees in repentance, crying out for mercy from God. But that is far from the case.

> But the rest of mankind, who were not killed by these plagues, did not repent of the works of their hands, that they should not worship demons, and idols of gold, silver, brass, stone, and wood, which can neither see nor hear nor walk. And they did not repent of their murders or their sorceries or their sexual immorality or their thefts (Revelation 9:20-21).

As believers, we all have experienced times in which we do our own thing. We have sin on our mind, and we don't think about the consequences. Eventually, the Lord disciplines us in one way or another and gets our attention. When that happens, we have a choice to make. We can ignore His warnings and pay a steep price. Or we can repent of our foolishness. When we repent, He is ready to forgive and restore our relationship with Him.

The unbelievers of the tribulation also have the option to turn to God for forgiveness. But their desire for sin outweighs the price they are paying. To them, the perceived benefit is worth the cost. Sadly, with the last trumpet preparing to sound, their window of opportunity for repentance is rapidly closing.

CHAPTER 10

THE SECOND INTERLUDE, PART 1: JOHN EATS THE BOOK

REVELATION 10

T oward the end of 2021, I released my first novel, *Operation Joktan*. It is a thrilling story of two Mossad agents, Nir Tavor and Nicole Le Roux, as they seek to thwart a devastating attack that would take thousands of lives in Dubai, UAE. One thing that I learned as I worked with my writing partner is the idea of pacing. After several scenes of heart-racing action, it's good to slow things down a bit. The reader must be allowed occasionally to stop and take a breath.

We've just read of horrific suffering and the deaths of billions of people during the first six trumpet judgments. With a perfect understanding of pacing, the Lord slows the action down before the seventh trumpet sounds. This interlude carries from 10:1–11:14 and is not wholly without its own violence and destruction. In it we observe a mighty angel, a little scroll, two witnesses in Jerusalem, and the second woe.

The Mighty Angel

A new angel comes on the scene who was magnificent in his appearance.

> I saw still another mighty angel coming down from heaven, clothed with a cloud. And a rainbow was on his head, his face was like the sun, and his feet like pillars of fire. He had a little book open in his hand. And he set his right foot on the sea and his left foot on the land, and cried with a loud voice, as when a lion roars (Revelation 10:1-3).

The first piece of information that stands out is that John has changed his location. Notice that the angel was "coming down" from heaven to earth. If John was still up in the throne room, the angel would be "going down" to earth. When exactly John made the trip is difficult to say, and we should not get too hung up on it. It's enough to recognize that John didn't just sit back in his reclining leather theater chair watching all this on a big screen. Instead, it appears that after the initial scenes were carried out in heaven, John was shuttled here and there to wherever he could best witness the action.

This angel that will arrive on earth will be huge. The description John gives does not lend itself to him simply standing on the shoreline, toes in the water, unsure if he really wants to wade in and get wet. This angel was standing on the sea, not just in the water. He was standing on the land, not just in the beachy sand. This depiction indicates an angel who is massive and reaches high into the sky.

His appearance also lends to his grandeur. Much of how he is described reflects the attributes of the Son of God—a rainbow around his head, a shining face, and fiery feet. However, this being is not divine; he is a servant of the divine. Once he is established on the planet, he lets out a terrifying cry. John compares it to a lion's roar designed to get the attention of the entire world.

> When he cried out, seven thunders uttered their voices. Now when the seven thunders uttered their voices, I was about to write; but I heard a voice from heaven saying to me, "Seal up the things which the seven thunders uttered, and do not write them" (Revelation 10:3-4).

The angel's cry certainly got the attention of the seven thunders.

This begs the obvious question: What are the seven thunders? Once again, we don't know for sure. Most likely they are angels with a unique message. The cry of the mighty angel will shake open the mouths of these thunders and they will begin talking. John, like a good scribe, will dip his pen in ink, but before he can write, a voice from heaven will stop him.

What did those thunders say? It's possible that they had messages of judgment, but that is just speculation. There are some secrets that God reveals to us in His Word, and there are others that He has chosen to keep to Himself. It's His book; therefore, He sets the rules. But we can't complain too much because through the huge angel's next actions, a mystery of God that had long been hidden is completed.

> The angel whom I saw standing on the sea and on the land raised up his hand to heaven and swore by Him who lives forever and ever, who created heaven and the things that are in it, the earth and the things that are in it, and the sea and the things that are in it, that there should be delay no longer, but in the days of the sounding of the seventh angel, when he is about to sound, the mystery of God would be finished, as He declared to His servants the prophets (Revelation 10:5-7).

For anyone on the earth who doubted that this was God's work, that suspicion could now be put to rest. What was taking place in all the nations with the death and destruction was exactly what God had promised would happen to those who turned their backs on Him in rebellion. The angel took a solemn oath on both the Creator and on all things created that this was true. When the seventh angel blew his trumpet, it would lead to the "mystery of God" coming to its conclusion.

Why was this called a mystery? To understand the "mystery of God," we first need to define the term *mystery*. A biblical mystery is not like a case that needs to be solved, like what you'd find in an Agatha Christie novel or a Scooby-Doo cartoon. Rather, it is a truth that up to a certain point has not yet been revealed. The word is used twenty-seven times in the New Testament and four times in Revelation. The mystery that had been pronounced long ago through the prophets was now being seen in its fulfillment.

Most likely the mystery here is referring to the many Old Testament references to the millennial reign of Christ spoken of in Revelation 20. Glimpses of this 1,000-year reign of the Lord on earth were given to the prophets Isaiah, Jeremiah, Daniel, Zechariah, and others. Satan's power in the world will come to an end, and the Messiah will take His proper place on His earthly throne. Then, what was once a mystery will be seen in its full reality.

In theological circles, this revealing of a little information at a time is known as progressive revelation. Just as we train up our children by teaching them a little at a time based on their ability to understand, so God has revealed to His people truth as they were able to comprehend it. The gradual communication of the truths about the millennial kingdom through the maturing of Israel can clearly be seen in Scripture beginning with the patriarchs:

> The scepter shall not depart from Judah,
> nor a lawgiver from between his feet,
> until Shiloh comes;
> and to Him shall be the obedience of the people
> (Genesis 49:10).

God began by informing us that the scepter would always belong to the tribe of Judah. Out of the twelve tribes, from which tribe does Jesus come? He is the Lion of Judah (Revelation 5:5).

> He who sits in the heavens shall laugh;
> the LORD shall hold them in derision.
> Then He shall speak to them in His wrath,
> and distress them in His deep displeasure:
> "Yet I have set My King
> on My holy hill of Zion" (Psalm 2:4-6).

God will place His King on His holy hill of Zion, which is Jerusalem.

Now we have a scepter, a king, and a location. And what about His royal lineage?

> Unto us a Child is born,
> unto us a Son is given;
> and the government will be upon His shoulder.
> And His name will be called
> Wonderful, Counselor, Mighty God,
> Everlasting Father, Prince of Peace.
> Of the increase of His government and peace
> there will be no end,
> upon the throne of David and over His kingdom,
> to order it and establish it with judgment and justice
> from that time forward, even forever.
> The zeal of the LORD of hosts will perform this
> (Isaiah 9:6-7).

From the prophet Isaiah we discover that this king with a scepter will not only rule from Jerusalem but will also sit on David's throne. To rightfully sit on David's throne, he must be a descendant of David. The genealogies of both Matthew and Luke make it quite clear that this is true of Jesus the Messiah.

> And in that day His feet will stand on the Mount of Olives,
> which faces Jerusalem on the east.
> And the Mount of Olives shall be split in two,
> from east to west,
> making a very large valley;
> half of the mountain shall move toward the north
> and half of it toward the south (Zechariah 14:4).

Finally, Zechariah tells us where the King will arrive when He returns to establish His kingdom. It will be the same location from which He left—the Mount of Olives (Acts 1:9-11). When we get to Revelation 19, we will see this prophecy of Zechariah come true.

Many other passages of Scripture could be added to the list of progressive revelations. In this case, the mystery of the Messiah King, the

Lord of lords, is about to come to pass. But before that happens, there is still more bitterness to endure.

The Bittersweet Scroll

What takes place next might have felt to John like playing out someone else's *déjà vu*. He knows that this has happened before; it just hasn't happened to him.

> Then the voice which I heard from heaven spoke to me again and said, "Go, take the little book which is open in the hand of the angel who stands on the sea and on the earth." So I went to the angel and said to him, "Give me the little book." And he said to me, "Take and eat it; and it will make your stomach bitter, but it will be as sweet as honey in your mouth" (Revelation 10:8-9).

The voice from heaven is back. This time, rather than prohibiting him from writing, it calls him to a task. "Go and take the little book from the big angel's hand," he is told. As he approaches the angel, the servant of God holds his hand down to John's level. The apostle takes the book, and as he does so, the angel gives him a curious command. Typically when someone gives you a book, their suggestion to you is to read it. Not this angel. He says to John, "Eat this book."

Let me take a moment to say that if the book that you are currently holding in your hands was given to you as a gift, and the person who gave it to you said, "When you are done with it, I would like for you to eat it," then I, as the author, give you full permission to ignore their suggestion. John, however, fully complied, even though the angel warned him that despite its sweet taste, it would soon have him reaching for the antacids. John ate the book because he knew that sometimes that is what prophets do:

> Now when I looked, there was a hand stretched out to me; and behold, a scroll of a book was in it. Then He spread it before me; and there was writing on the inside and on the outside, and written on it were lamentations

and mourning and woe. Moreover He said to me, "Son of man, eat what you find; eat this scroll, and go, speak to the house of Israel" So I opened my mouth, and He caused me to eat that scroll. And He said to me, "Son of man, feed your belly, and fill your stomach with this scroll that I give you." So I ate, and it was in my mouth like honey in sweetness (Ezekiel 2:9–3:3).

A scroll was given to Ezekiel, and the prophet had it for lunch. Did the scroll turn bitter after he ate it? It most likely did because afterward, the Holy Spirit transported him back to the exiles by the River Chebar, and he felt overwhelmed to the point of immobility for a week.

> So the Spirit lifted me up and took me away, and I went in bitterness, in the heat of my spirit; but the hand of the LORD was strong upon me. Then I came to the captives at Tel Abib, who dwelt by the River Chebar; and I sat where they sat, and remained there astonished among them seven days (Ezekiel 3:14-15).

In something like a recommissioning, here in Revelation 10, John was told to eat the book. This symbolized God's message becoming internalized in him. What he would write would not be his own words, but the words that God had put inside of him. While at first the message may seem sweet to those who are safe in the presence of the Savior, just a few moments of thinking about the devastation of God's wrath would be enough to turn the stomach.

> Then I took the little book out of the angel's hand and ate it, and it was as sweet as honey in my mouth. But when I had eaten it, my stomach became bitter. And he said to me, "You must prophesy again about many peoples, nations, tongues, and kings" (Revelation 10:10-11).

Even as I write this commentary on Revelation, I feel as though I am eating a bittersweet book. It is filled with wonderful news, and it is filled with tragedy. As part of the church, I know that I won't be here for the devastating judgments that will fall upon my own people Israel, as well as on all unbelieving Gentiles.

Removal before wrath—that is the sweet part of Revelation. But I ache for my people and for the rest of the world when I read what they will experience. My people will be deceived by the Antichrist. They will look to him as their Messiah until he sets himself up in the temple to be worshipped. Then my people will rebel, and they will feel the fury of this faux leader.

As for my Gentile friends, I ache for them also because they will taste God's wrath for seven years. Some of them will turn their hearts to God, and they will be violently martyred. Others will continue to reject Jesus as their Savior and will be sentenced to hell. As bitter a pill as that is for me to swallow, I cannot imagine the bitterness of those who realize too late that the Jesus whom they rejected truly is the King of kings and Lord of lords.

As the initial part of this second interlude concludes, we see a shift take place. Up to this point, the focus has been mostly on events connected with the breaking of the seal judgments and the sounding of the trumpets and the ensuing turmoil. From chapter 11 on, the emphasis moves more to individuals and groups, and we meet folk like the two witnesses, the woman and child and dragon, the Antichrist and false prophet, the harlot, and Jesus returning with His bride.

THE SECOND INTERLUDE, PART 2: THE TWO WITNESSES

REVELATION 11

Once again, we find ourselves facing a chapter that has often been abused with misidentification and misunderstanding. The two witnesses step forward to take their rightful place alongside the four horsemen and the 144,000 in the Revelation Misinterpretation Hall of Fame. Just who are these two perplexing men? Before we can deal with that question, John has some calculations to make.

Measuring the Temple

At this point, we zoom in on one section of Jerusalem, the temple. John was given a reed to measure with and told to determine the size of the temple.

> I was given a reed like a measuring rod. And the angel stood, saying, "Rise and measure the temple of God, the altar, and those who worship there. But leave out the court which is outside the temple, and do not measure it, for it has been given to the Gentiles. And they will tread the holy city underfoot for forty-two months" (Revelation 11:1-2).

The fact that we never are told the findings of John's surveying expedition tells me that the purpose is not so much the size of the temple but the fact that there is a temple in Jerusalem. What exactly is John measuring? There are two Greek words for temple. *Hieron* refers to the temple proper or the entire complex. The second word, *naos*, speaks specifically of the Holy of Holies. That is the word used in this passage. The angel wants John to focus on the place of God's presence because the rest has been corrupted by the Gentiles.

By the way, did you know that your body is the temple of the Holy Spirit? Paul wrote to the believers in Corinth, "Do you not know that your body is the temple of the Holy Spirit who is in you, whom you have from God, and you are not your own? For you were bought at a price; therefore glorify God in your body and in your spirit, which are God's" (1 Corinthians 6:19-20).

Which of the two words do you think the apostle Paul used when speaking about your body? It may surprise and even humble you to know that Paul used *naos*, the Holy of Holies. In other words, your physical body is to be a holy residence in which the Lord dwells. That is why Paul included a cause-effect relationship in his comments, saying that because your body is the Holy of Holies where the living God abides, "glorify God in your body."

John's words about the temple in Revelation 11:1-2 would have been significant, particularly to the Jewish readers. When John wrote this, there had not been a temple for two decades. In AD 70, the Tenth Roman Legion invaded Jerusalem, destroying both the city and the temple. Two thousand years later, there is still no temple in Jerusalem. In the current political climate, it seems impossible that the Muslim nations around the world would ever allow a third temple to be built on the Temple Mount alongside the al-Aqsa Mosque and the Dome of the Rock. It will take a man of peace to work out those delicate negotiations—a man like the Antichrist, who will win the hearts of the world, including the Jews, with his incredible political skills that he will employ to restore their presence on the holy mount.

However, before the tribulation begins and the Antichrist is revealed, Russia, Turkey, Iran, Sudan, Libya, and others will gather to invade Israel (Ezekiel 38–39). But before they can destroy God's people, He will intervene and destroy them. The bloodshed will be great, and it will pave the way for the Antichrist—the man of peace—to step forward on the world stage.

This third temple is not a new concept to Revelation. The prophet Daniel spoke of a time during the tribulation when temple sacrifices will be cut off (Daniel 9:26-27). Jesus taught of a future temple in the end times during His Olivet Discourse (Matthew 24:15-26). Paul talked about the tribulation temple, writing,

> Let no one deceive you by any means; for that Day will not come unless the falling away comes first, and the man of sin is revealed, the son of perdition, who opposes and exalts himself above all that is called God or that is worshiped, so that he sits as God in the temple of God, showing himself that he is God (2 Thessalonians 2:3-4).

There will be a temple during the tribulation, and it will play out significantly in the exposure of the true character of the Antichrist.

Two Witnesses and a Second Woe

Suddenly, two men will appear in Jerusalem. They will be a sight to behold:

> I will give power to my two witnesses, and they will prophesy one thousand two hundred and sixty days, clothed in sackcloth (Revelation 11:3).

While sackcloth was commonplace at the time John wrote this description, it's pretty much faded out of style. It's been quite a while since the latest sackcloth trends made news at Paris Fashion Week. When these two men show up on the streets of Jerusalem in their itchy, woven garments, people will take notice.

Why sackcloth? Wearing it was an outward demonstration of great inner mourning or distress. When King Hezekiah heard that Jerusalem was next on the list for the great Assyrian king Sennacherib's juggernaut, "he tore his clothes, covered himself with sackcloth, and went into the house of the LORD" (2 Kings 19:1). In wearing these clothes, it will be obvious to all that the message that these two witnesses are bringing is not one of comfort and joy.

There is much speculation concerning the identity of these two witnesses. I can remember one time, after delivering a message, a man approached me claiming that he was one of the two witnesses. Rather than letting him take the time to point out how he had significantly upgraded the material of his wardrobe, I politely excused myself and ran for the back room.

The two individuals most equated with these men are Moses and Elijah, for they had already appeared on the Mount of Transfiguration to speak to Jesus about His coming death (Luke 9:30). Two others often discussed are Enoch and Elijah, because neither of them ever died. Enoch walked with God when he was suddenly removed from the earth (Genesis 5:24). Elijah was strolling alongside Elisha when he was taken up to heaven by a chariot of fire (2 Kings 2:11-12). It is also possible that these witnesses are two people whom we have never heard of.

God does not tell us who they are, so our speculation can never be more than a fun mental exercise. If their identities really mattered, their names would be in the book. Unfortunately, it is too often what we don't know that attracts our attention instead of what we do know. Looking at the text, our questions should not be *who*, but *why* and *when*.

The first reason that we see these men show up in Jerusalem is that God always allows there to be a witness when Satan is running rampant throughout the world. God has already supplied 144,000 Jewish gospel-evangelists, and now He adds two more. This "light in the darkness" role is clearly seen by this description of them:

> These are the two olive trees and the two lampstands stand-
> ing before the God of the earth (Revelation 11:4).

This picture of olive trees and lampstands goes back to the days of the prophet Zechariah. Before we go further, we should review some history of Israel.

There have been two temples in Jerusalem. The first temple was known as Solomon's Temple, which was built by the king of the same name. The second temple was first known as Zerubbabel's Temple, but then became referred to as Herod's Temple after the king greatly expanded it. Solomon's Temple was destroyed in 586 BC by King Nebuchadnezzar, and most of the Jews in the city were taken captive to the region surrounding Babylon. This captivity took place in three waves. The first captivity occurred in 605 BC, when Daniel was taken. The second took place in 597 BC, when Ezekiel was exiled. The third captivity took place when Nebuchadnezzar had had enough of the rebellious Jews and wiped out the holy city.

Just as there were three captivities, there were three returns to Jerusalem. Cyrus of Persia gave an edict that allowed the people of Israel to go back home and rebuild their temple. The first return was under the direction of Zerubbabel in 538 BC. This group laid the foundation of the temple and eventually rebuilt it. Decades later, in 458 BC, a second company returned with Ezra the priest. Ezra restored the worship at the temple. A final assembly came with Nehemiah, the cupbearer to King Artaxerxes, in 445 BC. Nehemiah rebuilt the walls of the city.

Around the time of the first return, Zechariah had a vision in which an angel showed him a lampstand that was flanked on either side by an olive tree.

> I answered and said to him, "What are these two olive trees—at the right of the lampstand and at its left?" And I further answered and said to him, "What are these two olive branches that drip into the receptacles of the two gold pipes from which the golden oil drains?" Then he answered me and said, "Do you not know what these are?" And I said, "No, my lord." So he said, "These are the two anointed ones, who stand beside the Lord of the whole earth" (Zechariah 4:11-14).

Like the two anointed ones in Zerubbabel's time, so these two witnesses have been anointed by God to declare the gospel message from Jerusalem to the world. Israel was created to be a "light to the Gentiles," and these two witnesses will show up in the holy city to fulfill that role.

How long will they minister? John answers that question in Revelation 11:3. Their ministry in Jerusalem will last for 1,260 days. For those of you scrambling for your calculators, let me save you the time. Just like the Gentiles "will tread the holy city underfoot for forty-two months" (verse 2), the two witnesses will preach the gospel of repentance for those same initial three-and-a-half years of the tribulation.

If you have Jews and Gentiles walking around the city of God and two witnesses telling them that all the bad stuff that's going on is what they deserve for their sins, there are likely to be some serious conflicts. The two men will be mocked, cursed, and attacked. But it will not go well for their attackers.

> If anyone wants to harm them, fire proceeds from their mouth and devours their enemies. And if anyone wants to harm them, he must be killed in this manner. These have power to shut heaven, so that no rain falls in the days of their prophecy; and they have power over waters to turn them to blood, and to strike the earth with all plagues, as often as they desire (Revelation 11:5-6).

There will be a global hatred for these two. It's easy to picture protests and riots surrounding them. But after the first few attempts to harm them meet with fiery failure, no one will have enough courage to attack. At least not until the Antichrist rides into town.

> When they finish their testimony, the beast that ascends out of the bottomless pit will make war against them, overcome them, and kill them. And their dead bodies will lie in the street of the great city which spiritually is called Sodom and Egypt, where also our Lord was crucified. Then those from the peoples, tribes, tongues, and nations will see their dead bodies three-and-a-half days, and not allow their dead bodies to be put into graves. And those who dwell on the

earth will rejoice over them, make merry, and send gifts to one another, because these two prophets tormented those who dwell on the earth (Revelation 11:7-10).

Notice the timing of the murderous assault on the two witnesses: "When they finish their testimony." It wasn't until these two servants of God could stand in front of a giant "Mission Accomplished" banner that they became vulnerable to the power of evil. The parallels to Jesus' ministry on the earth are easily seen. Jesus came and was a testimony for truth. All during His ministry period, the Pharisees and religious leaders tried to bring Him down. Time after time they failed. Until the one time they didn't. They cheered and jeered as the Lord hung on the cross. Then He took His last breath. They truly thought they had scored a victory. Three days later, they learned how wrong they were. What they had thought was a victory turned out to be a game-changing defeat at the hands of the Almighty God.

When the two witnesses are slaughtered, there will be global cheering. People will exchange presents and "Happy Dead Witnesses Day" cards. They will think that they have truly scored a victory. Three-and-a-half days later, they will learn how wrong they are.

We don't know what will take place in the next scene, but I've watched enough movies to have an idea of how I would like to see it play out. The television cameras will be focused on the two bodies that have been left out in the street to rot. Some large-haired commentator will be giving his thoughts about how these two intolerant menaces to society deserved their violent end. Suddenly, the cameras will zoom in to the right hand of one of the bodies. The producer will yell at the cameraman to reestablish his shot, but the cameraman will reply through his headphones, "I saw movement."

The index finger twitches. "There," the cameraman yells. "There it is again!"

Another twitch. Then the hand moves, followed by the arm. Every channel across the globe breaks into their programming. All eyes are glued to the screen as first one witness, then the other, sits up and stretches. Screams of anger and despair echo from one end of the planet to the other. The first witness works his way to his feet, then reaches down and pulls his friend upright.

Then, looking right into the camera, the first witness says with a grin, "We're back."

Of course, we don't know what will actually happen, but we do know that these two who were fully dead will become fully alive again. But by this time, their purpose on earth will be done; they will have finished their testimony. So God will call them home.

> Now after the three-and-a-half days the breath of life from God entered them, and they stood on their feet, and great fear fell on those who saw them. And they heard a loud voice from heaven saying to them, "Come up here." And they ascended to heaven in a cloud, and their enemies saw them (Revelation 11:11-12).

In one more parallel to the earthly ministry of Christ, they will ascend to heaven. However, unlike Jesus' quiet departure, the witnesses will go out with a bang.

> In the same hour there was a great earthquake, and a tenth of the city fell. In the earthquake seven thousand people were killed, and the rest were afraid and gave glory to the God of heaven. The second woe is past. Behold, the third woe is coming quickly (Revelation 11:13-14).

A devastating earthquake will kill 7,000 people and wipe out 10 percent of the city of Jerusalem. Those who are left will recognize the divine origins of the witnesses and the earthquake, and will give "glory to the God of heaven." Sadly, on the part of the Jewish people of the city, this will be an empty gesture. It will be another three-and-a-half years before they will recognize their need for a Savior and turn to Him.

This kind of giving "glory" often happens during difficult times. People call out to God for help, praising Him and promising to live righteously and serve others if only He will get them out of their predicament. Then, when the danger has passed and life normalizes, those "foxhole commitments" are quickly forgotten.

This moment with the death and resurrection of the witnesses and the resulting earthquake will shake the world to such an extent that John declares it to be the second woe. Then, with blatant foreshadowing, he warns that the third woe is right around the corner.

The Seventh Trumpet Sounds

Before we talk about the seventh trumpet, we need to make a necessary distinction between it and the last trumpet that Paul wrote about to the Corinthians: "Behold, I tell you a mystery: We shall not all sleep, but we shall all be changed—in a moment, in the twinkling of an eye, at the last trumpet. For the trumpet will sound, and the dead will be raised incorruptible, and we shall be changed" (1 Corinthians 15:51-52).

Not all "last trumpets" are the same. And while there may be some similarities between the wording in 1 Corinthians and Revelation, each word or phrase must be interpreted within its context. *Similar* words and phrases are not *identical* words and phrases. Paul was talking to the church in Corinth about the rapture of the bride of Christ. But in this passage in Revelation, the rapture is three-and-a-half years past and we are now dealing with the final series of judgments.

> The seventh angel sounded: And there were loud voices in heaven, saying, "The kingdoms of this world have become the kingdoms of our Lord and of His Christ, and He shall reign forever and ever!" And the twenty-four elders who sat before God on their thrones fell on their faces and worshiped God, saying:
>
> "We give You thanks, O Lord God Almighty,
> the One who is and who was and who is to come,
> because You have taken Your great power and reigned.
> The nations were angry, and Your wrath has come,
> and the time of the dead, that they should be judged,
> and that You should reward Your servants the prophets
>   and the saints,
> and those who fear Your name, small and great,
> and should destroy those who destroy the earth" (Revelation 11:15-18).

When the seventh trumpet sounds, another worship service will break out in heaven. It will start with loud voices calling out, which will then be joined by the twenty-four elders. Seeing the end of the rule of the enemy on earth and the soon-coming reign of Christ, they cry out, "The kingdoms of this world have become the kingdoms of our Lord and of His Christ." This subjection to godly rule is not something that the nations will submit to willingly. They are used to following their master, the devil, and will not readily abandon that allegiance. David saw this when he penned:

> Why do the nations rage,
> and the people plot a vain thing?
> The kings of the earth set themselves,
> and the rulers take counsel together,
> against the LORD and against His Anointed, saying,
> "Let us break Their bonds in pieces
> and cast away Their cords from us" (Psalm 2:1-3).

But no matter how they may rage, God's plan will prevail. All the nations of the world banded together are no match for the power of the All-Powerful. God's reclamation of the earth and rule over it has been ordained and is absolute. And those who know God and His goodness can't help but rejoice at what will undoubtedly be the amazing results.

The second part of this wonderful doxology focuses on reward and loss. Believers will be rewarded and unbelievers will not only lose their earthly gains, but also the opportunity to spend eternity with the God who loves them so much that He died for them.

Inside the Heavenly Temple

As this chapter ends, John sees something in heaven that he would have read about years earlier in the letter to the Hebrews. The writer of that epistle spoke of the tabernacle that Moses built in the wilderness as a "copy and shadow of the heavenly things" (Hebrews 8:5). Even the beauty of Solomon's Temple was only a facsimile of the glory of the real thing. John now had the opportunity to see the genuine article.

> The temple of God was opened in heaven, and the ark of
> His covenant was seen in His temple. And there were light-
> nings, noises, thunderings, an earthquake, and great hail
> (Revelation 11:19).

Not only did the apostle see the beauty of God's heavenly temple, but he saw the ark of the covenant. With all that effort that Indiana Jones put into tracking down the ark, little did he know that he was only after a copy of the real thing. Along with the opening of the temple of heaven came the "sight and sound" formula showing the power and majesty of the Lord.

With the second interlude concluded and the seventh trumpet sounded, we now take a break from the narrative. When John wants something to be taken allegorically, he will tell us so. When we begin chapter 12, that's exactly what he does.

THE THIRD INTERLUDE, PART 1: THE INVISIBLE WAR

REVELATION 12

After stepping back into the judgment narrative with the seventh trumpet, John steps right back out. It's story time in heaven, and, while we're reading it in a book, he was watching it play out in the heavens.

I understand that there are those who will read the phrase *story time* and panic. "Amir, are you agreeing with those who treat Revelation like fiction or an allegory?" Definitely not. Most of the letter is apocalyptic narrative describing events that will take place during the day of the Lord. There are times, however, when that changes. Those who allegorize the book may respond, "But you are being inconsistent. Why do you get to pick and choose what is allegory and what is narrative?" My response is that I don't pick and choose. I read the text. John makes it perfectly clear that we are shifting gears with the first seven words of this chapter: "Now a great sign appeared in heaven…" (Revelation 12:1). John tells us he is about to see something that is a sign or a symbol of something else.

Remember how Jesus communicated with the multitudes? Often, he spoke to people by telling stories or parables. The word *parable* comes from two Greek words—*para*, which means "alongside of," and *ballo*, which means "to cast or throw." A parable is a story that comes alongside a truth to illustrate it. When a parable is understood, it can bring great depth of meaning and feeling. Think of the shepherd finding his lost lamb, or the woman finding her lost wedding coin, or the father welcoming home his lost son, all of which illustrate the heavenly joy over a lost sinner who receives salvation (Luke 15).

Sometimes, however, parables are difficult to understand if you don't have the key to unlock their meanings. Jesus explained many of His parables to His disciples, but not to the masses. When the disciples asked Him why He didn't open the meanings to everybody, He replied, "I speak to them in parables, because seeing they do not see, and hearing they do not hear, nor do they understand" (Matthew 13:13).

There are those who will look at these next few chapters in Revelation and throw their hands in the air, saying, "This is just too weird. There are so many possible interpretations, how can anyone know the truth?" But that is like saying, "God, hate to break it to You, but You kind of messed up this part. You made these chapters so confusing that we'll never know the truth. So, we're just going to skip them." God included this part for a reason. And, like every other part of Scripture, with careful interpretation and the guidance of the Holy Spirit, we can understand what it is that He wants to communicate to us.

The Dragon ID'd

In the opening pages of my novel *Operation Joktan*, I included a list of characters. I wanted to make sure that everyone could identify who was who, particularly as the story progressed. Looking at the sign John sees, it would be beneficial for us to determine its cast of primary characters. That way, we will know who we're dealing with. As we read, we will notice that there is one character who is identified directly, one who is identified indirectly, and one who has a few options. Let's begin with the direct:

> Now a great sign appeared in heaven: a woman clothed with the sun, with the moon under her feet, and on her head a garland of twelve stars. Then being with child, she cried out in labor and in pain to give birth. And another sign appeared in heaven: behold, a great, fiery red dragon having seven heads and ten horns, and seven diadems on his heads. His tail drew a third of the stars of heaven and threw them to the earth. And the dragon stood before the woman who was ready to give birth, to devour her Child as soon as it was born (Revelation 12:1-4).

Without any doubt, there are symbols and analogies throughout the book of Revelation. And yet many of them are interpreted directly by the apostle John or just by looking at the context and comparing the passage with the rest of the Bible. This is one of those cases.

The word "dragon" is used thirteen times in Revelation. Eight of those occasions are here in this chapter. While the identity of the dragon is fairly apparent, before we give a positive ID, we should look at the wider context.

In Revelation 13:2, we see the dragon giving power and authority to the Antichrist. That certainly narrows down the options. But for those who want something a little more concrete, John gives us a rock-solid identification in chapter 20:

> I saw an angel coming down from heaven, having the key to the bottomless pit and a great chain in his hand. He laid hold of the dragon, that serpent of old, who is the Devil and Satan, and bound him for a thousand years; and he cast him into the bottomless pit, and shut him up, and set a seal on him, so that he should deceive the nations no more till the thousand years were finished. But after these things he must be released for a little while (Revelation 20:1-3).

Mystery solved, case closed, suspect identified in a record time that would make Sherlock Holmes envious. The dragon is the devil, and he has wanted to destroy this child long before He was ever born.

The Child ID'd

When God confronted Adam and Eve with their sin in the garden, He also dealt with the serpent. He told him,

> I will put enmity
> between you and the woman,
> and between your seed and her Seed;
> He shall bruise your head,
> and you shall bruise His heel (Genesis 3:15).

From the beginning, God foretold the victory of the coming Messiah over the devil. Because of that, Satan tried to destroy the Jews in general throughout history and Jesus specifically once He arrived on earth. His first attempt at the Messiah was while He was still a babe in Bethlehem: "Now when [the wise men] had departed, behold, an angel of the Lord appeared to Joseph in a dream, saying, 'Arise, take the young Child and His mother, flee to Egypt, and stay there until I bring you word; for Herod will seek the young Child to destroy Him'" (Matthew 2:13).

Thirty-three years later, Satan finally did have what he perceived to be a great victory. Jesus was crucified on the cross and died. Three days later, that devilish dragon discovered that all his evil work had ended up playing right into the perfect, righteous plan of God the Father. It reminds me of the Old Testament story of Haman, who wanted to kill Mordecai the Jew so badly that he built a scaffold seventy-five feet high on which to hang him. It wasn't long, though, before his fail-proof plan failed so badly that Haman himself was impaled on the gibbet.

Even though Jesus is not mentioned by name, He is clearly the child mentioned in Revelation 12. If anyone is still not convinced, they just need to read how John describes Him in verse 5:

> She bore a male Child who was to rule all nations with a rod of iron. And her Child was caught up to God and His throne.

There is only one person who was "caught up" and who will rule the nations with an iron scepter, and that is the Lord Jesus Christ. There may be those who say, "Amir! There is the Greek word *harpazo*. You yourself said that it is the word for the rapture, so the passage must be talking about the church, not Jesus." First, let me compliment you on your Greek skills. But second, you need to read the whole verse. The church is never told that we will rule nations with an iron scepter. That role belongs only to Jesus Christ, the ruler of the nations and the scepter-wielding Lion of Judah:

> Ask of Me, and I will give You
> the nations for Your inheritance,
> and the ends of the earth for Your possession.
> You shall break them with a rod of iron;
> you shall dash them to pieces like a potter's vessel
> (Psalm 2:8-9).

> The scepter shall not depart from Judah,
> nor a lawgiver from between his feet,
> until Shiloh comes;
> and to Him shall be the obedience of the people
> (Genesis 49:10).

If there is still any doubt that Jesus is that ruler, we only need to look further into Revelation to find John's chill-inducing description of the Lord:

> Now I saw heaven opened, and behold, a white horse. And He who sat on him was called Faithful and True, and in righteousness He judges and makes war. His eyes were like a flame of fire, and on His head were many crowns. He had a name written that no one knew except Himself. He was clothed with a robe dipped in blood, and His name is called The Word of God. And the armies in heaven, clothed in fine linen, white and clean, followed Him on white horses. Now out of His mouth goes a sharp sword, that with it He should strike the nations. And He Himself will rule them with a rod of iron. He Himself treads the winepress of the fierceness and wrath of Almighty God (Revelation 19:11-15).

The child is Jesus the Messiah, and the dragon has been after Him from day one. These first two identifications have been fairly simple. Tracking down the identity of the woman is a little more challenging.

The Woman ID'd

It would be easy to say, "Well, if the child is Jesus, then the woman must be His mother, Mary." But remember that John labels this section as a sign. It is a parable of sorts that tells a bigger story. The Bible and history both inform us that Jesus was born of a virgin. Not only was she a virgin, though, she was a Jewish virgin. This ethnicity is key to the woman's identity.

After she gave birth to her child and the child was caught up to safety from the jaws of the dragon, she "fled into the wilderness, where she has a place prepared by God, that they should feed her there one thousand two hundred and sixty days" (Revelation 12:6). We know those numbers. Those are tribulation numbers—forty-two months; three-and-a-half years; time, times, and half a time. Placing Jesus' mother, Mary, into this scenario in the tribulation period makes little sense and doesn't fit with the overall grandeur of what is being described.

An important clue to the woman's identity can be discovered if we answer the question, Why did she flee? But before we can answer that, we must make a temporal jump. Between verses 5 and 6 there is a time lapse. This is common in prophetic statements. Reading this passage is like looking at a series of mountain peaks. From a distance, those peaks look like they are back to back to back. However, if you climb to the top of the first peak, you often discover that the second peak is miles away, and the third is even farther. The same is true about prophecy. You may have years, centuries, or millennia between one verse and the next.

For instance, when Isaiah wrote about the birth of the Messiah, he said,

> Unto us a Child is born,
> unto us a Son is given (Isaiah 9:6).

Seven hundred years before that incredible night in Bethlehem, the prophet told of the moment that the Messiah would come as a gift from the Father above. We read of that earth-shattering event in the Gospels of Matthew and Luke. But, if we keep reading in Isaiah, in the very next phrase, he jumps at least 2,000 years ahead to a period that has not yet come:

> And the government will be upon His shoulder.
> And His name will be called
> Wonderful, Counselor, Mighty God,
> Everlasting Father, Prince of Peace.
> Of the increase of His government and peace
> there will be no end,
> upon the throne of David and over His kingdom,
> to order it and establish it with judgment and justice
> from that time forward, even forever.
> The zeal of the LORD of hosts will perform this
> (verses 6-7).

In Revelation 12, John moves from the ascension of Jesus in verse 5 to the woman fleeing for the wilderness in verse 6. He jumps from sixty years before he received this vision to a time that has yet to happen. What is the reason for the woman's flight? That is described in the next seven verses.

> War broke out in heaven: Michael and his angels fought with the dragon; and the dragon and his angels fought, but they did not prevail, nor was a place found for them in heaven any longer. So the great dragon was cast out, that serpent of old, called the Devil and Satan, who deceives the whole world; he was cast to the earth, and his angels were cast out with him. Then I heard a loud voice saying in heaven, "Now salvation, and strength, and the kingdom of our God, and the power of His Christ have come, for the accuser of our brethren, who accused them before our God day and night, has been cast down. And they overcame him by the blood of the Lamb and by the word of their testimony, and they did not love their lives to the death. Therefore rejoice, O heavens, and you who dwell

in them! Woe to the inhabitants of the earth and the sea! For the devil has come down to you, having great wrath, because he knows that he has a short time." Now when the dragon saw that he had been cast to the earth, he persecuted the woman who gave birth to the male Child (Revelation 12:7-13).

An angelic war breaks out, with Michael and his angels on one side, and the dragon and his angels on the other. Michael prevails and Satan is cast out of heaven for good. The question is whether this has happened yet. Is this speaking of when the devil was cast down to earth for his prideful desire to usurp God's authority? I don't believe it is.

According to the book of Job, Satan continues to have access to God in heaven (1:6; 2:1). After this great angelic battle, however, no longer will there be "a place found for them in heaven." While there will be rejoicing in heaven, there will be great bitterness down below on earth. The devil, in defeat, will take out his anger on the woman, and he will persecute the woman who gave birth to the male child (Revelation 12:13). When will this happen? According to John F. Walvoord,

> The immediate aftermath of Satan's being cast out of heaven is his persecution of the woman which brought forth the man-child. This apparently is the beginning of the great tribulation of which Christ warned Israel in Matthew 24:15-22.[13]

When Walvoord speaks of "the great tribulation," he is talking of the second three-and-a-half years of the seven-year period. We'll deal with this a little more when we get to chapter 16 and the bowl judgments. This once again fits perfectly with the "one thousand two hundred and sixty days" of verse 6 and the "time and times and half a time" in verse 14.

With these clues, is there any other passage in Scripture that could aid us in identifying this woman? I believe there is. When Jesus spoke from the Mount of Olives, He said that when the Jews (the people whom He was addressing) saw in the temple the abomination that makes desolate that Daniel spoke of in his day, they should flee to the mountains. Most likely He was referring to the mountains in present-day Jordan. This probably includes Petra, a city cut out of stone. To enter it, you must navigate the Siq, a mile-long, narrow gorge with very high stone walls on either side. If you've watched *Indiana Jones and the Last Crusade*, you have seen Petra.

When you combine the devil, Jesus, and the one who gave birth to Jesus, it is not difficult to identify the woman. She is the nation of Israel. Ever since the first curse in Genesis, the devil has done all he could to destroy the advent and the sustaining of the Jewish people. At first, it was so he could stop the coming Messiah. Now it is so that he can thwart God's plans for His coming judgment on the world, including on Satan and his servants. In those final days of the tribulation, Satan will act purely out of spite in the hope that there will be no more Jews left. He wants to negate the promise that at the end, "all Israel will be saved" (Romans 11:26).

When we look at the sorrow and grief the devil causes today while he still has access to heaven, imagine what it will be like when he is locked out and he knows that his days are numbered. His fury will know no limits. It will be his demonic hordes that will pour out of the abyss to torment mankind for five months with the sting of a scorpion. It will be his four demonic spirits at the Euphrates River who will lead the 200 million troops to kill a third of mankind. And it will be the devil himself who will empower the Antichrist to carry out his schemes. This is what we will discover in the next chapter.

CHAPTER 13

THE THIRD INTERLUDE, PART 2: THE ANTICHRIST COMES TO POWER

REVELATION 13

The Antichrist. Is there any name on earth, other than Satan or Lucifer, that causes as much fear? For many, it is like saying, "Bath time" to a dog—the dog just wants to run and hide. And rightfully so. The Antichrist will fully live up to the hype that his name invites. He will be a servant of Satan, and he will serve his master well. It's no wonder that the name most often given for him is the quite descriptive moniker *beast*.

In fact, "beast" is found thirty-seven times in the book of Revelation and seven times in Daniel. With the Old Testament prophet, it will sometimes refer to a specific nation, other times, a person. In Revelation, "beast" is used exclusively of an individual.

> I stood on the sand of the sea. And I saw a beast rising up out of the sea, having seven heads and ten horns, and on his horns ten crowns, and on his heads a blasphemous name. Now the beast which I saw was like a leopard, his feet were like the feet of a bear, and his mouth like the mouth of a lion (Revelation 13:1-2).

The Arrival of the Antichrist

Many years ago, there was a movie made about a monster that came up out of the water and attacked people. This green *Creature from the Black Lagoon* looked to be part fish and part lizard, and sported lips that appeared to have been enhanced by the worst of California's plastic surgeons. If the Antichrist is going to use his looks and charisma to win the hearts of the world, then chances are his "rising up out of the sea" is going to look quite a bit different than that of the Hollywood monster.

What does John mean when he says that the beast will come out of the sea? Once again, we must compare scripture with scripture to understand the symbolism here. Daniel linked beasts and the sea when he wrote, "I saw in my vision by night, and behold, the four winds of heaven were stirring up the Great Sea. And four great beasts came up from the sea, each different from the other" (Daniel 7:2-3).

The four beasts Daniel saw are four Gentile empires—Babylon, Medo-Persia, Greece, and Rome. Once again, these kingdoms did not literally rise out of the water, particularly the first two, which were not seafaring by nature. A look back to Revelation helps us to understand both these nations' origins and the beast's. An angel who was explaining a vision to John said,

> The waters which you saw, where the harlot sits, are peoples, multitudes, nations, and tongues (Revelation 17:15).

The sea in Daniel 7 and the waters here in Revelation are the same thing. They are Gentile nations from which will come empires and the Antichrist. Each of the empires mentioned in the book of Daniel treated people in a beastly manner. They ruled the world brutally. Whatever their despots said was treated as law. This will be true of the beast who is yet to come.

Some may wonder, "Why does John call him the beast? It's not like he doesn't know the name Antichrist." That is a good question, especially considering that John wrote in his first letter, "Little children, it is the last hour; and as you have heard that the Antichrist is coming, even now many antichrists have come, by which we know that it is the last hour" (1 John 2:18). We need to remember that we are in a symbolic portion of Revelation, where John is seeing images that are representative of reality but not necessarily real themselves. When John is shown the Antichrist, he describes him as a beast because that is a perfect description of the character of this unholy person.

The beast that rose out of the sea was quite unusual in appearance. Like the dragon (12:3), he had seven heads and ten horns. This also hearkens back to a beast that Daniel wrote about who similarly had ten horns:

> After this I saw in the night visions, and behold, a fourth beast, dreadful and terrible, exceedingly strong. It had huge iron teeth; it was devouring, breaking in pieces, and trampling the residue with its feet. It was different from all the beasts that were before it, and it had ten horns (Daniel 7:7).

John, however, goes deeper in his description, saying the beast was "like a leopard, his feet were like the feet of a bear, and his mouth like the mouth of a lion" (Revelation 13:2). Once again, Daniel parallels the imagery. We saw Daniel's fourth beast with the ten horns. What about the previous three beasts?

> The first was like a lion, and had eagle's wings...And suddenly another beast, a second, like a bear. It was raised up on one side, and had three ribs in its mouth between its teeth. And they said thus to it: "Arise, devour much flesh!"...After this I looked, and there was another, like a leopard, which had on its back four wings of a bird (Daniel 7:4-6).

"But wait, Amir! Either Daniel or John got the order of the beasts wrong. They are exactly reversed." Once again, I must commend you for your astute observations. But remember that Daniel's vision looks forward. Babylon the lion had already come. The next to rise would be Medo-Persia the bear, then Greece the leopard, and finally the fourth beast with the ten horns, which was Rome. John, however, looks backward. This is not the future for him; it is history. So he starts with the most recent and lists the creatures in reverse.

What about the seven heads and the ten horns? Again, these are referring to Gentile nations. The seven heads are seven sequential kings, and the ten horns are a royal confederacy. How do we know that? Let's check our context. Later in Revelation, an angel speaks to John and says,

> Here is the mind which has wisdom: The seven heads are seven mountains on which the woman sits. There are also seven kings. Five have fallen, one is, and the other has not yet come. And when he comes, he must continue a short time. The beast that was, and is not, is himself also the eighth, and is of the seven, and is going to perdition. The ten horns which you saw are ten kings who have received no kingdom as yet, but they receive authority for one hour as kings with the beast (Revelation 17:9-12).

So we see that the Antichrist will rise out of the Gentile nations and will be given power by Satan himself, the dragon. He is symbolized as a beast due both to the unrighteousness of his character and the violence of his actions. The Antichrist is the final in a succession of secular rulers spoken of by both Daniel and John, and his kingdom will be the last before Jesus returns to earth to reign from Jerusalem.

The Fatal Wound

The fourth beast in Daniel is the Roman Empire. It was different from the others, and it is out of this empire that the horns arise (Daniel 7:7-8). In some manner or form, the power and influence of the Roman Empire is going to be revived at the time of the tribulation. It is from this coming European conglomeration that the Antichrist will emerge.

> I saw one of his heads as if it had been mortally wounded, and his deadly wound was healed. And all the world marveled and followed the beast. So they worshiped the dragon

who gave authority to the beast; and they worshiped the
beast, saying, "Who is like the beast? Who is able to make
war with him?" (Revelation 13:3-4).

Here we read about an incident with the beast that has caused much
speculation. One of its heads is fatally wounded, but then either he
somehow survives or is brought back to life. Does this mean that the
Antichrist himself will be wounded or killed in an assassination attempt?
Could this be some kind of fake death and resurrection in order to gar-
ner sympathy and support or to boost his credentials? Or could this be
saying that the revived Roman Empire will experience a fatal wound?

From the English text, it is difficult to tell. But the Greek wording
is very similar to what was said about the Lamb looking "as though it
had been slain" (Revelation 5:6). Jesus was literally slain and then resurrected from the dead. It is quite possible that the Antichrist will want
to mimic a similar event in order to gain the awe and reverence of the
masses, and through deception will accomplish this objective. There
is also a strong potential that the Antichrist will actually be killed and
later resurrected.

"How can that be?" you may ask. "Only God has the power to give
life to the dead." That is true. But remember what Jesus said to His disciples: "False christs and false prophets will rise and show great signs
and wonders to deceive, if possible, even the elect" (Matthew 24:24).

In the last days, there are going to be works and wonders so powerful that even the elect can be fooled. God has given power and authority on this earth to Satan for a time, and we don't know the extent of
what He has granted. It is certainly within the realm of possibility that
the alive/dead/alive scenario will be exactly what it appears to be.

This resurrection will cause the world to marvel at the beast and
eventually worship him. Strong delusion will penetrate the world and
the Jews in particular. People everywhere will become convinced that
this is the promised Messiah. They will raise up new gods to follow—
the dragon and the beast.

He was given a mouth speaking great things and blasphe-
mies, and he was given authority to continue for forty-two

months. Then he opened his mouth in blasphemy against God, to blaspheme His name, His tabernacle, and those who dwell in heaven. It was granted to him to make war with the saints and to overcome them. And authority was given him over every tribe, tongue, and nation. All who dwell on the earth will worship him, whose names have not been written in the Book of Life of the Lamb slain from the foundation of the world. If anyone has an ear, let him hear. He who leads into captivity shall go into captivity; he who kills with the sword must be killed with the sword. Here is the patience and the faith of the saints (Revelation 13:5-10).

Notice in this passage that the phrases "was given" and "was granted to him" are used multiple times. The Antichrist has no power in himself. He is not some demigod or mighty angelic being. Any authority and influence he has is only that which has been bestowed upon him, and it will only be for a time—forty-two months, or 1,260 days, or three-and-a-half years, otherwise known as time, times, and half a time. During that period, he will have the power to slander God and the saints in heaven (verse 6), make war against the saints on earth and conquer them (verse 7), and cause all the inhabitants of the earth to worship him (verse 8).

This authority will be allowed by God, but it will come directly from Satan. The Antichrist will be a puppet, controlled and empowered by the devil himself. It is during the first three-and-a-half years of the tribulation that he will come to power. The armies of Russia, Turkey, Iran, Sudan, Libya, and other nations that seek to plunder Israel will be defeated (Ezekiel 38–39). This great defeat will provide an opening for the Antichrist to come as a peacemaker. As a result, his dominion will be global.

During the final three-and-a-half years of the tribulation, the Antichrist will turn from a peacemaker to a peace-taker. He will set himself up in the new temple in Jerusalem and will demand worship from the citizens of the world. Who will fall for the lies of the Antichrist and bow down before him? The answer, quite simply, is everyone.

John wrote that everyone "whose names have not been written in the Book of Life of the Lamb slain from the foundation of the world" will take a knee before this global leader. What is the Book of Life? It is where God has listed all those who belong to Him, those who are part of His family. Isn't it amazing to think that if you have given your life to Jesus Christ, it is because your name was written in the Lamb's book before you were even born? What a blessed thought! As Paul wrote:

> Blessed be the God and Father of our Lord Jesus Christ, who has blessed us with every spiritual blessing in the heavenly places in Christ, just as He chose us in Him before the foundation of the world, that we should be holy and without blame before Him in love (Ephesians 1:3-4).

The False Prophet

At this point, for all those who thought that one beast was already more than enough, the world is about to get double the trouble. A new beast arrives on the scene:

> Then I saw another beast coming up out of the earth, and he had two horns like a lamb and spoke like a dragon. And he exercises all the authority of the first beast in his presence, and causes the earth and those who dwell in it to worship the first beast, whose deadly wound was healed. He performs great signs, so that he even makes fire come down from heaven on the earth in the sight of men. And he deceives those who dwell on the earth by those signs which he was granted to do in the sight of the beast, telling those who dwell on the earth to make an image to the beast who was wounded by the sword and lived. He was granted power to give breath to the image of the beast, that the image of the beast should both speak and cause as many as would not worship the image of the beast to be killed (Revelation 13:11-15).

It isn't until chapter 16 that we are given the identity of this new beast. He is the false prophet. This Beast 2.0 will come with great signs and wonders, even calling fire down from the sky. Humanity will *oooh* and *ahhh* and be ready to do whatever the false prophet tells them to do. Once the false prophet has them where he wants them, he'll give them two tasks. First, make an image of the Antichrist. Second, worship it. It is here that the rule of the Antichrist moves from autocracy to theocracy. No longer will he be content to be followed as a great man; he will now demand to be worshipped as the all-powerful god.

Beast worship will not be a choice. It will be demanded as the new one-world religion. Freedom of worship will be gone. Freedom of expression will be removed. Freedom of the press will no longer exist. Everyone will have to fall 100 percent in line with the demands of the government order as led by the Antichrist.

Imagine what it will be like for believers during that time. They will huddle up in their homes for secret worship services. Others will clandestinely meet out in the woods to express their praise to God. Countless thousands will lose their jobs. They will be reduced to begging on the streets, where they will be beaten and spit upon because they have not followed the government's orders. Though they will have much to look forward to after death, there will be very little to look forward to before death.

The Mark of the Beast

And now it comes—the moment we deal with the most infamous trio of numbers in the history of the world.

> He causes all, both small and great, rich and poor, free and slave, to receive a mark on their right hand or on their foreheads, and that no one may buy or sell except one who has the mark or the name of the beast, or the number of his name. Here is wisdom. Let him who has understanding calculate the number of the beast, for it is the number of a man: His number is 666 (Revelation 13:16-18).

So much has been speculated about when it comes to the mark of the beast. The number 666 is used throughout popular entertainment's horror genre. Goths paint it on their clothing, Satanists tattoo it on their knuckles, online preachers drop it into their sermon titles to boost their views. But what does that short sequence of numbers really mean? Let's look at the facts.

First, this is not speaking of a Roman emperor's name. There are those, many of whom are in the camp that says that Revelation took place around AD 70, who have looked at the numbers and sought to find their equivalent in Hebrew or Latin or Greek. They've then taken those letters, compared them with the emperors, then said, "Aha!" The problem is that like the historicists we spoke of in this book's welcome, if you put 12 numerologists in 12 different rooms, they'll come back with 12 different emperors. As we've said before, you just can't fit a backward-looking allegorical peg into a future-looking literal hole.

The context of this passage has its eyes on what is yet to come. There is nothing about a "one-religion, worldwide worship of an image representing a global leader" that even remotely fits any time in history. Twisting and contorting at that level is beyond even the most flexible of Olympic gymnasts. The number 666, or possibly 616 according to some early Greek manuscripts, is most likely referring to the future Antichrist. What exactly do those numbers mean? It's another one of the mysteries of this most intriguing of books. If God has left blank the final word in the sentence, "The 666 guy is _____," then we shouldn't waste too much brainpower in speculation.

Still, so many people run down the rabbit hole of this creepy number and miss the overall point of the passage. This chapter is about two people who will rise up and take over the world. Rather than turning people to the worship of the living God, they will force the worship of the Antichrist. Those who don't worship his image will be put to death.

To show loyalty to the beast, people will have to receive his mark. Without this identifier of allegiance to the Antichrist, a person will not be able to buy or sell. It will be a horrible time in which believers will suffer greatly through violence, poverty, and starvation. As for those who accept the mark, they will not only live under an oppressive government, but they will experience all the other judgments as God's wrath is poured out on the planet.

It is human nature to want to control others. There is no greater evidence of this than in governments. Governments want power, and they usually get it by force or, as in many democracies, by deceit and by making promises to people that they never plan on fulfilling. In this next chapter, we will see governmental power at its worst because the endgame is not just political but spiritual.

CHAPTER 14

THE THIRD INTERLUDE, PART 3: PREVIEWS OF THINGS TO COME

REVELATION 14

It's date night with your spouse. The last few weeks have been incredibly hectic, and you are looking forward to getting out and spending some time between just the two of you. A movie came out two weeks ago that had miraculously made both of your must-see lists, and you had already ordered your tickets for the theater with the reserved leather reclining seats. It was going to be a nice, casual night with the one you love.

Then the iron fizzled out in the middle of smoothing out your shirt. Your middle child somehow managed to run forehead-first into the corner of the door. The sister of your babysitter showed up thirty minutes late, saying your scheduled sitter had the flu but that she herself was feeling fine, sniffing as she said so. In a move that you would never have made when all you had was your first child but was a no-brainer now that you've had three, you gave the replacement sitter your contact numbers and rushed out the door.

Then you wondered if someone at the traffic department was out to get you because you missed every single green light. When you finally got to the theater, you ignored the line for the concessions, found your auditorium, crawled over the legs of a series of people whose irons hadn't broken down and whose babysitters didn't have the flu, and plopped down in your seats just as the lights dimmed.

You grinned at your spouse. Made it just in time.

But then a movie starts that is not your movie. Quickly you realize that it is not a movie at all. All your rushing did was get you there in time for the previews. For the next fifteen minutes you watch scenes from other films that you don't care about and that you will never see, all the while thinking, *We could have stopped for a big bucket of popcorn and a box of Raisinets.*

If you are reading only to hear about the next series of judgments, this is the time to grab your popcorn and a soda. John is about to treat us to a few coming attractions before we get to our main feature in chapters 15–18.

Preview One: The Redeeming Lamb and 144,000 Redeemed

The 144,000 are back. Or are they? Are these the same 12 x 12,000 that we saw before or are they a different group? And, come to think of it, the question isn't just *who* are they, but *where* are they? These first five verses in chapter 14 have quite a few well-respected theologians taking several different views.

> I looked, and behold, a Lamb standing on Mount Zion, and with Him one hundred and forty-four thousand, having His Father's name written on their foreheads. And I heard a voice from heaven, like the voice of many waters, and like the voice of loud thunder. And I heard the sound of harpists playing their harps. They sang as it were a new song before the throne, before the four living creatures, and the elders; and no one could learn that song except the hundred and forty-four thousand who were redeemed from the earth. These are the ones who were not defiled with women, for they are virgins. These are the ones who follow the Lamb wherever He goes. These were redeemed

from among men, being firstfruits to God and to the Lamb. And in their mouth was found no deceit, for they are without fault before the throne of God (Revelation 14:1-5).

The first time we heard about a group of 144,000 Jewish evangelists was back in chapter 7 when they were given their commission. Are these the same young men, and are they standing in heaven or on earth? Charles C. Ryrie believes this group is the same 144,000 and sees the action taking place in heaven:

> Some understand this to be anticipatory of the millennial state, making Zion mean the earthly Jerusalem as it sometimes does (2 Sam. 5:7; Isa. 2:3). But since Zion is used of the heavenly Jerusalem (Heb. 12:22) and since these 144,000 are before the throne (v. 3), it seems more natural to understand Zion as the heavenly city. The important point, however, is that the 144,000 are now with the Lamb. When the group was first introduced they were on earth (7:1–3), but now they are in heaven. Their work of witnessing must now be finished, for none will be able to slay them until then. That they are the same group as in chapter 7 seems clear because (1) the distinctive number is exactly the same, and (2) God's name is written on their foreheads.[14]

John F. Walvoord would agree and disagree with Ryrie. He believes it is the same group of witnesses but says that they are standing with the Lamb on the earthly Mount Zion in Israel.

> Preferable is the view that this is a prophetic vision of the ultimate triumph of the Lamb following His second coming, when He joins the 144,000 on Mount Zion at the beginning of His millennial reign.[15]

Tim LaHaye and Timothy E. Parker agree this takes place at the heavenly Mount Zion but see these as a different 144,000.

The 144,000 from Revelation 7 were from the tribes of Israel, and their activity was on earth. Also, the group from Revelation 7 is sealed with the seal of the Father, while the Revelation 14 group has upon their heads the name of both the Father and the Son. This leaves little doubt that the groups are separate.[16]

I see no reason to distinguish between this 144,000 and the evangelists we met in chapter 7. At that time, they received the seal of God on their foreheads. That seal represented God's protection through the tribulation. But as this chapter opens, we are getting a preview of the end of the seven years of God's wrath. These faithful young men have given their testimony and the seal of protection has kept them safe. However, once their task was completed, it is very likely they were allowed to be killed. This is similar to what happened earlier with the two witnesses. No one could harm them during the three-and-a-half years of their ministry, but "when they finish their testimony, the beast that ascends out of the bottomless pit will make war against them, overcome them, and kill them" (Revelation 11:7). Anyone who thinks that this is a cruel chain of events—serve God, then die—doesn't understand the extreme harshness of the conditions of the earth and the extreme joy of being in the presence of God.

The 144,000 are standing there with the Lamb on Mount Zion. But I agree with Ryrie that it is not the earthly Mount Zion, but the heavenly one. The writer of Hebrews describes it thus:

> You have come to Mount Zion and to the city of the living God, the heavenly Jerusalem, to an innumerable company of angels, to the general assembly and church of the firstborn who are registered in heaven, to God the Judge of all, to the spirits of just men made perfect, to Jesus the Mediator of the new covenant, and to the blood of sprinkling that speaks better things than that of Abel (Hebrews 12:22-24).

On earth is the shadow of the true Mount Zion, in heaven is the reality. The fact that the 144,000 "sang as it were a new song before the throne, before the four living creatures, and the elders" necessitates their throne room location (Revelation 14:3). Just before the music starts, a booming voice speaks from heaven. We are left in the dark as to what it says. Then the music starts.

Music is constantly evolving. Styles and genres come and go. Today, we are in the praise era of Christian music. It seems that every week there is a new worship song that sweeps through the worldwide church. While there are quite a few that can be reduced to three chords and four lines repeated over and over and over, there are also many that are deep and heartfelt and are effective at transporting a congregation or even an individual commuting to work right into the presence of God.

The now heaven-dwelling witnesses break out in a worship song that is specifically tailored to them and their experiences. As much as we would like to know what it is, it is not for us. We have our own stories and our own praises to offer to God. This particular song, sung to the accompaniment of virtuoso harpists, is truly and completely theirs.

Pure, truthful, and without fault before the throne of God, these men are described by John as the "firstfruits to God and to the Lamb" (verse 4). The concept of firstfruits comes from the Old Testament. The firstfruits of the harvest belonged to God. It was the first gleaning that was to be set aside before being presented to the Lord as an offering. As we discussed earlier, the fact that they are "first" fruits means that there are more to follow. This is the same hope we gain from the knowledge that Jesus is the firstfruits of the resurrection:

> Now Christ is risen from the dead, and has become the firstfruits of those who have fallen asleep. For since by man came death, by Man also came the resurrection of the dead. For as in Adam all die, even so in Christ all shall be made alive. But each one in his own order: Christ the firstfruits, afterward those who are Christ's at His coming (1 Corinthians 15:20-23).

Jesus died, then rose again in a body that is immortal and incorruptible. Thus, we can be assured that one day as "second" fruits we will be raised in the same kind of eternal body to live forever with our

Savior, the Lamb. I wonder what kind of song we will learn in that day. I would suspect it is very similar to the hymns of praise that we have enjoyed throughout this wonderful visit to heaven.

Now that the 144,000 are praising God before the throne, does that mean that there is no more witness of Christ on the earth? Is everyone left below who hasn't turned to the Lord doomed because the gospel has been removed? As John watched, another angel flew by in heaven bringing a message of reassurance that the salvation message is still being proclaimed on earth, but with a warning that the window for acceptance is drawing to an end:

> Then I saw another angel flying in the midst of heaven, having the everlasting gospel to preach to those who dwell on the earth—to every nation, tribe, tongue, and people—saying with a loud voice, "Fear God and give glory to Him, for the hour of His judgment has come; and worship Him who made heaven and earth, the sea and springs of water" (Revelation 14:6-7).

With this cliffhanger of an ending, the first preview concludes. The projector keeps rolling, and the second coming attraction runs.

Preview Two: The Fall of Babylon

This preview is short, but it packs enough in it to get at least a PG-13 rating.

> Another angel followed, saying, "Babylon is fallen, is fallen, that great city, because she has made all nations drink of the wine of the wrath of her fornication" (14:8).

The message is earthshaking. Who or what is Babylon? We will go much more in depth about this when we arrive at chapters 17 and 18. For now, it is enough to know that Babylon is both a religious and economic system. Again and again throughout Scripture, the demise of Babylon has been predicted. Isaiah prophesied the fall of the empire, and tacked on the addendum that it would never be rebuilt:

> Babylon, the glory of kingdoms,
> the beauty of the Chaldeans' pride,
> will be as when God overthrew Sodom and Gomorrah.
> It will never be inhabited,
> nor will it be settled from generation to generation;
> nor will the Arabian pitch tents there,
> nor will the shepherds make their sheepfolds there
> (Isaiah 13:19-20).

The Babylonian Empire fell to the Persians in 539 BC, and the city crumbled over time afterward. As God declared through Isaiah, it has never been restored. Saddam Hussein attempted it, but that didn't work out so well for him. His kingdom collapsed as do all works that originate in man's rebellion against what God has ordained.

The physical city may be gone; the Babylonian systems remain. These, too, are born out of rebellion against God and a craving to fulfill one's own desires. The angel declares that it is a fornication-based system, meaning that it is purely centered on people fulfilling their own longings. If you look around at culture today, that is exactly what you see. Our world is centered purely on satisfying one's passions and lusts, be they sexual, financial, experiential, or anything else that is self-centered. It becomes so engrossing that people can be said to be drunk with their need to fulfill their desires. That is the me-based system that is going to come crashing to the ground.

Preview Three: The Marked and the Unmarked

If you're getting antsy for the main feature, you're going to have to wait a little longer. There are still a few more previews to watch. The next one begins the same as the previous, but the content of the angel's words are much more picturesque:

> Then a third angel followed them, saying with a loud voice,
> "If anyone worships the beast and his image, and receives
> his mark on his forehead or on his hand, he himself shall
> also drink of the wine of the wrath of God, which is poured
> out full strength into the cup of His indignation. He shall

be tormented with fire and brimstone in the presence of the holy angels and in the presence of the Lamb. And the smoke of their torment ascends forever and ever; and they have no rest day or night, who worship the beast and his image, and whoever receives the mark of his name" (Revelation 14:9-11).

I'm betting that John was happy he only had to hear about this punishment instead of seeing it. The angel speaks about the judgment of those who have worshipped the beast and his image. They are the ones who received his mark on their forehead or hand. They had access to what food and medicines may have been available during that time. It was these men and women who persecuted those who refused to receive the mark. They were the ones cheering their executions or watching as they starved because they had no ability to buy or sell. These are the wicked followers of the beast who will experience the final series of judgments that are about to be poured out of the bowls.

No one is telling John to write the next words that we read. There is no angel showing him a new vision. The words flow from his pen and feel almost like a sigh amid all the carnage.

> Here is the patience of the saints; here are those who keep the commandments of God and the faith of Jesus (Revelation 14:12).

If you have ever bought a diamond, most likely the jeweler placed your stone on a background of black velvet. That is done to show off the brilliance of the diamond—the precision of the cut, the clarity of the stone, the sparkle as the light passes through. John, in one phrase, presents the startling beauty of the faithful saints as they play off the darkness of followers of the beast. The contrast that he presents is so powerful that it seems to move those in heaven.

> Then I heard a voice from heaven saying to me, "Write: 'Blessed are the dead who die in the Lord from now on.'"
> "Yes," says the Spirit, "that they may rest from their labors, and their works follow them" (14:13).

Wow! Not only does a voice from heaven respond, but the Holy Spirit Himself weighs in. These diamonds that are caught in the rough world of God's judgment may be enduring horrible suffering for the time being. But the day is soon coming when their bodies and spirits will find rest, and they will be rewarded for remaining true to their God.

Preview Four: The Great Harvest

I was never a fan of the horror genre of films or books. There is enough blood and gore in the real world. The movie that this last preview advertises has enough violence and death to make even the most jaded horror fan queasy.

> Then I looked, and behold, a white cloud, and on the cloud sat One like the Son of Man, having on His head a golden crown, and in His hand a sharp sickle. And another angel came out of the temple, crying with a loud voice to Him who sat on the cloud, "Thrust in Your sickle and reap, for the time has come for You to reap, for the harvest of the earth is ripe." So He who sat on the cloud thrust in His sickle on the earth, and the earth was reaped (Revelation 14:14-16).

The reel starts great. We see Jesus with a golden crown on His head and a sharp sickle in His hand. There are two words for a crown in biblical Greek. The first is one that we have talked about before—*stephanos*. This is the victor's crown. The second is *diadem*. This is the king's crown. We will see Jesus wearing the diadem in chapter 19 when He rides forward as King of kings and Lord of lords. Here He is wearing the *stephanos*, sitting on a cloud as the One who has won the right to serve as the Judge over the world.

Inside the temple waits an angel. When the time is right—possibly indicated by a word from the Father—he will come forth and signal to the Son that the time for reaping has begun. The earth is "ripe," a word that means that the harvest is long overdue and is bursting at the seams. The One like the Son of Man will thrust His sickle into the earth and reap. What is the harvest that is being realized? We'll have to wait to find out about that.

Next we see another angel coming out, and we read what seems to be a "second verse, same as the first."

> Then another angel came out of the temple which is in heaven, he also having a sharp sickle. And another angel came out from the altar, who had power over fire, and he cried with a loud cry to him who had the sharp sickle, saying, "Thrust in your sharp sickle and gather the clusters of the vine of the earth, for her grapes are fully ripe." So the angel thrust his sickle into the earth and gathered the vine of the earth, and threw it into the great winepress of the wrath of God. And the winepress was trampled outside the city, and blood came out of the winepress, up to the horses' bridles, for one thousand six hundred furlongs (Revelation 14:17-20).

The angel has a sharp sickle. Another angel comes and repeats nearly the same words that the earlier angel said to the Son of Man. However, there are a couple differences. First, we are no longer dealing with the Son of Man. This is a powerful angel who has the authority to bring great violence upon the earth. Second, while we don't know the crop of the first harvest, we hear very clearly that this is a grape harvest. The fruit will be harvested by the angel and thrown into the great winepress of the wrath of God.

This preview is for the upcoming Battle of Armageddon, which we'll read about two chapters from now. This is when the nations will gather in the Jezreel Valley right outside my house. Then they'll march up toward Jerusalem for the final battle of the tribulation. Judging by the carnage described, it is evident that the fight doesn't go well for them. The blood of men and animals will be splashed all the way up to the bridles of the horses for 200 miles all around.

Our previews have now come to an end, as has our third interlude. We now go back to the judgments, but before they begin, we once more will hear the beautiful voices of heaven singing a song of praise to the Lord God Almighty.

CHAPTER 15

A SONG FOR THE END

Many years ago, I was invited by one of the players on the Denver Broncos football team to attend a game. Since he was a friend, he provided good seats for me and those who were with me. We got there early and after we found our seats, we began to look for him out on the playing field. However, he wasn't easy to find because the field was full of people. Players were stretching and practicing plays. Coaches were running drills and going over strategies. Media people and cameramen were setting up their shots and doing pregame reports. Field crews were wandering around making sure that everything was perfect with the turf. Everyone was busy preparing for a single moment—kickoff.

As we approach chapter 15, we see similar activity. There are a lot of moving parts going about their business. John spots seven angels ready for action, tribulation saints engaged in worship, the heavenly temple opening, and one of the living creatures preparing to distribute the bowls. Everyone is working toward one thing—the kickoff of the final seven plagues upon humanity. The seals have been broken and the trumpets have been blown. The earth now awaits the coup de grace of God's wrath.

Preparation for Completion

The interludes are over and the action is about to pick up. Before John's eyes, the Lord reveals an awe-inspiring sight:

> Then I saw another sign in heaven, great and marvelous: seven angels having the seven last plagues, for in them the wrath of God is complete (Revelation 15:1).

This is the third sign that John saw. The first was that of a woman about to give birth to a male child (12:1-4). The second revealed a great red dragon waiting to devour her child as soon as he was born (12:3-5). While the first two may have been confusing or even frightening, John feels a different emotion over what he now sees. A remarkable display is presented before him. He doubles the superlatives—"great and marvelous"—and could probably add to them amazing, spectacular, and even epic!

What is it that has John's jaw dropping to the floor? Seven angels with seven plagues. Now, if you are like me, you may be thinking, "Really, John? You're calling the worst seven plagues this world has ever seen 'marvelous'?" There are a couple different ways to look at this. First, the Greek word here is *thaumazo* and has a range of meanings. When taken in tandem with the first word of the pair *mega*, or "great, huge," the word "marvelous" can take on the idea of awe-inspiring or breathtaking. So, rather than John saying, "Isn't all this destruction wonderful?" he would be saying, "This is so big and terrifying that it will knock your sandals off."

There is also a marvelous element to this first sentence. John informs us that when these bowls are emptied, "the wrath of God is complete." While the apostle understands the justice of all the wrath that God has carried out and the necessity of His plan, it would have to be a welcome relief for John to know that the destruction was finally coming to an end.

What we read in verse 1 is an initial summary statement—the seven angels have the last seven plagues. The rest of the chapter presents to the reader the events and ceremony that ultimately place the bowls of wrath in their hands.

Pre-Plague Worship

We are finally coming to the end of the tribulation. But before we get there, praise for the Lord God Almighty breaks out once again.

> I saw something like a sea of glass mingled with fire, and those who have the victory over the beast, over his image and over his mark and over the number of his name, standing on the sea of glass, having harps of God (Revelation 15:2).

This is not the first time that we have read about this sea of glass. When John was first transported to heaven, he described before the throne "a sea of glass, like crystal. And in the midst of the throne, and around the throne, were four living creatures full of eyes in front and in back" (4:6). So we know that this puts us in the throne room of God, where the Almighty sits and the four creatures minister to Him.

However, there has been an addition to the cast of characters from earlier. Now standing on the sea of glass are a group of people who had victory over "the beast, over his image and over his mark and over the number of his name." There are some who might say, "But if they are in heaven, doesn't that mean they are dead?" Absolutely! But their deaths are not tallied on the Antichrist's half of the scoreboard. Remember Paul's celebratory chorus over death's defeat?

> O Death, where is your sting?
> O Hades, where is your victory? (1 Corinthians 15:55).

The saints own this victory because the Antichrist and his minions threw everything they had at them but these men and women remained true to God. Executing these faithful followers was not a win but an admission by the bad guys that despite their best efforts, they had lost. What amazing courage, perseverance, and faithfulness! Now that these martyrs are in heaven and are free from suffering, they break out in praise.

> They sing the song of Moses, the servant of God, and the song of the Lamb, saying:

"Great and marvelous are Your works,
Lord God Almighty!
Just and true are Your ways,
O King of the saints!
Who shall not fear You, O Lord, and glorify Your name?
For You alone are holy.
For all nations shall come and worship before You,
for Your judgments have been manifested"
(Revelation 15:3-4).

A song of Moses and the Lamb. How did Moses suddenly get in here? Doesn't he belong in the front part of the Bible? Many don't realize this, but Moses was a songwriter. The Torah—the first five books of the Bible—was not the only great work to come from his pen. Scattered in Scripture we find several songs from the great prophet, one of them even making it into that great hymnal, the book of Psalms (Psalm 90). But what does he have in common with these tribulation saints that would cause his music to be sung? Two words—*deliverance* and *praise*.

In Exodus, we find the first of Moses's songs. It is a celebration of God's having delivered the Hebrews from the hand of Pharaoh. The Israelites had left Egypt, but the king began having second thoughts. He still had some major building projects going and no one to make the bricks! He went after his departing slave force to bring them back. When it looked like he had them cornered up against the Red Sea, God parted the waters and the Hebrews walked across on dry ground. When Pharaoh chased after, the Lord closed up the waters and the Egyptian army was drowned. A deadly enemy, God's deliverance, praise the Lord!

I will sing to the LORD,
for He has triumphed gloriously!
The horse and its rider
He has thrown into the sea!
The LORD is my strength and song,
and He has become my salvation;

He is my God, and I will praise Him;
my father's God, and I will exalt Him (Exodus 15:1-2).

Moses's song was born out of redemption from physical bondage. The Lamb rescued us from spiritual bondage. Moses sustained his people with manna and water from a rock. The Lamb sustains us with the bread and water of life. Moses's song looks forward to the Promised Land. The Lamb's song anticipates an eternal kingdom in which the Savior is reigning from His throne.

At this point in the tribulation, the contrast between heaven and earth is staggering. In the presence of God, there is joy and celebration. In the presence of the beast, there is misery and the devastation that will be poured out of the bowls. This leads me to another pattern that I find interesting. Prior to each series of judgments upon the earth, there is praise in heaven. In chapter 5, the four living creatures, the twenty-four elders, and thousands upon tens of thousands of angels sang praise to the Lamb. Then the first seal was broken. In chapter 7, we witnessed the tribulation saints in heaven praising God and the Lamb. Then, in chapter 8, the first trumpet sounded. Now, once again, we hear God's people lifting His name and celebrating His actions. What comes next will complete the triple cycle of wrath.

Out from the Temple

After the songs of worship before the throne of God, John sees movement at the temple.

> After these things I looked, and behold, the temple of the tabernacle of the testimony in heaven was opened. And out of the temple came the seven angels having the seven plagues, clothed in pure bright linen, and having their chests girded with golden bands. Then one of the four living creatures gave to the seven angels seven golden bowls full of the wrath of God who lives forever and ever. The temple was filled with smoke from the glory of God and from His power, and no one was able to enter the temple

till the seven plagues of the seven angels were completed (Revelation 15:5-8).

The doors open wide and the seven angels that he mentioned in verse 1 now exit the building. Why is it important to see the temple involved in the judgments?

In Exodus, the Lord instructed Moses to build a tabernacle, which would serve as a visual representation of the fact that God was always with His people. In that tabernacle, Moses was to place the ark of the covenant. In that ark, Moses placed three items that were testimonies to the faithfulness of God: the tablets with the Ten Commandments, Aaron's rod that budded, and a jar of manna (Hebrews 9:4). Often, we think of the judgments of Revelation coming from Jesus Christ, the Lamb, who opens the seals. But the "temple of the tabernacle of the testimony in heaven" is the domain of the Father, whose place was upon the mercy seat.

The angels were sent out of the temple by the Lord Almighty. Then He dispatched one of the four living creatures. This creature passed out the bowls that were full of the wrath of God, giving them one by one to the seven angels. We don't know exactly what was in those bowls, but we do know that it was immensely powerful. The outpouring of God's glory into those vessels of wrath caused smoke to billow throughout the temple. The cloud was so thick and the grandeur was so great that the doors of the temple became impassable for the duration of the devastation.

What we are about to read in the next chapter is terrifying and tragic. But I once again must remind you that we, as the church, will not be on earth at this time. I am writing this as a comfort and as a motivation. As a comfort, it should give you peace that you will not experience even one of these three series of judgments. As a motivation, it should remind you that you have friends and loved ones who will.

CHAPTER 16

THE POURING OF THE BOWLS

REVELATION 16

Before we begin talking about this worst of all judgments, I want to quote to you three words that we will come to in verse 17—"It is done!" If it has felt to you like this book has seen plague after plague and devastation after devastation, that's because it has. After starting with the letters to the church and then enjoying a glorious worship service in heaven, the seals were opened. Then the trumpets were sounded. Now the bowls are about to be poured. But once the seventh angel empties the contents of his vessel, a voice from the throne will finally say, "It is done!" The Lord Himself will declare that the rightful and justified suffering of humanity on this earth is coming to an end.

The Wrath of God

The seven angels have departed from the temple and are all lined up. One of the four living creatures has distributed the bowls "full of the wrath of God who lives forever and ever" (Revelation 15:7). Then the word comes that it's time.

> I heard a loud voice from the temple saying to the seven angels, "Go and pour out the bowls of the wrath of God on the earth" (16:1).

These seven bowls contain "the wrath of God." That is why some commentators refer to this period as the Great Tribulation, in comparison to the first three-and-a-half years. There are two Greek words that are translated as "wrath." The first is *thumos*, which is used eight times in Revelation. The second is *orge*, which is used five.

In his classic dictionary of Old and New Testament words, W.E. Vine makes the following distinction between these two Greek words:

> *Thumos*, "wrath" (not translated "anger"), is to be distinguished from *orge*, in this respect, that *thumos* indicates a more agitated condition of the feelings, an outburst of wrath from inward indignation, while *orge* suggests a more settled or abiding condition of mind, frequently with a view to taking revenge. *Orge* is less sudden in its rise than *thumos*, but more lasting in its nature. *Thumos* expresses more the inward feeling, *orge* the more active emotion. *Thumos* may issue in revenge, though it does not necessarily include it. It is characteristic that it quickly blazes up and quickly subsides, though that is not necessarily implied in each case.[17]

When John, in his Gospel, wrote of the spiritual situation of the unbeliever, he used the word *orge*: "He who believes in the Son has everlasting life; and he who does not believe the Son shall not see life, but the wrath of God abides on him" (John 3:36).

This is a slow, long-suffering wrath that will one day find its expression. The apostle Paul used the same word when he spoke of the condition we were in before we came to Christ:

> You He made alive, who were dead in trespasses and sins, in which you once walked according to the course of this world, according to the prince of the power of the air, the spirit who now works in the sons of disobedience, among whom also we all once conducted ourselves in the lusts of our flesh, fulfilling the desires of the flesh and of the mind, and were by nature children of wrath, just as the others (Ephesians 2:1-3).

As we enter these final judgments, the wrath of God has finally stewed to a point that it is no longer *orge*. It has now become *thumos*, a boiling over type of anger. The long-suffering patience of the Lord has come to an end, replaced with a virtuous fury over the brazen sin and contemptuous rebellion of those left on the earth. Who is about to feel His righteous rage?

> Then a third angel followed them, saying with a loud voice, "If anyone worships the beast and his image, and receives his mark on his forehead or on his hand, he himself shall also drink of the wine of the wrath of God, which is poured out full strength into the cup of His indignation. He shall be tormented with fire and brimstone in the presence of the holy angels and in the presence of the Lamb" (Revelation 14:9-10).

While the tribulation saints will experience the wrath of the Antichrist, those who follow the Antichrist will experience the wrath of God.

The Pouring of the Bowls

> The first went and poured out his bowl upon the earth, and a foul and loathsome sore came upon the men who had the mark of the beast and those who worshiped his image (Revelation 16:2).

When Satan asked for permission to test the faithfulness of Job, God told him that he could touch anything Job had but not the man himself. Satan took away everything that belonged to Job, including his children, but the man of God stood by his Lord. Satan went back for a second round and was given permission to afflict Job physically but not take his life. Job was afflicted from head to toe with painful sores. His suffering was tremendous, and all he could do for relief was to scrape himself with broken pottery as he sat among the ashes. Still, he kept his eyes on the Lord.

Now, in a reversal, we see God pouring that same type of plague out upon those who were faithful to the beast. Will they follow Job's path and look to God for relief in their suffering? Of course not. They will remain in their unholy rebellion.

Rather than hearkening back to Job, the next two bowls look to Pharaoh.

> Then the second angel poured out his bowl on the sea, and it became blood as of a dead man; and every living creature in the sea died. Then the third angel poured out his bowl on the rivers and springs of water, and they became blood (16:3-4).

When the second and third trumpets were blown, one third of the saltwater and freshwater were either bloodied or tainted. This time, the rest of the water is turned to blood. Imagine placing a glass under the faucet in the kitchen, turning the handle, and watching bloody water flow out. Those with even a rudimentary knowledge of the Bible will remember that there was something in there about God turning water to blood. This will clearly be a divine judgment. But still, no one will turn to the Lord.

At least, no person will. Two angels, however, turn their faces toward Almighty God and once again affirm the justice and righteousness of His actions:

> I heard the angel of the waters saying:
> "You are righteous, O Lord,
> the One who is and who was and who is to be,
> because You have judged these things.
> For they have shed the blood of saints and prophets,
> and You have given them blood to drink.
> For it is their just due."
>
> And I heard another from the altar saying, "Even so, Lord God Almighty, true and righteous are Your judgments" (Revelation 16:5-7).

We must never forget that sin has consequences. Often we treat sin as if it is no big deal. Everybody sins. We can't help it, can we? Besides, God has promised that all I have to do is confess my sins and I'll be good. So if all I have to do is say a few words when I do something wrong, then obviously that means God doesn't take sin too seriously either, right?

If that is your attitude toward sin, then let me counter with two facts. First, the forgiveness of sins came at a severe price. God Himself became one of us, then allowed Himself to be tortured and crucified so that you can pray that prayer of confession and receive forgiveness. Second, all the judgments from the seals, trumpets, and bowls are appropriate punishments for sin. And they don't even cover the cost, because for all those who remain in their sins, there is an eternity in hell waiting for them when this hell on earth concludes. The angels of the water and the altar remind us of that truth.

> Then the fourth angel poured out his bowl on the sun, and power was given to him to scorch men with fire. And men were scorched with great heat, and they blasphemed the name of God who has power over these plagues; and they did not repent and give Him glory (Revelation 16:8-9).

As someone who spent time in Jericho while in the Israeli Defense Forces, I know hot. There were days that I had sweated through my uniform within five minutes of walking outside. But what I experienced then is nothing compared to what is awaiting the world's population when the fourth bowl is emptied. People will not just be sunburned, they will be sun-scorched. Their reddened skin will become blistered and eventually turn into first-degree, then second-degree, then third-degree burns.

John reminds us that these suffering sinners know the source of their misery. But rather than repent, they "blasphemed the name of God who has power over these plagues." Rather than seeking the mercy and forgiveness that was right there for the asking, they chose to take the advice of Job's wife to "curse God and die!" (Job 2:9). Then, in the midst of this incredible suffering, the lights will go out.

The fifth angel poured out his bowl on the throne of the beast, and his kingdom became full of darkness; and they gnawed their tongues because of the pain. They blasphemed the God of heaven because of their pains and their sores, and did not repent of their deeds (16:10-11).

There are some who may think, *Darkness? Is that all? Nothing wrong with a little isolated lights-out time now and then.* It is interesting that darkness won't come until the fifth bowl. Even in Egypt, it wasn't until eight other plagues had passed in the ever-increasing crescendo of plagues that God said to Moses, "Stretch out your hand toward heaven, that there may be darkness over the land of Egypt, darkness which may even be felt" (Exodus 10:21). We've all experienced darkness before, but this was something else. Not only could no one see each other, but the darkness was so heavy that no one "[rose] from his place for three days" (verse 23). This future darkness will be immobilizing. There will be nothing in the people's surroundings to stimulate their senses other than the pain-filled cries of others in the blackness around them. All that people will be able to do day and night is experience every lightning bolt of agony that the nerves in their body radiate with no ability to see what is going on around them.

Once again, though, we find that the response will not be one of repentance but of blasphemy. People won't turn to God for help, but to one another. But they will find no answers from those who have no wisdom. The most brilliant minds will be dumbfounded. There will be no medications that can bring relief. In the darkness people will stew in their anger, and their desire for vengeance will burn. They will want to make someone pay for this. They will get so riled up that when the lights come back on, they will be ready to come out fighting. This anger will be good for the beast and his false prophet, because they will have just the target.

The Gathering

In the 1930s, Germany's economy was collapsing. Much of this was due to the reparations the nation owed following their signing of the

Treaty of Versailles. The fact that the world was in an economic depression didn't help matters at all. The German people were desperate for a strong leader, someone who could bring back their financial solvency and once again restore their pride among the nations. They found that person in Adolf Hitler. He was able to turn around the economy and national morale in three ways: ignore the nation's financial commitments, rebuild the military, and offer a scapegoat for all the country's problems. Who did he find to be the national whipping boys? The Jews.

As we've seen, those left in the world toward the end of the tribulation will not be accepting any credit for their misery. Who will they say is responsible for the suffering and the destruction worldwide? Once again, the people will turn toward the race who always seems to be on the opposite end of everyone's pointing fingers—the Jews.

> Then the sixth angel poured out his bowl on the great river Euphrates, and its water was dried up, so that the way of the kings from the east might be prepared. And I saw three unclean spirits like frogs coming out of the mouth of the dragon, out of the mouth of the beast, and out of the mouth of the false prophet. For they are spirits of demons, performing signs, which go out to the kings of the earth and of the whole world, to gather them to the battle of that great day of God Almighty (16:12-14).

In an earlier chapter, we looked at the Euphrates River, which flows through several Middle East countries. We learned about the four angels that were bound at the river until it was time for God to use them to bring about judgment. Now we find ourselves back at what was previously the Euphrates River, but is now the Euphrates "long, dried-up stretch of dirt." Maybe the water dried up when it turned to blood. Maybe God stopped the flow of the water. While we don't know the *how* the Euphrates became dry, we do know the *why*.

In verse 12, John wrote the words "so that." Anytime you see a "so that," you're going to learn a reason for something. Why was the Euphrates dry? So that the kings from the East would have an easy time getting to where they wanted to go. Where did they want to go? Let's hold off on that for just a second. We need to deal with some frogs first.

The evil triumvirate was gathered: the dragon, who is Satan; the beast, who is the Antichrist; and the false prophet. In an event that makes me thankful that the Bible is only written and not on video, three frog-like demonic spirits come out of their mouths—one from each of them. If there was ever any doubt that the Antichrist and the false prophet were demon-possessed, that uncertainty is gone.

The fact that these evil spirits exit their mouths means that they are taking the words of these three with them. They are messenger-frogs on a special mission. They will go to the kings of the nations and recruit them for an undertaking. Any hesitancy in the minds of the national leaders will be removed by these demonic beings, who will convince them—through miraculous signs—that joining the coalition is better than staying behind. The kings will call together their armies and march out toward a gathering place.

Demonically led forces will stream across the Euphrates. Their destination will soon become clearer to those who are reading John's letter. Many would now be on the edge of their seats waiting. Their hands would be clasped; their eyes would be wide.

But before the target is revealed, something very interesting happens. Jesus breaks into the narrative.

> Behold, I am coming as a thief. Blessed is he who watches, and keeps his garments, lest he walk naked and they see his shame (Revelation 16:15).

It is as if the Savior knew that His people would need some reassurance at this point. The world is breaking apart, but Jesus says, "Don't worry, I'm watching. I've got this whole thing planned out." Isn't that so like Him? We know that we can always turn to Him and He will be there to reassure us and remind us of His presence.

There are also times, like here in Revelation, when He knows we need to hear from Him even before we realize it ourselves. His comfort may come in a verse we read or an encouraging thought during our prayers. It might be a phone call from a friend or an apropos message from a pastor. As long as we are watching and striving for righteousness, we know that we will be safe in His care.

Back to the action. The kings of the earth are all congregating in one place—a place I can see as I stand on my back porch.

> They gathered them together to the place called in Hebrew, Armageddon (Revelation 16:16).

The place of gathering is called *Har Megiddo*. The Hebrew word *har* means "mount." Megiddo is a city on the west side of the Valley of Jezreel. *Jezreel* mean "God sows," and this area is the beautiful breadbasket of Israel, as well as for many other places around the world. I live right at the western edge of this fertile region.

The valley is about 14 miles wide and 67 miles long, which works out to about 1,000 square miles. Many battles have been fought here. Barak and Deborah fought the Canaanites here (Judges 4). Gideon fought the Midianites in Jezreel (Judges 6–7). Both King Saul and King Josiah died in this valley.

The city of Megiddo was strategically located between the north-south and east-west crossroads. Egyptian King Thuthmose III (1504–1450 BC) said that the one who conquers Megiddo conquers a thousand cities. Napoleon saw the Jezreel Valley as the most natural location on earth for battles. It was there that he scattered the Ottomans in 1799.

The cities around Armageddon have been destroyed and rebuilt fifteen different times, according to archaeologists who have discovered that many layers of civilization. Megiddo itself was built, destroyed, and rebuilt twenty times. In King David's day, the Megiddo he knew was already the sixteenth layer of that city.

There was someone else who knew that valley. Ten miles across from Megiddo was a small place called Nazareth. There, as a small boy, then a teenager, then a man, Jesus would be able to come to the pinnacle of the town and look down at this gathering place.

One day, all that lush green will be turned to brown mud as army after army rolls into the valley. I won't be here to see that, thankfully, because it would absolutely break my heart to watch what takes place.

The Battle of Armageddon

The Battle of Armageddon is really a misnomer. There is nowhere in Scripture that those words are used together. John, in verse 14, calls this war the battle of that great day of God Almighty. Armageddon is simply the rally point; the target is Jerusalem.

Although Revelation 16 is the only place where Armageddon is mentioned, the gathering of the armies and the assault on Jerusalem can be found throughout Scripture. Joel spells out some of the reasons for this great battle. Notice that it all comes back to how the nations treat God's people, Israel:

> Behold, in those days and at that time,
> when I bring back the captives of Judah and Jerusalem,
> I will also gather all nations,
> and bring them down to the Valley of Jehoshaphat;
> and I will enter into judgment with them there
> on account of My people, My heritage Israel,
> whom they have scattered among the nations;
> they have also divided up My land.
> They have cast lots for My people,
> have given a boy as payment for a harlot,
> and sold a girl for wine, that they may drink (Joel 3:1-3).

I would be remiss to not once again remind you that the only way to understand biblical prophecy, particularly when it comes to the fate of the nations, is to look through the lens of Israel. This point is made in Zechariah as well:

> Behold, the day of the LORD is coming,
> and your spoil will be divided in your midst.
> For I will gather all the nations to battle against Jerusalem;
> the city shall be taken,
> the houses rifled,

and the women ravished.
Half of the city shall go into captivity,
but the remnant of the people shall not be cut off from the city.
Then the LORD will go forth
and fight against those nations,
as He fights in the day of battle (Zechariah 14:1-3).

In the Zechariah passage, another key element is introduced. It will not be the Jews who fight against the massive army. Left on their own, they would be squashed like a bug. But they don't have to fight this battle because they will have Someone standing between them and this massive horde.

> "Behold, I will make Jerusalem a cup of drunkenness to all the surrounding peoples, when they lay siege against Judah and Jerusalem. And it shall happen in that day that I will make Jerusalem a very heavy stone for all peoples; all who would heave it away will surely be cut in pieces, though all nations of the earth are gathered against it. In that day" says the LORD, "I will strike every horse with confusion, and its rider with madness; I will open My eyes on the house of Judah, and will strike every horse of the peoples with blindness. And the governors of Judah shall say in their heart, 'The inhabitants of Jerusalem are my strength in the LORD of hosts, their God'" (Zechariah 12:2-5).

Jehoshaphat was a wise and faithful king over Judah (2 Chronicles 17–20). During his reign, a large army from Ammon, Moab, and Mount Seir united against him. Did Jehoshaphat panic? Did he run around like his hair was on fire, crying out, "What should I do? What should I do?" Absolutely not. This godly king called his people together and, as a group, they sought the Lord. God rewarded their faithfulness, assuring them that this battle was to be His and not theirs. So Jehoshaphat led his people to the battlefield not with the soldiers out front, but the praise team. They marched forward led by worship and not swords. Meanwhile, God brought panic into the enemy armies, and they turned upon one another and slaughtered each other. I think that this is likely what will happen as the Armageddon armies march on Jerusalem. That is why the bloodshed will spread for "one thousand six hundred furlongs" (Revelation 14:20), which is about 180 miles.

Even though Israel has a handful of friends on the world scene today, at that future time in God's chronology, the nation will find itself abandoned and alone. No country will want to warm up to her. Even the United States, her closest friend, will no longer support her. Their only friend will be God, yet the people of Israel will remain blinded to the truth found in the Messiah. It is only when their eyes look up and they see the Lord descending from heaven that they will mourn as one who has lost her only child.

The Seventh Bowl

In the Zechariah 14 passage above, the prophet wrote, "The LORD will go forth and fight against those nations, as He fights in the day of battle" (verse 3). On paper, it won't be a fair fight—one against a thousand or a million or, as in the case of Armageddon, tens and tens of millions. But God is omnipotent, which means "all-powerful." Men fight with guns, tanks, planes, and bombs—weapons that can wipe out entire cities at a time. But humanity is limited to the natural. God fights with the supernatural. Sometimes the supernatural means using natural phenomena like earthquakes and meteors and hundred-pound hailstones. Sometimes it's sowing the seeds of confusion so the armies destroy each other. Sometimes it's simply God revoking people's license to breathe.

All-powerful means exactly what it sounds like. God chose when to begin the time of wrath. God laid out the methodology for the wrath through the seals, trumpets, and bowls. And God will decide when enough is enough. When the seventh bowl is poured out, God will say, "Enough!"

> The seventh angel poured out his bowl into the air, and a loud voice came out of the temple of heaven, from the throne, saying, "It is done!" (Revelation 16:17).

How good those words will sound to all who hear them. But before heaven and earth can breathe a sigh of relief, there is one more flourish. Like the finale of a fireworks show, a grand display will rock the earth.

> There were noises and thunderings and lightnings; and there was a great earthquake, such a mighty and great earthquake as had not occurred since men were on the earth. Now the great city was divided into three parts, and the cities of the nations fell. And great Babylon was remembered before God, to give her the cup of the wine of the fierceness of His wrath. Then every island fled away, and the mountains were not found. And great hail from heaven fell upon men, each hailstone about the weight of a talent. Men blasphemed God because of the plague of the hail, since that plague was exceedingly great (Revelation 16:18-21).

A global earthquake will convulse the planet, causing entire cities to collapse. Islands will disappear due to the resulting tsunamis and mountains will break apart and crumble. For those who managed to survive the destruction, hailstones the size of baby hippos will fall from the sky. There will be no place to hide because the buildings have all been destroyed by the earthquake, and any that somehow have managed to survive need only a couple hippo-strikes to bring them down the rest of the way.

But still—and this makes me shake my head—humanity will refuse to repent, choosing instead to blaspheme God. Their hearts are hardened, their eyes are blinded, and their ears are deaf. They will not be able to hear the voice of the Holy Spirit because they refuse to listen.

At this point, God's wrath will be done. I feel exhausted from having been immersed in all this during these past weeks of writing. I cannot imagine seven years of enduring the judgment of God. The writer of Hebrews was so right when he wrote, "It is a fearful thing to fall into the hands of the living God" (10:31).

You have a choice: You can either fall into the hands of the living God, or you can fall into the arms of the loving Savior. You can continue to rebel and turn your back on the Lord's salvation, or you can accept the free gift that He is holding out to you. Enduring the tribulation is a choice. By closing this book without dealing with your eternal standing with God, you are making that choice. His arms are open; He's inviting you in. Surrender to Him, accept His love and forgiveness, receive His salvation, live for Him.

For anyone who has received Jesus as their Savior yet still feels scared when reading these judgments, let me implore you to bask in the peace that God gives to you. Jesus said, "Peace I leave with you, My peace I give to you; not as the world gives do I give to you. Let not your heart be troubled, neither let it be afraid" (John 14:27). He was giving that promise to His disciples, but that promise is for us too. Our peace comes from knowing that through our Savior we are fully exempt from the wrath of God because Jesus already paid the price.

Be a light. Share the gospel. Serve the Lord. Follow the Holy Spirit's lead. But do not be afraid, because the perfect love of Jesus has cast out fear (see 1 John 4:18).

CHAPTER 17

THE FALL OF BABYLON

REVELATION 17–18

One of the rites of academic passage in many parts of the world is when a student is assigned to read Homer's epic poems *The Iliad* and *The Odyssey*. While there are certainly those youth who have excitedly awaited their opportunity to delve into these grand works of Greek literature, I'm guessing that they are few and far between. Most teens receive the mandatory assignment with a groan. Why? Because for so many, these two classics are nearly impossible to understand. Thankfully, there are those literary scholars who understand this situation, thus an enormous number of tools have been published to assist the students in their comprehension. If the reluctant students will avail themselves of these literary keys, they'll be able to unlock the secrets to grasping what are really quite amazing works.

For the reader of Revelation, it would be easy to look at the first six verses of chapter 17 and say, "Uh, I think I'll pass. I truly have no clue what is going on here." They may even pick up their copy of *The Iliad* for some comparatively easy reading. But don't give up. The Lord knew that what John saw when he was transported away was bizarre and almost impossible to understand. So he sent a literary key—an angel—to reveal to the writer, and ultimately to the reader, the fact that this was, in actuality, an incredibly powerful and profound vision.

The Background of Babylon

In these next two chapters, we will see two entities—both given the name Babylon. Babylon is initially illustrated by a great harlot (17:1). However, as we read, we discover that it is actually a "great city" (17:18; 18:16, 19). What makes it great? It rules over the world (17:18). In a sense, it is the anti-Jerusalem. When Christ comes, He will rule the world from the holy city. Now, however, the world is controlled by the devil, who does everything exactly the opposite of God. And here, we see that he has established his headquarters in the harlot-city Babylon.

Before we launch into this wild vision, let's lay a foundation. To do this, we must go back to the origin of Babylon. There was a time when humanity spoke one language. All people were the descendants of Noah, and not enough time had passed nor had there been enough spread of people across the earth to allow for the changing of language naturally. As the population multiplied, it spread to the east. Eventually, there developed a large settlement in a plain in the land of Shinar.

Content with this location, the people decided to build both a city and a tall tower.

> They said to one another, "Come, let us make bricks and bake them thoroughly." They had brick for stone, and they had asphalt for mortar. And they said, "Come, let us build ourselves a city, and a tower whose top is in the heavens; let us make a name for ourselves, lest we be scattered abroad over the face of the whole earth" (Genesis 11:3-4).

What was wrong with that? There were three issues. The first was that they decided to reach for the heavens not by God's provision but by man's own effort. It is man's nature to try to get to heaven on his own terms. In fact, all religions other than Christianity are based on a works system designed to attain salvation. It all began with Cain when he brought the best of his agricultural success as an offering to God. The Lord rejected Cain's "me-based" offering, but accepted Abel's offering of a blood sacrifice. The tendency of humanity is to say, "Yes, Lord, I'd love to spend eternity with you in heaven. Let me tell you how I'm going to get there."

The second issue the people in Shinar had was that rather than doing something for the glory of God, they wanted to make a name for themselves. They wanted people to look at how wonderful they were. This is similar to our TikTok, Facebook, Instagram generation. Everyone wants to be a social media star. People become societal influencers because they have gathered millions of followers just by posting short videos of themselves. Our world has forgotten that we are here to reflect the glory of Christ, not to make a name for ourselves.

Finally, the people at Shinar did not want to follow God's directive to multiply and spread across the earth. They were tired of traveling and finding new places to settle. This felt like home to them, and home they would stay. So God intervened. He brought confusion among them. They began speaking different languages. Clans and families were divided as people scrambled to find others whom they could understand. Once they were grouped together by comprehension, they set off. Through their example, we see that it makes no sense to rebel against God. God is going to accomplish His plan no matter what. It's so much easier for us to just do what God asks.

Where did all this take place? In the city of Babel, which means "confusion." Babel eventually morphed to Babylon. To understand this city even more, we need to look at its original founder—the self-sufficient ringleader of the "we'll do it our way" group. His name was Nimrod, and he was a mighty hunter. He was the architect of the "mystery religions" of that area.

Nimrod had a wife named Semiramis, who was a high priestess of idol worship. Her followers believed that she had miraculously conceived a son. His name was Tammuz, and he was born to be a savior of his people. Soon a religion developed around these two, with people worshipping both mother and child. Tammuz worship continued in various forms over the centuries, eventually reaching even into the

temple in Jerusalem, where, in a vision, Ezekiel saw women "sitting
there weeping for Tammuz" (Ezekiel 8:14).

Babylon was always deeply involved in astrology, sorceries, and
magic. Isaiah emphasized this focus on the occult when he pronounced
God's judgment upon the city:

> Therefore evil shall come upon you;
> you shall not know from where it arises.
> And trouble shall fall upon you;
> you will not be able to put it off.
> And desolation shall come upon you suddenly,
> which you shall not know.
> Stand now with your enchantments
> and the multitude of your sorceries,
> in which you have labored from your youth—
> perhaps you will be able to profit,
> perhaps you will prevail.
> You are wearied in the multitude of your counsels;
> let now the astrologers, the stargazers,
> and the monthly prognosticators
> stand up and save you (Isaiah 47:11-13).

Meeting the Harlot

With this background, we can now begin to interpret these next
two chapters. The scene begins with one of the bowl angels speaking with John before the angel carries the apostle away into the
wilderness.

> Then one of the seven angels who had the seven bowls came
> and talked with me, saying to me, "Come, I will show you
> the judgment of the great harlot who sits on many waters,
> with whom the kings of the earth committed fornication,
> and the inhabitants of the earth were made drunk with
> the wine of her fornication." So he carried me away in the
> Spirit into the wilderness. And I saw a woman sitting on a
> scarlet beast which was full of names of blasphemy, having

seven heads and ten horns. The woman was arrayed in purple and scarlet, and adorned with gold and precious stones and pearls, having in her hand a golden cup full of abominations and the filthiness of her fornication. And on her forehead a name was written:

MYSTERY, BABYLON THE GREAT,
THE MOTHER OF HARLOTS
AND OF THE ABOMINATIONS
OF THE EARTH.

I saw the woman, drunk with the blood of the saints and with the blood of the martyrs of Jesus. And when I saw her, I marveled with great amazement (Revelation 17:1-6).

In the wilderness, John is confronted with the vision of a woman. She is dressed in an outfit that many would consider "not church-going clothes." Under her is the multiheaded beast, and in her hand is a cup "full of abominations and the filthiness of her fornication." She is drunk with the blood of the martyrs and the saints, indicating that she is not only in agreement with their deaths but likely has a hand in their executions.

On her forehead, she's got a name written: "Mystery, Babylon the Great, the Mother of Harlots and of the Abominations of the Earth." Now, if we were at a business conference and a woman walked up to us with that spelled out on her "Hi, My Name Is..." sticker, we'd probably give her a wide berth, thinking, *Wow, a little too much information.* For us, though, this is a very helpful clue to her identity. The fact that the words "Mystery, Babylon" are included tells us that she is not representing the physical city of Babylon, but something symbolized by Babylon. Typically, the city is used to represent two aspects of the world system—the religious arena and the political and financial facet.

When the true church is raptured prior to the tribulation, into the vacuum will flow an apostate church. This false religion represented by Babylon will persecute those who have found Christ as their Savior. It won't preach the gospel of Christ's death, burial, and resurrection. It certainly will never mention His return to earth at the second coming. Religion will be much more external, with the focus on appearance and personal achievement rather than on the reality of the spiritual world. It will center on ritual rather than revival.

It isn't difficult for us to imagine this kind of religious system. Even today, we see theological deterioration within Christendom. Denominations are compromising on the moral qualifications of the clergy they are willing to ordain. Some well-known Christian writers, preachers, and teachers are no longer communicating a clear gospel. Others don't believe in a literal hell. Still others claim that Jews can be saved not by placing their faith in the Lord Jesus Christ but by other means. Fewer and fewer seminaries teach about prophecy. They want to focus on the here and now rather than on God's plans for the future. Therefore, students graduate either without taking a course on prophecy or they have been given a wide variety of viewpoints and told to figure it out for themselves. This leads to congregations around the world being left ignorant of the truth regarding God's prophetic statements.

John saw the unexpected sight of this woman and "marveled with great amazement." I love that phrase. It tells me that I shouldn't feel bad about having no clue as to what is going on with this beast-riding harlot. John was blown away too. Thankfully, the angel saw John standing there astonished and bewildered.

> The angel said to me, "Why did you marvel? I will tell you the mystery of the woman and of the beast that carries her, which has the seven heads and the ten horns" (Revelation 17:7).

There have been men and women in my life who were great teachers. They were the ones that I could turn to, particularly earlier in my Christian walk, when a biblical passage or a doctrinal thought just wasn't coming together. We would sit down together or talk over the phone, and they would explain the Scriptures to me and all would become clear. This is the role that the angel now took with John.

Riding the Beast

Mystery Babylon had a beast saddled up, and she was moseying along on this creature. What is this beast? When the angel describes him, his identity quickly becomes clear:

> The beast that you saw was, and is not, and will ascend out of the bottomless pit and go to perdition. And those who dwell on the earth will marvel, whose names are not written in the Book of Life from the foundation of the world, when they see the beast that was, and is not, and yet is (Revelation 17:8).

It's none other than the Antichrist, the one who ascended out of the abyss. For him to be accepted by the people, he will feign loyalty to religious leadership. For a while, all will go great as they work in tandem. But eventually, hard feelings will develop between the two, particularly when the Antichrist decides that the object of everyone's veneration should be him. Their parting will not be an amicable one.

The beast is depicted with seven heads and ten horns. Let's start with the angelic explanation about the heads:

> Here is the mind which has wisdom: The seven heads are seven mountains on which the woman sits. There are also seven kings. Five have fallen, one is, and the other has not yet come. And when he comes, he must continue a short time. The beast that was, and is not, is himself also the eighth, and is of the seven, and is going to perdition (Revelation 17:9-11).

There are some who equate the seven mountains to Rome. This is possible, but not definite. Of more importance are the kings. They could be seven Roman emperors or seven world empires. From John's perspective, five of them had already passed. The one that "is" is the current empire in his time, Rome, or the current emperor, likely Domitian. Then there is one yet to come from his historical perspective but is already in the past from ours. Finally, there is an eighth king; he is the Antichrist himself.

In case you are not yet "kinged out," we discover even more of them when we come to the horns.

> The ten horns which you saw are ten kings who have received no kingdom as yet, but they receive authority for one hour as kings with the beast. These are of one mind, and they will give their power and authority to the beast. These will make war with the Lamb, and the Lamb will overcome them, for He is Lord of lords and King of kings; and those who are with Him are called, chosen, and faithful (Revelation 17:12-14).

In the future, there will be ten more kings who will reign simultaneously with the Antichrist. They will all rule, but he will rule the rulers. What is their purpose in aligning together? This is the foundation of the great army. Who can possibly stand against eleven kings and their vast military? The answer: one Lamb. As we saw before, all the natural in the world cannot compete against one supernatural God. To paraphrase the old parental line: God brought everyone into existence, and He can take everyone back out.

The End of the Harlot

Although we will read more about this great downfall in the next chapter, here we see the end of the harlot:

> Then he said to me, "The waters which you saw, where the harlot sits, are peoples, multitudes, nations, and tongues. And the ten horns which you saw on the beast, these will hate the harlot, make her desolate and naked, eat her flesh and burn her with fire. For God has put it into their hearts to fulfill His purpose, to be of one mind, and to give their kingdom to the beast, until the words of God are fulfilled. And the woman whom you saw is that great city which reigns over the kings of the earth" (Revelation 17:15-18).

Earlier, I said that Babylon is both a religious entity and a political one. Here, we see the end of spiritual Babylon. While the woman is riding the beast at the beginning, the beast doesn't want to remain in his subservient position. He's probably thinking, *I'm the Antichrist. She should be carrying me around.* In John's vision, the woman is on the waters. The angel informs John that those waters represent multitudes and nations and languages. Her religious reach touched every corner of the globe. But that would not be enough to save her.

Under the direction of the beast, the ten kings will turn on the harlot and destroy her. Who will step up in her place? The angel tells John that the kings were of one mind "to give their kingdom to the beast." The Antichrist is now fully in charge. Not only does the world follow him politically, but they will worship him too.

Moving to the Next Mountain

As we begin chapter 18, we come to another one of those prophetic mountaintops. Remember, we learned earlier that there are passages in which a prophecy is like a series of mountaintops one right after the other. But when you reach one summit, you often find that the next mountain is miles away. In biblical prophecy, the distance can be centuries or millennia. Between chapters 17 and 18, we are talking about a gap of only three-and-a-half years.

In fact, to find the antecedent to chapter 18, we need to go back to the end of chapter 16.

> Now the great city was divided into three parts, and the cities of the nations fell. And great Babylon was remembered before God, to give her the cup of the wine of the fierceness of His wrath. Then every island fled away, and the mountains were not found. And great hail from heaven fell upon men, each hailstone about the weight of a talent. Men blasphemed God because of the plague of the hail, since that plague was exceedingly great (Revelation 16:19-21).

When we remember this passage, we can understand how chapter 18 can say that "in one hour she is made desolate" (verse 19). When the religious system collapses in chapter 17, it is both a gradual process and human-caused—"the ten horns which you saw on the beast, these will hate the harlot, make her desolate and naked, eat her flesh and burn her with fire" (verse 16). The devastation at the end of chapter 16 and in chapter 18 takes place in the span of sixty minutes and is the result of the angel pouring out the seventh bowl.

Walvoord describes the distinction between chapters 17 and 18, writing,

> The Destruction of Babylon in chapter 18 should be com-
> pared with the preceding announcement in 16:19 where
> the great city is divided and the cities of the Gentiles fall.
> This event comes late in the great tribulation, just prior to
> the second coming of Christ, in contrast to the destruc-
> tion of the harlot of chapter 17 which seems to precede the
> great tribulation and paves the way for the worship of the
> beast (13:8).[18]

Fallen, Fallen

As chapter 18 opens, John sees another angel coming down to earth from heaven. This angel is intriguing in that his authority was evident to the apostle, and the glory of this messenger of God illuminated the earth.

> After these things I saw another angel coming down from
> heaven, having great authority, and the earth was illumi-
> nated with his glory. And he cried mightily with a loud
> voice, saying, "Babylon the great is fallen, is fallen, and has
> become a dwelling place of demons, a prison for every foul
> spirit, and a cage for every unclean and hated bird! For all
> the nations have drunk of the wine of the wrath of her for-
> nication, the kings of the earth have committed fornication
> with her, and the merchants of the earth have become rich
> through the abundance of her luxury" (18:1-3).

The message of the angel is emphatic, twice repeating the fact that Babylon the great is fallen. Interestingly, this is the exact wording that is found in Isaiah when a chariot with horsemen reported, "Babylon is fallen, is fallen!" (Isaiah 21:9). All is about to change because the nations of the world all knew her, caroused with her, and became wealthy through her. Now, that is all gone.

Who or what is being talked about here? Is this a literal city or is it a symbol of the political and economic system of that time? Throughout the Bible, Babylon is used both literally and figuratively. Often it refers to the literal city along the Euphrates River. However, Peter also uses it to refer to the capital city of the Roman Empire, writing, "She who is in Babylon, elect together with you, greets you" (1 Peter 5:13). There are many commentators who fall on either side of the literal/symbolic line, with some believing that the Babylon of Revelation 18 is an actual rebuilt Babylon. Others believe it is Rome, which allows those who make their living from the sea to view the destruction from their ships (18:17-18), something impossible to do if the city is in central Iraq, where the literal Babylon is located.

Charles Ryrie believed Babylon to be both a literal city and an economic system. He wrote: "Babylon involves a city (evidently Rome and perhaps Babylon on the Euphrates) and a system."[19]

Tim LaHaye and Timothy Parker put forth another view of chapters 17 and 18: "Chapter 17 refers symbolically to the religious Babylon, while chapter 18 refers to the commercial and political systems of Babylon. Chapter 18 describes destruction that will rid the world of devastating evils that have plagued mankind for thousands of years."[20]

Charles Swindoll considers the Revelation Babylon to represent the false religious system at the time of the tribulation: "This means that the false religious system she represents will lead to the zealous persecution and slaughter of countless true servants of God."[21]

As I've already mentioned, I personally hold to these two chapters speaking of a religious and an economic system that are both godless and worldwide. However, I've also promised to tell you when the Scriptures are not clear, and this is one of those times.

What *is* clear in this chapter is that God is calling out to the believers of that time not to compromise. He's saying that they may feel as though the system is all-powerful, but it is not. The destruction of Babylon and salvation for the saints are on the way. Don't compromise.

Don't get sucked up into the mob mentality. Don't partake of the current worldview or involve yourself in its practices. These clear commands hearken back to a very similar message that the prophet Jeremiah gave to the people of his time when they faced the literal Babylon:

> Flee from the midst of Babylon,
> and every one save his life!
> Do not be cut off in her iniquity,
> for this is the time of the LORD's vengeance;
> He shall recompense her.
> Babylon was a golden cup in the LORD's hand,
> that made all the earth drunk.
> The nations drank her wine;
> therefore the nations are deranged.
> Babylon has suddenly fallen and been destroyed.
> Wail for her!
> Take balm for her pain;
> perhaps she may be healed (Jeremiah 51:6-8).

Then, as now, as in the future, the Lord allows those within the political and economic system to continue feeling protected. They live in their wealth, popularity, and satisfaction, but destruction is on the way. This is one of the reasons Jesus said that it is so hard for a rich man to enter the kingdom of God. His sense of well-being comes from his wealth or his popularity or his own wisdom. He is totally unaware of the spiritual world that surrounds his physical world. He has eyes that cannot see, ears that cannot hear. There will come a day when, in one hour, any safety he may have left will be taken from him.

It's All Gone

After the world has been wrecked, people will still hold on to hope. They will believe that someday, all the bad will pass. Somehow things will all get better again. They think they will be able to pick up the pieces and rebuild. Why do they think this? Because their guy is still in charge. They've still got their systems in place.

Then, everything will collapse.

> The fruit that your soul longed for has gone from you, and all the things which are rich and splendid have gone from you, and you shall find them no more at all. The merchants of these things, who became rich by her, will stand at a distance for fear of her torment, weeping and wailing, and saying, "Alas, alas, that great city that was clothed in fine linen, purple, and scarlet, and adorned with gold and precious stones and pearls! For in one hour such great riches came to nothing." Every shipmaster, all who travel by ship, sailors, and as many as trade on the sea, stood at a distance and cried out when they saw the smoke of her burning, saying, "What is like this great city?" They threw dust on their heads and cried out, weeping and wailing, and saying, "Alas, alas, that great city, in which all who had ships on the sea became rich by her wealth! For in one hour she is made desolate" (Revelation 18:14-19).

We all want security. We look for it in our marriage, our job, our bank account, our house, and in so many of the things that we own. Yet all that security can disappear in a moment. The only guaranteed security we have is in our relationship with God through Jesus Christ. That relationship is eternal. It doesn't depend on whether we have a job or a bank account or a spouse. That security comes from the very character of the Almighty.

God told His people through the prophet Jeremiah, "I know the thoughts that I think toward you, says the LORD, thoughts of peace and not of evil, to give you a future and a hope" (Jeremiah 29:11). Those thoughts come with a purpose. They are plans for your life. And we know that if they come from God, then they are good.

In Revelation 18, everything that people had left to depend on will suddenly be gone. Any future they thought they had will evaporate into the air. When Babylon falls, there will be a worldwide economic collapse. Banks will close; stockbrokers will jump out of windows if there happen to be any high-rises still left standing. Thousands will have heart attacks and strokes because all their security was wrapped up in what they owned. All of it will be gone, with no help coming.

As so often happens in Revelation, amid the misery there is rejoicing.

> Rejoice over her, O heaven, and you holy apostles and prophets, for God has avenged you on her! (Revelation 18:20).

Why are the apostles and prophets told to rejoice? Because this is the system that persecuted them and took their lives. These are the ones who mocked their words instead of listening to the truth. God promised justice according to His time line, and that time has come.

There is more in this chapter, but it is all according to the same theme. Babylon is at an end. Digging too deeply into the details will only muddy the main point. Besides, we have been on a very dark journey for many chapters. Looking ahead, I see some very bright light at the end of this tunnel. In fact, it is so bright that it can only be coming from the One who said, "I am the light of the world" (John 8:12). There's also another group that's going to make an appearance in the next chapter, and if you look closely, you just might see yourself in the crowd.

PART FOUR

THE REIGN
OF THE KING
(Revelation 19–20)

CHAPTER 18

THE RETURN OF THE KING

REVELATION 19

L et me give you a heads up on this next chapter. There is a lot going on, and it is all good! And for any of you who have been tapping your fingers and thinking, *It's been interesting reading about what all those left behind will go through, but when do we see the church again?* get ready to do your happy dance. The bride of Christ is on her way, and she is coming with her Groom! If that isn't reason enough for a spontaneous worship service, then I don't know what is. And that is exactly what we get in chapter 19.

As I travel from country to country and church to church, I am amazed at the different ways that Christians express their worship. In some churches, the people love to cry out, "Hallelujah!" Others shout, "Amen!" Some churches are not as demonstrative on the outside, but their hearts are right there in the throne room with God praising His holy name.

Whatever you do in your services here the earth, when we get to heaven, we will all be doing a lot of shouting, bowing, praising, and lifting our hands to the One who saved us and called us to be part of the family of God. How do I know this? As we continue our end-times tour with the apostle John in this chapter, we're going to hear the voices of a great multitude. What will they be crying out? "Alleluia…Alleluia…Alleluia…Alleluia!" (verses 1, 3, 4, 6).

A Praise Recap

The writer side of me loves these first verses of chapter 19. So much of wordsmithing is trying to find creative ways to repeat yourself, whether it is revisiting an important point or trying to make sure that you don't use the same word two sentences in a row. As this chapter begins, the Holy Spirit is bringing the reader up to speed with what just happened in order to transition into the amazing events that are about to take place. Rather than saying, "So this happened, then this happened, then this happened," He lets the recap come in worship form.

> After these things I heard a loud voice of a great multitude in heaven, saying, "Alleluia! Salvation and glory and honor and power belong to the Lord our God! For true and righteous are His judgments, because He has judged the great harlot who corrupted the earth with her fornication; and He has avenged on her the blood of His servants shed by her." Again they said, "Alleluia! Her smoke rises up forever and ever!" And the twenty-four elders and the four living creatures fell down and worshiped God who sat on the throne, saying, "Amen! Alleluia!" Then a voice came from the throne, saying, "Praise our God, all you His servants and those who fear Him, both small and great!" (Revelation 19:1-5).

God's righteous judgments have come. The great harlot is dead. Everything is fantastic—"Amen! Alleluia!" Of course, there's still that huge Armageddon army lurking out there with the devil, the Antichrist, and the false prophet, but that's no big deal. The returning Messiah will have that little issue mopped up by the end of this chapter. Our job as "His servants and those who fear Him" is to let Him worry about fighting while we focus on the praise!

Having had our melodic review, we can now look forward to the next major happening, which is the second coming of Christ. However, before we go there, we need to answer the foundational *why* question: Why is Jesus coming back? Is He returning for a final judgment of mankind before we transition into eternity? Or is He coming to set up a literal, physical kingdom in Jerusalem, from which He will reign? The answer to that question will determine how we interpret the rest of this chapter. There are three major views that attempt to answer the why question.

The pre-millennialist believes in a literal kingdom in which Jesus will reign from Jerusalem for 1,000 years. This period will begin at the conclusion of the tribulation, when Jesus returns. At that time, God will pour out His Holy Spirit upon the Jewish nation. The Jews will recognize Jesus as their Messiah and will individually give themselves to the Lord. Contrary to the accusations of many who hold to other views, there is no salvation of the Jews simply because they are Jews. Salvation does not come because you are part of a certain ethnicity. Every Jew who receives Jesus as their Savior will do so the same way that you and I have done. The uniqueness of that Romans 11:26 moment in time is that it is the only instance in which the Holy Spirit will move the hearts of an entire people group to individual repentance and salvation. This will signify the fulfillment of the promise for a new covenant with Israel, as promised in Jeremiah 31:31.

The post-millennialist believes that we are currently in the millennium. *When did the 1,000 years start?* you wonder. Well, it's difficult to answer your question because to them, it is based on a false premise. The 1,000 years of the millennium is not really 1,000 years, they say, and the reign of Christ is spiritual rather than literal. The world today is not great, and it has never been all that godly. But there will come a day when this will turn around. Post-millennialists are optimistic about our future, and they work toward ushering in a golden age of righteousness before Jesus returns. When we can accomplish that, He will be back and bring with Him the final judgment. Then He will reign in the New Jerusalem for eternity.

Amillennialism is similar to post-millennialism, but without the optimism. Like the post-millennialists, they take a nonliteral view of the 1,000 years and believe that Jesus is already ruling over the affairs of mankind. They do not, however, see a future period of a triumphant church prior to the physical return of Jesus. When the Lord does come back, He will create a new heavens and new earth, and will usher in eternity.

As a biblical literalist myself, the pre-millennial position is clear to me in the Scriptures. Jesus Christ will physically reign from a physical throne in the physical city of Jerusalem on this physical earth. Not only does that scenario fit the overall context of prophecy and the character of God, but it also fits the words that are clearly typed out on the pages of the Bible. In particular, the repetition of the phrase "thousand years" in the future-focused narrative of the next chapter of Revelation necessitates a literal 1,000 years. The only way to interpret it differently is to filter it through a preconceived ideology and say that the words do not mean what they clearly mean.

The Return of the Bride

A multitude begins singing, and their song is loud and true. Who is this mass of mankind? Most likely the tribulation saints who were martyred by the religious and political systems during the tribulation. What do they sing? The heavenly praise version of "Here Comes the Bride"!

> I heard, as it were, the voice of a great multitude, as the sound of many waters and as the sound of mighty thunderings, saying, "Alleluia! For the Lord God Omnipotent reigns! Let us be glad and rejoice and give Him glory, for the marriage of the Lamb has come, and His wife has made herself ready." And to her it was granted to be arrayed in fine linen, clean and bright, for the fine linen is the righteous acts of the saints. Then he said to me, "Write: 'Blessed are those who are called to the marriage supper of the Lamb!'" And he said to me, "These are the true sayings of God." And I fell at his feet to worship him. But he said to me, "See that you do not do that! I am your fellow

servant, and of your brethren who have the testimony of
Jesus. Worship God! For the testimony of Jesus is the spirit
of prophecy" (Revelation 19:6-10).

What is the "marriage of the Lamb"? As we learned earlier, on the
night before Jesus was crucified, He told His disciples that He was
going away "to prepare a place for you. And if I go and prepare a place
for you, I will come again and receive you to Myself; that where I am,
there you may be also" (John 14:2-3). That promise will be fulfilled at
the rapture of the church.

After the Bridegroom comes for His bride, He will take her back
to His Father's house. There, the marriage of the Lamb and the church
will take place. The "marriage supper of the Lamb" refers to the wedding feast and not the marriage itself. What is to take place on the earth
is the grand celebration of the Father's perfect plan that united in matri-
mony His Son and those who had been promised to Him through the
sealing of the Holy Spirit during the church age on earth.

The bride is beautiful. She has "made herself ready," and the clothes
that she is wearing are made of the fine linen of all her acts of love and
devotion over 2,000 years. "But Amir, isn't the church imperfect today?
Aren't hypocrisy and immorality and apathy rampant?" Sadly, it's true.
But if you are waiting for a day when there will be no more sin in the
church, you'll be waiting a long time. The church is made up of people, and there will never be a time when we of our own accord will be
good enough and pure enough and holy enough. And I hate to tell you
post-millennialists that there will never be a golden age of righteousness as long as we are living in this flesh.

Thankfully, while striving for holiness is part of what demonstrates
our genuine faith, it is not our responsibility to make ourselves worthy
enough to be the bride. Paul wrote,

> Husbands, love your wives, just as Christ also loved the
> church and gave Himself for her, that He might sanctify
> and cleanse her with the washing of water by the word,
> that He might present her to Himself a glorious church,

not having spot or wrinkle or any such thing, but that she
should be holy and without blemish (Ephesians 5:25-27).

After the first four words of that passage, who becomes the active
party? It's Christ. He gave Himself, He sanctifies, He cleanses, and He
presents her to Himself. There is not one thing listed that we are responsible for other than to stand there in faith to be cleansed by His blood,
washed by the Word, and presented spot- and wrinkle-free, holy and
without blemish. That is how we have "made [ourselves] ready" as a
church. It's the same way we made ourselves ready as individuals for eternity. We repented of our sins, we accepted Christ's forgiveness, we committed to serving Him as our Lord, and we let Him take care of the rest.

Because the marriage occurs after we are raptured, that means we
are now in the engagement period. The Lord has given us the guarantee
of His Holy Spirit as a down payment for what is yet to come (Ephesians 1:13-14). After the rapture will come the marriage and the judgment seat of Christ. That time of judgment is for reward; it is not an
adjudication about heaven or hell. Our eternal destiny has already been
taken care of by Christ. This is the *bema* that we spoke of in chapter 3,
when the motives for our works will be put through the fire.

Now that the matrimonial ceremony is complete and the judgment is done, it is time for the banquet. The Bridegroom and the bride
will both return to the earth because the guests to the feast will not be
angelic beings but the people belonging to God who survive to the end
of the tribulation, including the recently "revivaled" Jews.

The Return of the King

In the first ten verses of chapter 19, John "heard" (verse 1) the statements of a great multitude, then the twenty-four elders and the four
creatures. Then a voice came from the throne, followed by a return of
the multitude, then the voice of a fellow servant who stood next to him.
Now there is a shift from what John "heard" to what he "saw."

Now I saw heaven opened, and behold, a white horse.
And He who sat on him was called Faithful and True, and

in righteousness He judges and makes war. His eyes were like a flame of fire, and on His head were many crowns. He had a name written that no one knew except Himself. He was clothed with a robe dipped in blood, and His name is called The Word of God. And the armies in heaven, clothed in fine linen, white and clean, followed Him on white horses. Now out of His mouth goes a sharp sword, that with it He should strike the nations. And He Himself will rule them with a rod of iron. He Himself treads the winepress of the fierceness and wrath of Almighty God. And He has on His robe and on His thigh a name written:

KING OF KINGS AND LORD OF LORDS (Revelation 19:11-16).

This is not the first time that we've seen a rider on a white horse. If you'll recall, when the Lamb opened the first seal, a white horse came forward. The rider who sat on it "had a bow; and a crown was given to him, and he went out conquering and to conquer" (6:2). What was he conquering? The hearts and minds of the people, because eventually he would be calling for them to worship him. This new rider also comes forward as a conqueror. But this time when people fall to worship Him, it will be because He is worthy. It will not be because they've been forced or coerced.

The description that John gives of the rider is one of the greatest depictions of a warrior hero ever written. It is nearly impossible to read the words without feeling awe, fear, and an overwhelming gratitude that He is on your side.

Who is this rider? There can be no doubt that it is Jesus Christ returning to usher in His kingdom. In fact, every one of John's descriptions can be found elsewhere in Scripture referring to the conquering Savior. He is called Faithful and True (Revelation 3:14); His eyes are like a flame of fire (Revelation 1:14); His robe has been dipped in blood (Isaiah 63:2); His name is the Word of God (John 1:1); a sharp sword proceeds from His mouth (Revelation 1:16; 2:12); He will rule the nations with a rod of iron (Psalm 2:8-9; Revelation 12:5); and He is called the King of kings and Lord of lords (1 Timothy 6:15).

I love that last title—King of kings and Lord of lords. It brings to my mind Handel's *Messiah*, when the singers call out those titles and echo "Hallelujah! Hallelujah!" in praise. When Paul wrote to his protégé Timothy, he used this same majestic moniker in his good confession:

> I urge you in the sight of God who gives life to all things, and before Christ Jesus who witnessed the good confession before Pontius Pilate, that you keep this commandment without spot, blameless until our Lord Jesus Christ's appearing, which He will manifest in His own time, He who is the blessed and only Potentate, the King of kings and Lord of lords, who alone has immortality, dwelling in unapproachable light, whom no man has seen or can see, to whom be honor and everlasting power. Amen (1 Timothy 6:13-16).

What a glorious event! What a grandiose celebration! Jesus Christ is returning to rule over all the kingdoms of the world. As He returns to earth, He will come not as He first did when He was weak, humble, helpless. This time as He rides in, He will do so as God in all His glory—all-powerful deity, general of righteous armies, leader of angelic forces, the one true ruler over all things. For centuries, the promise of Jesus' return has been preached throughout the world. Nations, tribes, families, and individuals have anticipated the day. It is coming!

Who will return with Him? Who are the "armies of heaven" that ride at His back? Are they angelic beings like the ones Elisha saw during the siege of Dothan (2 Kings 6)? The context makes clear their identity. Looking at their description, we read that they are "clothed in fine linen, white and clean" (verse 14). Six verses earlier, the description John gave of the bride said that she was "arrayed in fine linen, clean and bright, for the fine linen is the righteous acts of the saints" (verse 8). Not only are we returning as the bride; we are coming back as the army of God.

"But Amir, I don't want to be part of an army! I don't even kill spiders when they come into my house!" Fear not, there is only one righteous Warrior who will fight in this battle, and it is not you. Your job will to be to ride behind your King, which is exactly where you will want to be. In fact, there will be only two options on the day of Christ's return—you will either see Jesus' face or His back. In that day of His judgment, it will be much better to be riding behind Him than fleeing from in front of Him.

The Army of the Bad Guys

If the Warrior Jesus is riding forth to battle with a sword to strike the nations, who are the armies that have gathered to fight Him? These are the kings of the earth who were enticed by the frog-like demons who went forth with the beguiling words of the devil, the Antichrist, and the false prophet.

> I saw an angel standing in the sun; and he cried with a loud voice, saying to all the birds that fly in the midst of heaven, "Come and gather together for the supper of the great God, that you may eat the flesh of kings, the flesh of captains, the flesh of mighty men, the flesh of horses and of those who sit on them, and the flesh of all people, free and slave, both small and great." And I saw the beast, the kings of the earth, and their armies, gathered together to make war against Him who sat on the horse and against His army. Then the beast was captured, and with him the false prophet who worked signs in his presence, by which he deceived those who received the mark of the beast and those who worshiped his image. These two were cast alive into the lake of fire burning with brimstone. And the rest were killed with the sword which proceeded from the mouth of Him who sat on the horse. And all the birds were filled with their flesh (Revelation 19:17-21).

These verses pick up where Revelation 16:16 left off: "And they gathered them together to the place called in Hebrew, Armageddon." We are at the end of the tribulation. The Jews have now come to realize that the one they thought was their Messiah is actually an anti-Messiah, demanding worship from all the nations of the world. Under devilish deception, these nations have gathered to destroy Jerusalem, but before they can do so, there is a loud noise and a bright light. They look up toward the heavens and realize that this is not going to go well for them.

The prophet Zechariah describes the scene:

> Behold, the day of the LORD is coming,
> and your spoil will be divided in your midst.
> For I will gather all the nations to battle against Jerusalem;
> the city shall be taken,
> the houses rifled,
> and the women ravished.
> Half of the city shall go into captivity,
> but the remnant of the people shall not be cut off from the city.
> Then the LORD will go forth
> and fight against those nations,
> as He fights in the day of battle.
> And in that day His feet will stand on the Mount of Olives,
> which faces Jerusalem on the east.
> And the Mount of Olives shall be split in two,
> from east to west,
> making a very large valley;
> half of the mountain shall move toward the north
> and half of it toward the south (Zechariah 14:1-4).

The armies will immediately be put to death by Christ, and the beast and the false prophet will be thrown into the lake of fire. That is the last we will ever see of them. I believe that one of the reasons the devil does not want people reading the book of Revelation is because he wants them to think he has greater power than he actually does. He talks a big game, and he has power here on the earth. But when Jesus joins in the fight, Satan is shown to be just another created being who is no match for his Creator.

CHAPTER 19

WRAPPING THINGS UP

In the military, authority is determined by rank. While I was in the Israeli Defense Forces, I had my commander, and he had his commander. On up the chain it went until it reached the one man who was ultimately in charge—the general over all others. If your direct commander is a difficult person, then life can be miserable. You will be so wrapped up fulfilling the demands of your immediate supervisor that you don't have the time nor the inclination to consider that there is anyone else higher up. To you, anybody farther up the chain is utterly irrelevant because you must "serve your master." They become the end-all and be-all of your personal authority structure.

This is how it is for unbelievers today. They are serving the evil authority structure of the world, the flesh, and the devil. When these authorities say jump, they ask how high. When these leaders say sin, they say you bet. This triumvirate of iniquity is so demanding and their devotees are so committed that following them becomes all-encompassing. Who can possibly see that there is a higher authority who is ready to give peace, hope, and forgiveness when their attention is taken up by the sinful sergeant who is screaming in their ear to drop down and give them twenty?

What would happen if some of those influences were taken away? Would people become more attentive to the Commander-in-Chief if one or, even two, of the sergeants were put away in the brig? In this very full chapter, we are going to see what happens when the influences of the world, the flesh, and the devil are trimmed down to just the flesh. Will the momentary temptation-relief lead to long-term righteous success? Or will humanity fall right back into the same old patterns that led to the day of the Lord?

Satan Shut Away

One day, David was in a poetic mood. He picked up his pen to write, and moved by the Holy Spirit, he scratched out the following words: "The LORD said to my Lord, 'Sit at My right hand, till I make Your enemies Your footstool'" (Psalm 110:1).

In Revelation 20, this messianic prophecy is fulfilled. The typical English Bible translation does not do this passage justice. The Hebrew text says, "Yahweh said to my Adonai." This is the Father speaking to the Son. He is saying that there will come a time when You will rule with Me and all those who have fought against You will be vanquished. It is the time when the Father hands over the nations to Jesus the Messiah as His inheritance, along with the ends of the earth for His possession. The rightful King will come to take up residency on this planet and restore that which was lost in the Garden of Eden. Genesis is the book of "Paradise Lost" and Revelation is the book of "Paradise Found."

For this to happen, though, the one to whom temporary authority of the world had been given needs to be removed. That is exactly what happens.

> Then I saw an angel coming down from heaven, having the key to the bottomless pit and a great chain in his hand. He laid hold of the dragon, that serpent of old, who is the Devil and Satan, and bound him for a thousand years; and he cast him into the bottomless pit, and shut him up, and set a seal on him, so that he should deceive the nations no more till the thousand years were finished. But after

these things he must be released for a little while (Revelation 20:1-3).

Satan is powerful, but he is not all-powerful. All it takes is one angel acting in the strength of God to bind up the devil and throw him into the abyss, which, if you will remember, is the place of demons and dark forces. It is the bottomless pit from which the demonic locusts poured forth when the fifth trumpet was sounded (9:1-3). It is the ideal locale for the prince of all demons to spend an extended stay.

Back to the sin sources of the world, the flesh, and the devil. At this point in chapter 20, Jesus is reigning over the earth from His throne in Jerusalem. That eliminates the evil world system. The devil is chained up and stewing in the abyss. No longer can anyone say, "The devil made me do it." All that's left is the flesh. Surely that alone isn't enough to lead the world back down the wrong path, is it? Jesus' brother, James, answered this question when he wrote:

> Let no one say when he is tempted, "I am tempted by God"; for God cannot be tempted by evil, nor does He Himself tempt anyone. But each one is tempted when he is drawn away by his own desires and enticed. Then, when desire has conceived, it gives birth to sin; and sin, when it is full-grown, brings forth death (James 1:13-15).

The only ones left on earth will be God and man—both those who have been resurrected and those still in the corruptible flesh. God doesn't tempt toward sin, so if sin exists, it is a human issue. Sadly, even with the worldly system and the devil gone, the inherited sin-taint of corruptible flesh will be strong enough to draw people away from righteousness. When the devil is released after the 1,000 years, he will not have to look hard to find those who are ready to follow him in rebellion against the rule of Jesus.

The Millennium or "the Millennium"

In this chapter and throughout this book, I've spoken of the millennium, also known as the 1,000-year reign of Christ on the earth.

Yet, once again, we have a doctrine labeled by a word that many claim is not in the Bible. And, once again, that is not true. The Greek word translated "thousand" is *chilioi*, from which we get the metric prefix *kilo*. But, before some form of "kiloyear" could catch on, the Bible was translated into Latin. The Greek *chilioi* became the Latin *mille*, to which was added *ennium* from the word *annus*, which means "year." So, just like *rapture* traces its origins through Latin to the original Greek, so too does *millennium*.

The question that is up for debate for many is whether 1,000 years really means 1,000 years. Isn't John simply using a big number to speak of a long time? He never really meant for "a thousand" to be taken literally, some say. To bolster their point, they turn to Peter, who wrote that "with the Lord one day is as a thousand years, and a thousand years as one day" (2 Peter 3:8). See? Not even God considers 1,000 years to really be 1,000 years. In Revelation, "a thousand years" is simply a biblical literary device used to refer to an extended period.

I will readily agree that Peter uses that phrase as a tremendously effective literary device to demonstrate the long-suffering nature of God. However, just because the words "a thousand years" are used in one place as a literary device doesn't mean that elsewhere, they are considered off-limits for denoting real time. Otherwise, the prophetic phrase "day of the Lord" would negate any possible usage of the word "day" to refer to a twenty-four-hour period. And forget any literal use of the word "soon"!

Ultimately, it once again comes down to how you interpret Scripture. Do you take a literal approach to the Word of God unless a passage is clearly meant to be taken otherwise based on its context and verbiage? Or do you approach Scripture with an allegorical bent, always on the hunt for the supposed deeper meaning behind the words? There are plenty of theologians on either side of this coin.

The late Grant R. Osborne was a professor of New Testament at Trinity Evangelical Divinity School for many years. His view was that the 1,000 years should be taken symbolically:

> The question for us is whether this should be seen as a literal period of time or a symbolic use of numbers. Numbers

in Revelation tend to be symbolic, and that is likely the case here. As the half-hour in Revelation 8:1 and the hour in Revelation 18:9-19 refer to very short periods, this likely connotes a lengthy period of time. Note the contrasts between the short period of the antichrist's reign (42 months) and the very long period of Christ's reign here.[22]

First, note Osborne's use of the words "tend" and "likely." Such words are not the foundations upon which to build theological doctrine. The bigger question to put to this statement taken from his commentary is whether his conclusions are the result of careful exegesis (drawing truth out of the text) or eisegesis (reading meaning into the text). You would think that with his credentials and background, Osborne would be an excellent exegete—and he might be in other parts of Scripture. But he tipped his hand early on in his book when he wrote,

> We must understand Revelation as John wrote it, and he understood all the symbols through his first-century Jewish perspective. Background knowledge of the first century will unlock the symbols of Revelation, and we will sift through the possible understandings to determine the most likely background.[23]

Looking through a Reformed lens, Osborne approached Revelation believing that John used his understanding of Jewish apocalyptic literature as a basis for the "symbols" that are mentioned in the book. But how do we know that? And how does this jibe with the Holy Spirit revealing truth for John to see, hear, and copy down? For John to filter his text through his knowledge of first-century Jewish thinking would entail him saying, "Okay, this is what I am seeing, which reminds me of this representation that I've read before. So, rather than writing what I actually see, I'm going to communicate it using what is more familiar to me." Or, we can just make the assumption that God revealed His truth to John using only Jewish apocalyptic concepts and symbols. But how would that make sense when the letter is being sent to primarily

Gentile churches? It is a major step to say, without any clear textual backing, that rather than interpreting a biblical text as it is clearly written, "I am going to filter it through other sources and seek to find its real meaning."

Jesus is the One who said to John, "Write the things which you have seen, and the things which are, and the things which will take place after this" (Revelation 1:19). I agree that we must recognize the culture of the first century when interpreting Scripture, but we must also be careful not to impose that culture on the sacred text in places where it doesn't belong.

The allegorical approach essentially says that the numbers in Revelation should be interpreted symbolically rather than literally unless it is obvious that they are literal—for example, the seven churches. The literalist, however, says that the numbers in the book of Revelation should be interpreted literally rather than symbolically unless it is obvious that they are symbolic.

The literal approach is used by Bible teachers and scholars like David Jeremiah, Charles Swindoll, John Walvoord, Charles C. Ryrie, Tim LaHaye, and Hal Lindsey. They, and I, all agree that when Revelation 20 says that Satan will be bound for 1,000 years, then Satan will be bound for 1,000 years. When John wrote that Christ will reign on earth for those same 1,000 years, then Christ will reign on the earth for those same 1,000 years. Why is this so difficult to accept and understand? Why must there be a hidden meaning? The only reason is to force a theological presupposition into a passage that, when taken literally, contradicts what a person has already decided must be true.

Reigning with the King

Now we come to one of the most interesting periods in all human existence—a time when God rules on the earth, and mortal and immortal humanity will inhabit the same space for 1,000 years. Reading that last sentence, I can sometimes understand why there are those who try to find a different explanation for the millennium. Because when it is looked at as described in the Scriptures, it is going to be one unusual time.

I saw thrones, and they sat on them, and judgment was committed to them. Then I saw the souls of those who had been beheaded for their witness to Jesus and for the word of God, who had not worshiped the beast or his image, and had not received his mark on their foreheads or on their hands. And they lived and reigned with Christ for a thousand years. But the rest of the dead did not live again until the thousand years were finished. This is the first resurrection. Blessed and holy is he who has part in the first resurrection. Over such the second death has no power, but they shall be priests of God and of Christ, and shall reign with Him a thousand years (Revelation 20:4-6).

Who enters the millennial kingdom of Christ? First, there will be those who are still alive on earth in their physical bodies. These are believers who have not worshipped or accepted the mark of the beast and who survived the persecutions and the devastation of the tribulation. This will also include all the surviving Jewish people who gave themselves to Jesus upon His return. Second, there will be the tribulation martyrs. They will have been given their resurrection bodies—more about that in just a moment—and will reign with Christ. At this time, the Old Testament saints will also be resurrected. Finally, there will be the church, the bride of Christ, who will reign with the Bridegroom, according to the promise that Jesus gave to the disciples: "Assuredly I say to you, that in the regeneration, when the Son of Man sits on the throne of His glory, you who have followed Me will also sit on twelve thrones, judging the twelve tribes of Israel" (Matthew 19:28).

What does reigning with Christ during the millennium look like? We really don't know. First, we have no idea how many mortal survivors there will be who need judging or reigning over. Undoubtedly, though, as time passes, that number will grow. The world population in the year AD 1000 was around 310 million. Now there are over eight billion. Can you imagine the population explosion that will take place on earth over a period of 1,000 years in a world without the diseases, natural disasters, and violence of our current times? Chances are our "ruling" workload will greatly increase as the years slide by.

It is exciting to think about the fact that we will have responsibilities in the kingdom of God. As someone who loves to work, the idea of a 1,000-year vacation is enough to give me the shakes. But ten centuries to labor at something, honing my skills as I serve the Lord? Sign me up for that!

The Resurrections

The prophet Daniel wrote: "Many of those who sleep in the dust of the earth shall awake, some to everlasting life, some to shame and everlasting contempt" (Daniel 12:2).

There are those who read that passage and see in it one big resurrection. However, when you study through the rest of Scripture, you'll find two resurrections broken down into several different events. In Revelation 20, John mentions the first resurrection, then says, "Blessed and holy is he who has part in the first resurrection" (verse 6). Those two adjectives make it clear that the first resurrection is a believer's resurrection. At no point could anyone who has not been washed clean by the blood of the sacrificial Lamb be considered "blessed and holy."

While the second resurrection will happen all at once, the first resurrection will have approximately 2,000 years or more between its onset and its completion. It began at the tomb of Joseph of Arimathea one Sunday morning. A group of women had gone to tend to Jesus' body, but found the stone rolled away. Rather than seeing their Savior, they discovered two men shining brightly who asked, "Why do you seek the living among the dead? He is not here, but is risen! Remember how He spoke to you when He was still in Galilee, saying, 'The Son of Man must be delivered into the hands of sinful men, and be crucified, and the third day rise again'" (Luke 24:5-7). Jesus the Messiah, who was crucified on the cross, was raised on the third day. According to Paul, this was the advent of something new—something that would affect the eternities of every person from all time.

> Christ is risen from the dead, and has become the firstfruits of those who have fallen asleep. For since by man came

death, by Man also came the resurrection of the dead. For as in Adam all die, even so in Christ all shall be made alive. But each one in his own order: Christ the firstfruits, afterward those who are Christ's at His coming. Then comes the end, when He delivers the kingdom to God the Father, when He puts an end to all rule and all authority and power (1 Corinthians 15:20-24).

Because Jesus is the firstfruits, there are two truths we can be certain of. As we mentioned earlier, if He is first, then that means that there will be more to come. Second, because the firstfruits are the initial gleaning of a crop, then it is expected that everything harvested after that will be a similar crop. You don't gather firstfruits from your apple tree, then harvest the rest from your banana tree. You glean the firstfruits of your apples, then gather the rest of your apples. You harvest the firstfruits of your bananas, then gather the rest of the bananas. If we want to know what our bodies will be like at our resurrection, we only need to look at Jesus' body at His resurrection. In that same chapter of 1 Corinthians, Paul compares Adam, the man of dust, and Jesus, the heavenly man:

The first man was of the earth, made of dust; the second Man is the Lord from heaven. As was the man of dust, so also are those who are made of dust; and as is the heavenly Man, so also are those who are heavenly. And as we have borne the image of the man of dust, we shall also bear the image of the heavenly Man (verses 47-49).

Jesus' resurrection body was incorruptible. It was not bound by physics. It was capable of survival both on earth and in heaven. Beyond that, we don't know what our immortal bodies will be like, except that all the aches and pains and illnesses of our present bodies will be no more. With the back issues that I've had over the years, I cannot wait to get my upgrade!

The first resurrection began with Jesus, but it has been on a two-millennia pause. The next time that the resurrection will kick in will be that wonderful day when we will meet our Savior in the clouds.

> For the Lord Himself will descend from heaven with a shout, with the voice of an archangel, and with the trumpet of God. And the dead in Christ will rise first. Then we who are alive and remain shall be caught up together with them in the clouds to meet the Lord in the air. And thus we shall always be with the Lord (1 Thessalonians 4:16-17).

This is the rapture of the church, and it could come any day now. The Lord will come to the clouds, then "in a moment, in the twinkling of an eye…the trumpet will sound, and the dead will be raised incorruptible, and we shall be changed" (1 Corinthians 15:52). First will be the dead brought back to life, followed immediately by those of us who are still alive. But that is not the end of the first resurrection. It is only the church—those saved under the new covenant—who are raptured; there are still more who will need to be rebodied.

Several chapters back, we witnessed another event in the first resurrection. The two witnesses had completed their mission. The Antichrist was allowed to attack and kill them. However, three-and-a-half days later, there was a stirring in the bodies that had been left to rot in the open air. "The breath of life from God entered them, and they stood on their feet," much to the dismay of the onlookers (Revelation 11:11). A voice from heaven called them up, and they ascended in a cloud.

There is one more grand event in the first resurrection. This takes place at the end of the tribulation and is what we read about in Revelation 20:4-6. At this resurrection, all the believers who had been martyred during the seven years of wrath or had been killed through the devastation will receive their resurrection bodies. Along with them will be the saints of the Old Testament. They have been patiently waiting all this time, and now they will finally receive this glorious reward. This is the time that Jeremiah spoke of when he said that, after the period of "Jacob's trouble," the people shall "serve the LORD their God, and David their king, whom I will raise up for them" (Jeremiah 30:9). Jesus the Messiah will be ruler over the world from Jerusalem, while the resurrected David will once again be the king of Israel.

There is a second resurrection, but we will deal with that in a few moments. First, it seems that the clock has kept running. The 1,000 years are now over, and someone is about to get paroled.

Back on the Streets

Every day for a millennia, the devil had been scratching a hash mark on the wall of the abyss. Lucky for him it's a bottomless pit, so there's room for a lot of hashmarks. One morning, he scratches number 365,250 (he had to account for the leap years), the pit opens, his chains drop off, and he's free.

> Now when the thousand years have expired, Satan will be released from his prison and will go out to deceive the nations which are in the four corners of the earth, Gog and Magog, to gather them together to battle, whose number is as the sand of the sea. They went up on the breadth of the earth and surrounded the camp of the saints and the beloved city. And fire came down from God out of heaven and devoured them. The devil, who deceived them, was cast into the lake of fire and brimstone where the beast and the false prophet are. And they will be tormented day and night forever and ever (Revelation 20:7-10).

When Satan gets out, he will move with purpose. He will have had quite a bit of time on his hands to formulate a plan. Whether it's because he thinks he can actually pull this off or he just wants to take as many as he can down with him, he gathers up an army and takes one last shot at God. When he goes recruiting, he doesn't have difficulty finding volunteers. As we said earlier, you don't need the devil or a corrupt world system to desire to sin. The devil will find an army "whose number is as the sand of the sea" ready to break the rule of righteousness. We, the saints, will gather in Jerusalem. Whether God has called us in or we have made our way back over time as sin once again has deteriorated humanity, we don't know. As the dark army surrounds us, I suspect we will be distracted in a great worship service. We've all seen the Father by now; we're in the presence of the King of kings and Lord of lords. I don't expect there will be any worry or concern on our part.

As soon as the devil's troops launch their attack, fire will come down from heaven and that's it. Game over. The devil will once again be captured. This time he will be tossed into the lake of fire to join his old buddies, the beast and the false prophet.

A common trope is that Satan rules hell. It's portrayed as his headquarters from which he controls all his demonic legions. When new souls are sent there, he is ready to welcome them and takes great joy in arranging their suffering. The truth is that the devil is a victim of hell just as all are who rebel against God and reject His grace. There will be no joy, no relief, no mercy—only an expectation of eternal torment as the just reward for his sins.

For a short time, there will just be the three-person Axis of Evil in hell. But they will soon be joined by others. And that is when our narrative gets truly heartbreaking.

The Great White Throne Judgment

Most people do not believe in a literal hell. They may not have a clue as to what happens after they die, but the one thing they feel certain of is that they won't go to hell. Even if by some crazy chance there is an actual place of eternal torment, they are sure that they have never done anything bad enough to go there. You'd have to be a Hitler or a Stalin or a Bundy or a Dahmer to go there. Sadly, for so many, there will come a day when they will be confronted with the truth that when our beliefs and reality diverge, it is reality that wins out.

> Then I saw a great white throne and Him who sat on it, from whose face the earth and the heaven fled away. And there was found no place for them. And I saw the dead, small and great, standing before God, and books were opened. And another book was opened, which is the Book of Life. And the dead were judged according to their works, by the things which were written in the books. The sea gave up the dead who were in it, and Death and Hades delivered up the dead who were in them. And they were judged, each one according to his works. Then Death and Hades were

cast into the lake of fire. This is the second death. And anyone not found written in the Book of Life was cast into the lake of fire (Revelation 20:11-15).

In between verses 10 and 11 of Revelation 20, an event occurs. It is the second resurrection. All the mortal believers who died during the millennium will be raised, as will all unbelievers from all time. You see, it is not only Christians who will face resurrection; it is everyone. When the Jews were challenging Jesus in John 5, He let them know that He had been given authority to judge (verse 22). They shouldn't be shocked, He said, "For the hour is coming in which all who are in the graves will hear His voice and come forth—those who have done good, to the resurrection of life, and those who have done evil, to the resurrection of condemnation" (verses 28-29). A body of flesh is mortal and could not stand the fires of hell. The resurrection body that is destined for condemnation is designed to suffer the everlasting consequences of sin.

Those who experience the second resurrection will line up before the judgment throne of Christ. One by one they will come before Him. If they gave their lives to Jesus during the 1,000 years of the Lord's rule, they will be ushered into their eternal reward. However, if their name is not found written in the Book of Life that records all those who belong to the family of God through repentance and forgiveness, then the verdict will be "Guilty." The person will be cast into the lake of fire, where they will spend eternity.

This is difficult for me to write. Being a Jew living in Israel, I have so many family and friends who are either secular in their thinking or are committed to an old covenant doctrine of works. If they stand before that throne and plead a commitment to the law as their defense, their case will not stand. The reality of hell stays with me wherever I go. It is at the gatherings I join, at the school events I attend, along the streets as I walk. Yes, there will come a day when all Israel will be saved, but two-thirds of those whom I see every day will not make it that far.

My friend, hell is real. The good news is that the only way that you will end up there is if you choose to go. Do not fall victim to the second death. The first death separates you from your physical life. The second will remove you from the Source of Life for eternity. Decide today that you will receive the grace and forgiveness that God is offering you.

For those of you who have nonbelieving family and friends, let this motivate you. The only eventuality worse than them having to endure the tribulation is knowing that they have judgment and the lake of fire waiting for them when it is over. Don't let fear or apathy or past failures hold you back. This is too important. This isn't just life and death, it is eternity.

PART FIVE

ETERNITY
(Revelation 21–22)

CHAPTER 20

ALL THINGS NEW

I t's over. The wrath is done. The reign is established. The judgment is complete. The punishments have been enacted. The old has passed away. Behold, the new has come.

What will it be like? Of course, we can only speculate. For years there had been so much activity with reigning and judging. Then there was the big flurry at the end with the release of the devil, followed by the final battle. When the time comes for the Great White Throne judgment, I don't know what we will be doing. I can't imagine watching because it would be so heartbreaking. It's possible that we will have such a clear understanding of God's holiness that we can compartmentalize our sorrow over others' suffering in favor of our understanding of God's justice. But to me it is that empathy we feel at others' pain that, in part, expresses our *imago dei*, the image of God in us. But that is a tangent.

Now that the judgment is all done, what's left are the people who love God and have committed themselves to Him. While our eternal life began when we received Jesus as our Savior and Lord, this is when eternity truly starts.

The New Heaven and New Earth

Not long ago, I watched a video from China. There were fifteen unfinished high-rise buildings that were sitting on a property. From what I could glean, the new owner of the property wanted them gone so that he could erect his own development. As I watched, charges exploded at the bases of the buildings, and one after another, they toppled to the ground. Soon, all that could be seen was a massive cloud of dust.

God spares us the details of the demolition of the original heaven and earth, although I am thinking that it will be even more spectacular to watch than the destruction of those fifteen Chinese buildings. Instead, God jumps John forward to the pulling of the great curtain and the unveiling of the new heaven and the new earth.

> Now I saw a new heaven and a new earth, for the first heaven and the first earth had passed away. Also there was no more sea. Then I, John, saw the holy city, New Jerusalem, coming down out of heaven from God, prepared as a bride adorned for her husband (Revelation 21:1-2).

A new beginning—how wonderful! Sometimes something is just so far gone that there is nothing left to do except start over. In Greek, there are two words that can be translated "new." One is *chronos* and it primarily refers to something that is "new in time." You used to drive an old car, but now you drive a new car. The second word is *kainos* and it means "new in kind." This is what we find John using in this passage.

The new heaven and the new earth are not only more recent, but, more importantly, they are superior in quality to the old. These will never perish, as did the old ones. This new creation has not been infected with sin, nor will it ever be. Death will never be seen in God's upgraded handiwork. When the old goes and the new comes, everything will be made better.

Just because the new is improved it doesn't mean that the old was bad. When God created everything, He declared it to be good. It's when we got our sinful little hands on what God had made that it all deteriorated. There is precedent for God looking around and deciding to start over.

While creation began with a close relationship between God and the first two humans, the moment sin entered the world, the corrosion began. If there is one activity that people excel at, it is rebellion. As the generations following Adam and Eve expanded and multiplied, so did their capacity and creativity for sin. By the time Noah came along, everything was irrevocably out of hand.

> Then the Lord saw that the wickedness of man was great in the earth, and that every intent of the thoughts of his heart was only evil continually. And the Lord was sorry that He had made man on the earth, and He was grieved in His heart. So the Lord said, "I will destroy man whom I have created from the face of the earth, both man and beast, creeping thing and birds of the air, for I am sorry that I have made them." But Noah found grace in the eyes of the Lord (Genesis 6:5-8).

The hope of mankind appears in that last line. The righteousness of that one man is the reason why you and I are alive today. God saw that He had to get rid of the old before He could create the new, so He sent a flood to destroy everything except for what was in the ark. Once the flood subsided and Noah again stood on solid ground, he experienced God's new beginning.

When humanity sinned against God, it brought death. This mortality was not just for living creatures but for nature as well. The prophet Isaiah alluded to this fact:

> Lift up your eyes to the heavens,
> and look on the earth beneath.
> For the heavens will vanish away like smoke,
> the earth will grow old like a garment,
> and those who dwell in it will die in like manner;
> but My salvation will be forever,
> and My righteousness will not be abolished (Isaiah 51:6).

That will be the state of the earth after the tribulation. It will be old and torn up, like a shirt that is stained, fraying at the seams, and full of holes. No amount of loving care and careful tailoring can restore it. It's best to break down and buy a new shirt. Isaiah tells us that is exactly what God says He will do: "Behold, I create new heavens and a new earth; and the former shall not be remembered or come to mind" (Isaiah 65:17). The apostle Peter also refers to this new creation, even giving us a possible look into what the demolition of the old might look like:

> Therefore, since all these things will be dissolved, what manner of persons ought you to be in holy conduct and godliness, looking for and hastening the coming of the day of God, because of which the heavens will be dissolved, being on fire, and the elements will melt with fervent heat? Nevertheless we, according to His promise, look for new heavens and a new earth in which righteousness dwells (2 Peter 3:11-13).

Like in Noah's time, God will protect the righteous from the destruction of the old and will release us onto the solid ground of His new beginning.

As John checks out God's new creation, he notes that there is no sea. "Amir, how can this be heaven? I can't imagine never wiggling my toes in the sand of the beach or watching the sun set over the ocean." First, we're nearing the "no more sun" part of chapter 21, so you're about to be doubly disappointed. But, second, this is where you need to trust God and the amazingness of what He will do. What the great Creator has planned for His new heaven and new earth will make you forget sandy toe-wiggling ever existed.

The question remains: Why is there no sea? We don't know. However, before those of you who crave a thinly sliced tuna sashimi get too worked up, notice that John says there will be "no more *sea*." He doesn't say that there will be no more bodies of water. Currently, a majority of the earth is covered by saltwater. It is possible that God is simply reworking that water-to-land ratio.

Then the loud voice from the throne speaks once again:

> I heard a loud voice from heaven saying, "Behold, the tabernacle of God is with men, and He will dwell with them, and they shall be His people. God Himself will be with them and be their God. And God will wipe away every tear from their eyes; there shall be no more death, nor sorrow, nor crying. There shall be no more pain, for the former things have passed away" (Revelation 21:3-4).

This will be a world of Emmanuel—God with us! No longer will our prayers be just spirit to Spirit or heart to heart but face to face. Imagine that! It is no wonder that there will be no tears or sorrow. We will be in the presence of the Almighty! And, of course, there will be no more death or pain. We'll be sporting our incorruptible resurrection bodies.

New bodies equal physical peace.

Presence of God equals spiritual peace.

Lord, I am so ready for this day!

A Message from the Throne

Then God speaks. Imagine the stillness in all creation as the voice of the Creator booms forth:

> Then He who sat on the throne said, "Behold, I make all things new." And He said to me, "Write, for these words are true and faithful." And He said to me, "It is done! I am the Alpha and the Omega, the Beginning and the End. I will give of the fountain of the water of life freely to him who thirsts. He who overcomes shall inherit all things, and I will be his God and he shall be My son. But the cowardly, unbelieving, abominable, murderers, sexually immoral, sorcerers, idolaters, and all liars shall have their part in the lake which burns with fire and brimstone, which is the second death" (Revelation 21:5-8).

The Lord introduces a summary statement when He says, "Behold." This essentially means "Pay attention! You need to hear what I am about to say." What does He want everyone to know? That His work is complete. He has finished His re-creation, and inherent in His words is the declaration "And it is good!" This is the statement that He is giving to all who are with Him in His new heaven and new earth, including the future us.

But then He has something else to say—this time, to the present us. To demonstrate this transition, God speaks directly to John, which probably made the scribe's knees begin to wobble a bit. Remember, John's purpose is to bring what he has written back to the church. This is His fourfold message to us.

First, God's judgment is for a reason and only for a season. It must be accomplished because sin demands a recompense. For those who accept the payment that Jesus made for their sins, there is no more price that needs to be paid. For those who reject His gift of salvation, then the wages of their sin is death—eternal separation from God. But there will come a time when God's plan is completed and He will say, "It is done!"

Second, we can be assured that the plan that God has laid out in this book will come to pass. Why? He is the Alpha and the Omega, the Beginning and the End. He is the sovereign One who has the power to carry out His designs as well as the wisdom and goodness to ensure that it is a righteous and perfect plan.

Third, for those of us who commit ourselves to following God, all the good stuff found in the previous twenty chapters of the book belongs to us. We are His family, and we will inherit all things, just as Paul wrote to the Galatians: "You are no longer a slave but a son, and if a son, then an heir of God through Christ" (Galatians 4:7). This includes eternal life, and the new heaven and new earth.

Finally, for those who are still living in their sinful ways, all the bad stuff found in the previous twenty chapters of the book belongs to them. Wrath, judgment, and eternal punishment is reserved for those who make the God-rejecting decision to trust themselves for their eternity. They will get exactly what their rebellion deserves.

The New Jerusalem

When God finished saying what He had to say, one of the bowl angels came back to carry John away.

> Then one of the seven angels who had the seven bowls filled with the seven last plagues came to me and talked with me, saying, "Come, I will show you the bride, the Lamb's wife." And he carried me away in the Spirit to a great and high mountain, and showed me the great city, the holy Jerusalem, descending out of heaven from God, having the glory of God. Her light was like a most precious stone, like a jasper stone, clear as crystal (Revelation 21:9-11).

From John's angel-designated vantage point, he sees something amazing. A city descending from the sky. It is massive! It's not normal city big or even country big. It's continent big. It's wider than Europe from London to Kiev. Whatever mountaintop John was standing on had to have some serious elevation for him to be able to see more than just one small portion of one enormous wall. And, oh, is it beautiful! Like the most perfect of gemstones are its walls and its foundations and its gates and its streets.

For the next twenty-two verses, John presents a description of the New Jerusalem that is dressed as a beautiful bride would be for her husband. Why does God provide these details? Maybe it is because He wants to create a bit of anticipation for our future home. If He gives too much detail, our focus might excessively shift to the future and we will be of no use serving Him today. If He gives too little detail, there will be no anticipation. So like a parent who covers a Christmas gift with festive paper and elaborate bows to excite the imagination of a child, God presents us with just enough of a picture to stir our fancies and build our expectations.

As we already mentioned, John starts by telling us of the city's size. There was a time when Jerusalem was a great city. When King Solomon took control of Israel from his father, David, the Lord blessed him with wisdom, power, and wealth. The capital city drew people from many nations who came simply to hear the words of the king and witness the beauty of the city. But then under Solomon's son, Rehoboam, the kingdom split and Jerusalem has never been the same since. Even today, while it may be "great" in its regional influence, it cannot be considered so in its size and wealth.

What John saw descending from the sky is beyond superlatives. I am not a fan of made-up words like *ginormous*, but in this case I might have to make an exception. Because the New Jerusalem cannot be accurately described even by phrases like "super massive" and "really, really big," God decided to provide a number. John describes the scene: "[The angel] who talked with me had a gold reed to measure the city, its gates, and its wall. The city is laid out as a square; its length is as great as its breadth. And he measured the city with the reed: twelve thousand furlongs. Its length, breadth, and height are equal" (Revelation 21:15-16). Twelve thousand furlongs works out to around 1,380 miles. Again, continent big. But not only is this square city that big on each side, it is also that high.

"You see, Amir, that's when you know that these are symbolic numbers. They're just too big." I agree, my allegorically inclined friend, that they are huge numbers. But to say that it is ridiculous for the city to literally be that big, as some do, is to diminish the God who has just completed His second creation of a perfect heaven and perfect earth. I will not put my God in a box, nor will I put His acts of creation in a box that says, "This big, but no bigger." You can set up your eternal household in whatever tiny outlying hamlet you want. I'm going to be looking for a nice four-bedroom flat somewhere around the 240,000th floor of a New Jerusalem high-rise. Great view; hopefully fast elevators.

The next fact we learn about the New Jerusalem is that it is beautiful beyond words. If we've already made a once-in-a-lifetime exception for *ginormous*, then maybe we need to coin a new term like *gi-gorgeous*. As John tried to describe the brilliance of the colors he saw, he resorted to comparisons to what are most beautiful and valuable—gemstones.

The construction of its wall was of jasper; and the city was pure gold, like clear glass. The foundations of the wall of the city were adorned with all kinds of precious stones: the first foundation was jasper, the second sapphire, the third chalcedony, the fourth emerald, the fifth sardonyx, the sixth sardius, the seventh chrysolite, the eighth beryl, the ninth topaz, the tenth chrysoprase, the eleventh jacinth, and the twelfth amethyst. The twelve gates were twelve pearls: each individual gate was of one pearl. And the street of the city was pure gold, like transparent glass (Revelation 21:18-21).

It is quite possible that each foundation layer was exactly what John said it was—a massive, miraculously created gemstone. But it is the "gold, like transparent glass" that makes me think that maybe he is just a guy who is confronted with something so amazing that the Greek language simply fails him.

As John looks around, he realizes something is missing. How can this be the city of God if there is no temple in which to worship? A temple, or a desire for a temple, has been a defining factor of Jerusalem ever since the time of David's plans and Solomon's build. But now in this final and permanent city, the holy building is missing. Quickly, though, John realizes what is going on and explains that "the Lord God Almighty and the Lamb are its temple" (verse 22). Why is it necessary to have a structure that represents the presence of God in the city when you have God Himself in the city? Everyone will have ready access to the Father and to the Lamb, and there will be no need for sacrifices because sin and death have been done away with.

There is a change also in the heavens, so that the sun and the moon are no longer needed. John wrote, "The city had no need of the sun or of the moon to shine in it, for the glory of God illuminated it. The Lamb is its light" (verse 23). The light for the world will come from the Light of the World. "Ummm, Amir, I have a hard time sleeping unless it is really dark. I'm going to turn into a sleepless zombie." I understand, but remember that you will have your resurrection body. It will not run down the way your flesh does now. So don't worry if you don't get your eight hours. And, if you want to take a nap just because you like to sleep, try pulling the blinds.

John is then struck by one more truth. The holy city is finally quite literally the holy city. There will be no sin or darkness in it. There will only be righteousness. That is because the only ones who will live inside its walls are "those who are written in the Lamb's Book of Life" (verse 27). How can John be sure of that? Because that is all who are left. Everyone whose name was not in that book—a volume identified here as belonging to the Lamb—has already been judged and is tragically experiencing their punishment.

The River and the Tree

One of the sons of Korah penned a prophetic psalm. In it, he wrote of the city of God and a waterway:

> There is a river whose streams shall make glad the city of God,
> the holy place of the tabernacle of the Most High.
> God is in the midst of her, she shall not be moved;
> God shall help her, just at the break of dawn (Psalm 46:4-5).

For most of Jerusalem's existence, there was one major water source known as the Gihon Spring. At the second coming, when Jesus returns at the end of the tribulation, Ezekiel tells us that water will flow out from under the temple and will eventually turn into a river. But both of those sources only produced regular old water. Flowing in the New Jerusalem will be a new river with a special kind of water.

> He showed me a pure river of water of life, clear as crystal, proceeding from the throne of God and of the Lamb. In the middle of its street, and on either side of the river, was the tree of life, which bore twelve fruits, each tree yielding its fruit every month. The leaves of the tree were for the healing of the nations. And there shall be no more curse, but the throne of God and of the Lamb shall be in it, and His servants shall serve Him. They shall see His face, and

His name shall be on their foreheads. There shall be no night there: They need no lamp nor light of the sun, for the Lord God gives them light. And they shall reign forever and ever (Revelation 22:1-5).

The water of life flows out from the Source of Life, God Himself. As it pours down the street, it brings nourishment to the tree of life, which stands majestically straddling the flow of water. The tree bears fruit, and its leaves are for healing. Why is healing needed if there is no sickness or death? The word itself isn't limited to the idea of being healed of an illness. It can also speak of therapeutic healing, which fits into the whole tree of life and water of life motif. While it is possible that these all refer to some physical necessity our resurrected bodies will have—that is, to be nourished and refreshed to maintain their vitality—that doesn't appear to be the case because of our bodies' incorruptible nature.

Many explanations have been offered, but none fully satisfy. As a result, we should be content to take this for what it is—a marvelous concluding statement offered by God to spark our imaginations about what He has waiting for us, while still holding most of the details back because He knows that no language spoken on earth could possibly describe the wonderful eternity He has waiting for us.

CHAPTER 21

EVEN SO, COME

REVELATION 22:6-21

We are finally at the end of our tour of the sixty-sixth book of the Bible. I'm reminded of what we read in the first chapter about God's blessing for those who read, hear, and apply the truths of this book to their lives. I know that I have been blessed as I have written this book, and I know that you have been blessed as you have read it. How do I know? Because God promised it, and here at the end of the letter He promises it once again. First, though, we read these words:

> Then [the angel] said to me, "These words are faithful and true." And the Lord God of the holy prophets sent His angel to show His servants the things which must shortly take place (Revelation 22:6).

The angel who is giving John this tour—who was among the angels who had poured out the seven bowls—assured him of the truthfulness of what he had heard and seen. You would think that because the Lord brought about the whole tour, this affirmation wouldn't have been necessary. But, as we've talked about already and as we see today, there are many who are quick to say, "Yeah, the words may be faithful and true, but the words themselves don't really mean what they normally mean." The angel here counters that by saying, with all certainty, that what you are reading is truly what you are reading.

Jesus Breaks In

Suddenly, Jesus breaks into the conversation, saying, "Behold, I am coming quickly! Blessed is he who keeps the words of the prophecy of this book" (Revelation 22:7). This is the first of four instances in this last chapter that the Lord inserts Himself (verses 7, 12-13, 16, 20). In three of the four, His opening words are "I am coming quickly!" If you are saying, "Quickly? A week, a month, a year, even a decade is quickly! Two thousand years? That's not quickly!" then let me remind you that you should be so very thankful that God's definition of *quickly* is very different than yours. If He limited His meaning to our earthly, temporal definition rather than looking at it through the lens of eternity, then He would have returned long ago. That means you would not exist. You would not have had the opportunity to experience the joys of this life, the blessed hope of salvation, the glories of an eternity with God, and the freedom to complain about the "slowness" of the Lord's return.

The second part of Jesus' statement is where we find the promised blessing of Revelation. But in reminding us, the Lord also reiterates that reading Revelation is not a spectator sport. We are to keep the words that we read. That means we learn from Jesus' words to the churches in chapters 2 and 3, ensuring that we keep our first love strong, that we stand strong in the midst of persecution, that we protect our congregations from heresy and immorality, and that we don't allow ourselves to fall into the nauseating state of lukewarm faith.

We also learn from the judgments that we need to trust that God will carry out His perfect plan in His perfect time, that we can love our enemies knowing that He will bring justice in His time, and that because time is short, we must be a light to our unbelieving friends and family and anyone else that He puts us in contact with.

Finally, these last few chapters remind us of our future reward, which helps us to realize that this short life we live on the earth is not about us. We are here as servants. We are called to sacrifice ourselves and follow and carry out whatever the Lord calls us to do, knowing that from an eternal perspective, our years here on earth are just a blip when compared to the forever that we will spend enjoying the rewards of our faith and service.

John Gets Confused

We don't know how much time went by from the moment that Jesus appeared to John on Patmos to the wrapping up of the revelation. But after so many wild visions and up-and-down emotions and transports from here to there and back again—all the while having to scribble down everything that he witnessed—this old disciple momentarily lost it.

> Now I, John, saw and heard these things. And when I heard and saw, I fell down to worship before the feet of the angel who showed me these things. Then he said to me, "See that you do not do that. For I am your fellow servant, and of your brethren the prophets, and of those who keep the words of this book. Worship God." And he said to me, "Do not seal the words of the prophecy of this book, for the time is at hand. He who is unjust, let him be unjust still; he who is filthy, let him be filthy still; he who is righteous, let him be righteous still; he who is holy, let him be holy still" (Revelation 22:8-11).

Worshipping an angel? It would be easy to chastise John, but I can't imagine having been in his place. I appreciate how the angel handled the awkward situation. He corrected but didn't condemn. He stopped John and told him why what he was doing was wrong. Then he told him what he should be doing instead. "Don't worship me. I'm just a fellow servant. Worship God."

How much more grace and mercy would there be in the church if we were to treat each other this way? Instead, the attack culture has become entrenched in the bride of Christ. If you could see only a handful of the emails and social media comments that I receive every day from "church people" who viciously attack me because they disagree with my theology or my personal decisions, I think you would be surprised. Even worse, those who are in the church do the same thing to those who are outside the family of God—they are flinging words of darkness at others when they should be shining the light of Christ.

There is one other lesson to learn from this incident. We live in a personality-driven culture. Young people can develop followings numbering into the millions on their social media. This also happens within the church. Pastors, speakers, and ministries all have their followings. This is not bad in and of itself. But we must beware of two possible consequences. We must not let these followings divide the church, and we must never allow our admiration for a person to eclipse our focus on the Lord, whether intentionally or unintentionally. This is what happened in the church at Corinth. The congregation began to choose sides over their favorite Christian leader. Rather than celebrating their position as followers of Christ, they called themselves followers of Apollos or followers of Paul. Soon, divisions opened in the church. Paul quickly shut this down, saying, "Let no one boast in men. For all things are yours: whether Paul or Apollos or Cephas, or the world or life or death, or things present or things to come—all are yours. And you are Christ's, and Christ is God's" (1 Corinthians 3:21-23).

I am very thankful for the great following with which God has blessed Behold Israel. My prayer, though, is that the ministry never becomes about a person, unless that person is Jesus Christ, the true Messiah, the King of kings and Lord of lords, the Savior of the world. I am blessed to be a simple servant, as are all of you, just following the call that he has placed on my life.

Back in his right mind, John writes down the rest of the message. The angel tells John to make sure the words of the message he has written get disseminated throughout the church—quickly, because the time is short. This is another reminder that this book is for all people. It should not be sealed up only for the theologian and the prophecy teacher and the pastor and the seminary professor. Like the rest of the Bible, it is written for all people to read, to learn from, and to use as a template for how to live.

Jesus Breaks in Again!

Once again, Jesus jumps into the conversation. He starts as we expect:

> Behold, I am coming quickly, and My reward is with Me, to give to every one according to his work. I am the Alpha and the Omega, the Beginning and the End, the First and the Last (Revelation 22:12-13).

Jesus is coming, and He is bringing His reward with Him. What is that reward? It is to go to the place that He has prepared for us, and there to experience the *bema* seat judgment, during which we will be recompensed for our faithful service here on the earth. Remember, He is not coming to take us to a judgment of salvation. That's not necessary, because if you are not a believer in Christ, you will not be going with Him. When we lift off from this earth, there is nothing but good waiting for us for the rest of eternity.

Blessings of the Book

John once again reminds the reader that this is a book with applications. Do what it says, and you will be blessed:

> Blessed are those who do His commandments, that they may have the right to the tree of life, and may enter through the gates into the city. But outside are dogs and sorcerers and sexually immoral and murderers and idolaters, and whoever loves and practices a lie (Revelation 22:14-15).

The blessing that John presents here is the last of seven blessings that we have come across as we have gone through this book.

> Blessed is he who reads and those who hear the words of this prophecy, and keep those things which are written in it; for the time is near (1:3).

> "Blessed are the dead who die in the Lord from now on." "Yes," says the Spirit, "that they may rest from their labors, and their works follow them" (14:13).

> Blessed is he who watches, and keeps his garments, lest he walk naked and they see his shame (16:15).

> Blessed are those who are called to the marriage supper of the Lamb! (19:9).

> Blessed and holy is he who has part in the first resurrection. Over such the second death has no power, but they shall be priests of God and of Christ, and shall reign with Him a thousand years (20:6).

> Blessed is he who keeps the words of the prophecy of this book (22:7).

> Blessed are those who do His commandments, that they may have the right to the tree of life, and may enter through the gates into the city (22:14).

Before you opened this book, did you have any idea that Revelation is a book of such blessing? Most see it as only doom and gloom. However, the Bright and Morning Star shines through the dark night of wrath. Jesus Christ is our hope, our joy, our peace, our salvation!

Again, Jesus Breaks in Again

Jesus reminds us that He is the Author of this book, the angels have been the tour guides, and John is just the scribe.

> I, Jesus, have sent My angel to testify to you these things in the churches. I am the Root and the Offspring of David, the Bright and Morning Star (22:16).

This is the first time we see any mention of the church since chapter 3. Once again, for those who are so desperate to find the church in the tribulation, it is not there. The tribulation is not an amorphous "spiritual testing" period of the new covenant people of God over a long stretch of time, as some say. It is also not a seven-year purifying of the bride, as others assert. The tribulation is not for the church! There are only two purposes for the period during which God's wrath will be poured out on the earth: the discipline of unbelieving Israel, and the punishment of unbelieving Gentiles. If you are unhappy with that statement, I must say that I don't get you. Not only does what I say line up with what we've seen biblically, but it makes for a much happier outlook for the future.

Come!

When my wife, Miriam, and I were engaged to be married, I cherished every moment I had with her. Being with her just felt right. We were complete. In those times that we were apart, I could not wait until we were united once again. Our desire to be together was based on love and joy and the knowledge that God was calling us to be joined as one. It is that same kind of emotion that I feel when I read these next words:

> And the Spirit and the bride say, "Come!" And let him who hears say, "Come!" And let him who thirsts come. Whoever desires, let him take the water of life freely (Revelation 22:17).

These words are packed with passion. Sometimes I hear preachers read these words in the biblical monotone that is used in so many religious services. I want to jump up and ask, "Do you realize what you are reading?" The Holy Spirit, who knows the plans that the Father has for the church, calls for the Bridegroom to come. The bride, whose love for her betrothed is so deep that one could write a sequel to the Song of Songs based on it, cries out for the Son to retrieve her and take her with Him to the home He has prepared.

Then John looks to you, the one who has heard these words, who has read this letter, with the full expectation that your response will equal that of the Spirit and the bride. "Come!" you cry. "Lord, I am so ready to see you! Come! Take me to be with you! Come, Lord Jesus, come!"

If you are not ready to cry out for the return of Christ, John has a word for you too. If you have not drunk deeply of the water of life, come. It is there for you—come. It costs you nothing of any worth—come. It will give you everything that really matters—come. If your desire is to spend eternity with God in the new heaven and the new earth, drink of the water, my friend. Receive Jesus as your Savior. Follow Him as your Lord. Drink freely of the Water of Life, and He will make you His own.

A Warning

As the letter comes to a close, John gives a warning. He knows the nature of the prophecies in the letter. He knows that the deceiver is already at work in the church trying to destroy what God had established through his apostles. He knows that the last thing that Satan wants is for people to know that the "rumors" of his future demise are not at all exaggerated, but dead-on accurate. So John lets people know that it would be in their own best interest to not tamper with the text.

> I testify to everyone who hears the words of the prophecy of this book: If anyone adds to these things, God will add to him the plagues that are written in this book; and if anyone takes away from the words of the book of this prophecy, God shall take away his part from the Book of Life, from the holy city, and from the things which are written in this book (Revelation 22:18-19).

This is not the first time that a biblical writer has given a warning like this. Moses wanted to make sure that no one after him would look at the Torah and start shifting things around, so he wrote, "You shall not add to the word which I command you, nor take from it, that you may keep the commandments of the LORD your God which I command you" (Deuteronomy 4:2). Agur, in the book of Proverbs, gave a general warning not to mess with the words of God, saying, "Every word of God is pure; He is a shield to those who put their trust in Him. Do not add to His words, lest He rebuke you, and you be found a liar" (Proverbs 30:5-6).

Revelation, like the rest of the Bible, is a gift given to mankind. God wanted to give us a peek into the bigger picture from before time began to when time will be no more, so He commissioned the Holy Spirit to move faithful men to write down His story. That is exactly what is found from Genesis to Revelation. Every book, every division, every verse has its purpose and has been given for a reason. Imagine how in the dark we would be about all that really matters in this world if we hadn't been blessed with this precious book.

Again, Jesus Breaks in Again...Again

One last time, our loving Bridegroom reminds us that He's coming for us:

> He who testifies to these things says, "Surely I am coming quickly" (Revelation 22:20).

If you ever have wanted to see the heart of Jesus Christ, just look at His threefold reminder in this chapter that it won't be long until we see Him. Any time we doubt, any time we want to cry out, "How long, O Lord?" we just need to remember these words. Just like how those moments when I was finally reunited with Miriam would erase the memory of the time we were apart, so the thrill of finally seeing our Savior's face will be so joy-inspiring that the long wait for His arrival will fade to nothing.

Thus, when Jesus tells us that He is coming quickly, we echo the closing words of John's letter and use them to conclude this book:

> Amen. Even so, come, Lord Jesus! The grace of our Lord Jesus Christ be with you all. Amen (verses 20-21).

NOTES

1. Paige Patterson, *Revelation*, ed. E. Ray Clendenen (Nashville, TN: B&H, 2012), introduction, Logos Bible Software.

2. Stanley Toussaint, *Revelation*, a video class for alumni of the Dallas Theological Seminary, media .dts.edu.

3. Toussaint, *Revelation*.

4. Robert L. Thomas, *Revelation 1–7: An Exegetical Commentary, Vol. 1* (Chicago, IL: Moody, 1992), Kindle locations 9216-9219.

5. Toussaint, *Revelation*.

6. "Did Israel get all of the good land?" *Israel Advocacy Movement*, www.israeladvocacy.net.

7. "Israel's population up to 9.25 million, though growth rate, immigration down," *The Times of Israel*, September 16, 2020, https://www.timesofisrael.com/israels-population-up-to-9-25 -million-but-growth-rate-immigration-down/.

8. John F. Walvoord, *The Revelation of Jesus Christ* (Chicago, IL: Moody, 1989), 142.

9. Thomas, *Revelation 1–7: An Exegetical Commentary*, 476-477.

10. Albert Barnes and Ingram Cobbin, *Barnes' Notes on the New Testament* (Naples, FL: GraceWorks Multimedia, 2008), Kindle location 100000.

11. Charles C. Ryrie, *Revelation* (Chicago, IL: Moody, 2018), Kindle location 72.

12. Chris Baraniuk, "What It's Like to Sail a Giant Ship on Earth's Busiest Seas," *BBC Future*, BBC, November 26, 2016, https://www.bbc.com/future/article/20161128-what-its-like-to-sail -colossal-ships-on-earths-busiest-sea.

13. Walvoord, *The Revelation of Jesus Christ*, 194.

14. Ryrie, *Revelation*, Kindle location 121.

15. Walvoord, *The Revelation of Jesus Christ*, 214.

16. Tim LaHaye and Timothy E. Parker, *The Book of Revelation Made Clear* (Nashville, TN: Thomas Nelson, 2014), Kindle location 118.

17. W.E. Vine, Merrill F. Unger, and William White Jr., *Vine's Complete Expository Dictionary of Old and New Testament Words* (Nashville, TN: Thomas Nelson, 1996), 26-27.

18. Walvoord, *The Revelation of Jesus Christ*, 259.

19. Ryrie, *Revelation*, Kindle location 145.

20. LaHaye and Parker, *The Book of Revelation Made Clear*, Kindle locations 146-147.

21. Charles R. Swindoll, *Charles R. Swindoll's New Testament Insights: Insights on Revelation* (Grand Rapids, MI: Zondervan, 2001), 230.

22. Grant R. Osborne, *Revelation Verse by Verse* (Bellingham, WA: Lexham Press, 2016), Kindle locations 314-315.

23. Osborne, *Revelation Verse by Verse*, Kindle location 12.

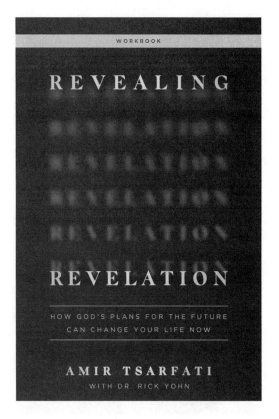

This companion workbook to *Revealing Revelation*—the product of many years of careful research in Bible prophecy—offers you a clear and exciting overview of God's perfect plan for the future. Inside you'll find...

- principles from the Bible that equip you to better interpret the end-times signs and occurrences Revelation describes

- explorations of other key prophecy passages in Scripture that bring clarity to the teachings in Revelation

- insights that provide you with practical wisdom about how the message of Bible prophecy is relevant to your life today

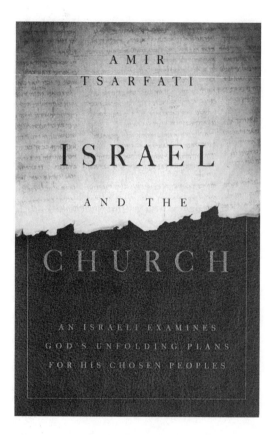

AMIR TSARFATI

ISRAEL

AND THE

CHURCH

AN ISRAELI EXAMINES
GOD'S UNFOLDING PLANS
FOR HIS CHOSEN PEOPLES

In *Israel and the Church*, bestselling author and native Israeli Amir Tsarfati helps readers recognize the distinct contemporary and future roles of both the Jewish people and the church, and how together they reveal the character of God and His perfect plan of salvation.

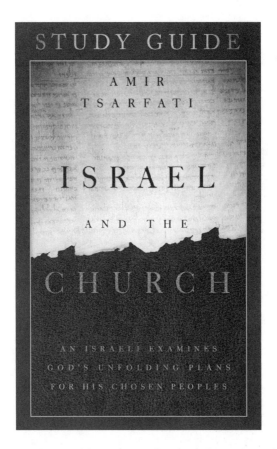

STUDY GUIDE

AMIR TSARFATI

ISRAEL

AND THE

CHURCH

AN ISRAELI EXAMINES
GOD'S UNFOLDING PLANS
FOR HIS CHOSEN PEOPLES

To fully grasp what God has in store for the future, it's vital to understand His promises to Israel. The *Israel and the Church Study Guide* will help you do exactly that, equipping you to explore the Bible's many revelations about what is yet to come.

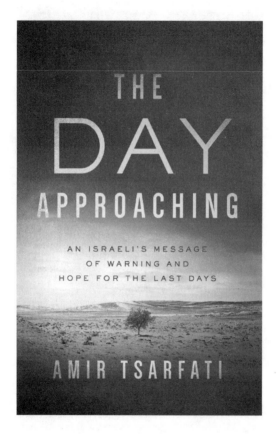

As a native Israeli of Jewish roots, Amir Tsarfati provides a distinct perspective that weaves biblical history, current events, and Bible prophecy together to shine light on the mysteries about the end times. In *The Day Approaching*, he points to the scriptural evidence that the return of the Lord is imminent.

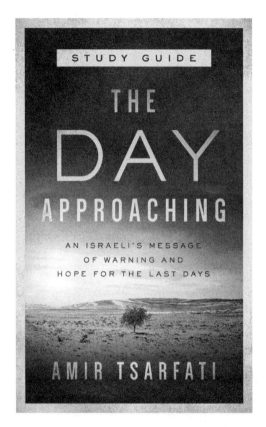

Jesus Himself revealed the signs that will alert us to the nearness of His return. In *The Day Approaching Study Guide*, you'll have the opportunity to take an up-close look at what those signs are, as well as God's overarching plans for the future, and how those plans affect you today.

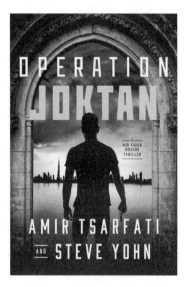

"It was the perfect day—until the gunfire."

Nir Tavor is an Israeli secret service operative turned talented Mossad agent.

Nicole le Roux is a model with a hidden skill.

A terrorist attack brings them together, and then work forces them apart—until they're unexpectedly called back into each other's lives.

But there's no time for romance. As violent radicals threaten chaos across the Middle East, the two must work together to stop these extremists, pooling Nicole's knack for technology and Nir's adeptness with on-the-ground missions. Each heart-racing step of their operation gets them closer to the truth—and closer to danger.

In this thrilling first book in a new series, authors Amir Tsarfati and Steve Yohn draw on true events as well as tactical insights Amir learned from his time in the Israeli Defense Forces. For believers in God's life-changing promises, *Operation Joktan* is a suspense-filled page-turner that illuminates the blessing Israel is to the world.